Introduction to

Web 2.0

Introduction to

Web 2.0

Alan Evans | **Diane Coyle**

Prentice Hall

Boston   Columbus   Indianapolis   New York   San Francisco   Upper Saddle River
Amsterdam   Cape Town   Dubai   London   Madrid   Milan   Munich   Paris   Montreal   Toronto
Delhi   Mexico City   Sao Paulo   Sydney   Hong Kong   Seoul   Singapore   Taipei   Tokyo

VP/Editorial Director: Natalie E. Anderson
Editor-in-Chief: Michael Payne
Associate VP/Executive Acquisitions Editor: Stephanie Wall
Director, Product Development: Pamela Hersperger
Product Development Manager: Eileen Bien Calabro
Editorial Project Manager: Meghan Bisi
Development Editor: Box Twelve Communications, Inc.
Editorial Assistant: Terenia McHenry
AVP/Director of Online Programs, Media: Richard Keaveny
AVP/Director of Product Development: Lisa Strite
Editorial Media Project Manager: Alana Coles
Production Media Project Manager: John Cassar
Marketing Manager: Tori Olson Alves
Marketing Coordinator: Susan Osterlitz
Marketing Assistant: Angela Frey
Senior Managing Editor: Cynthia Zonneveld
Associate Managing Editor: Camille Trentacoste
Production Project Manager: Rhonda Aversa and Mike Lackey
Manager of Rights & Permissions: Charles Morris
Senior Operations Specialist: Nick Sklitsis
Operations Specialist: Natacha Moore
Senior Art Director: Jonathan Boylan
Art Director: Anthony Gemmellaro
Interior Design: Anthony Gemmellaro
Cover Design: Anthony Gemmellaro
Cover Illustration/Photo: Shutterstock Images
Manager, Cover Visual Research & Permissions: Karen Sanatar
Composition: Black Dot Group
Full-Service Project Management: Black Dot Group
Printer/Binder: Webcrafters Inc.
Typeface: 11/12 Garamond 3

Credits and acknowledgments borrowed from other sources and reproduced, with permission, in this textbook appear on page 289.

Microsoft® and Windows® are registered trademarks of the Microsoft Corporation in the U.S.A. and other countries. Screen shots and icons reprinted with permission from the Microsoft Corporation. This book is not sponsored or endorsed by or affiliated with the Microsoft Corporation.

Many of the designations by manufacturers and seller to distinguish their products are claimed as trademarks. Where those designations appear in this book, and the publisher was aware of a trademark claim, the designations have been printed in initial caps or all caps.

Library of Congress Cataloging-in-Publication Data
Evans, Alan (Alan D.)
  Introduction to Web 2.0 / Alan D. Evans, Diane M. Coyle.
    p. cm.
  ISBN-13: 978-0-13-507403-9
  ISBN-10: 0-13-507403-7
  1. Web 2.0. I. Coyle, Diane II. Title.
  TK5105.88817.E93 2009
  006.7--dc22
                          2009004344

Prentice Hall
is an imprint of

www.pearsonhighered.com

10 9 8 7 6 5 4 3 2 1
ISBN-13: 978-0-13-507403-9
ISBN-10: 0-13-507403-7

About the Authors

Alan Evans, MS, CPA
aevans@mc3.edu

Alan is currently a faculty member at Manor College and Montgomery County Community College teaching a variety of computer science and business courses. He holds a B.S. in Accounting from Rider University and an M.S. in Information Systems from Drexel University as well as being a Certified Public Accountant. After a successful career in business, Alan finally realized his true calling was education. He has been teaching at the collegiate level since 2000. Alan enjoys giving presentations at technical conferences and meets regularly with computer science faculty and administrators from other colleges to discuss curriculum development and new methods of engaging students.

Dedication: For my students, who constantly inspire me to expand my knowledge....just to keep up with them!

Diane M. Coyle
dcoyle@manor.edu

Diane is a faculty member at Manor College and Montgomery County Community College. Diane frequently incorporates Web 2.0 projects into her face-to-face and online classes in computer concepts, Microsoft Office, and Web design. She also teaches computer literacy courses for at-risk and unemployed clients for several social service programs and has a successful freelance business providing marketing, editorial, and computer training services. Diane values networking and interacting with other educators and students and is currently the Secretary for the Pennsylvania Community College Computer Consortium—a group dedicated to encouraging interest and improving education in computer science and information and related technology disciplines.

Dedication: As always, I'm grateful to my family and friends for their support and encouragement. You guys are the best!

Contents

Visual Walk-Through

Many of today's introductory computing courses are moving beyond coverage of just the traditional Microsoft® Office applications. Instructors are looking to incorporate newer technologies and software applications into their courses, and on some college campuses new alternative courses based on emerging technologies are being offered.

The NEXT Series was developed to provide innovative instructors with a high-quality, academic teaching solution that focuses on the next great technologies. There is more to computing than Microsoft® Office, and the books in *The NEXT Series* enable students to learn about some of the newer technologies that are available and becoming part of our everyday lives.

The NEXT Series…making it easy to teach what's *NEXT!*

▶ Whether you are interested in creating a new course or you want to enhance an existing class by incorporating new technology, *The NEXT Series* is your solution.

Included in this series are books on alternative productivity software application products, **Google Apps** and **OpenOffice.org**, as well as new technologies encompassed in **Web 2.0** such as social networking sites, information sharing, and collaboration tools.

▶ *Introduction to Web 2.0* is a teaching and learning tool that was designed for use in a classroom setting, encouraging students to learn by using these new technologies hands-on.

The text includes in-chapter Hands-On Exercises, end of chapter exercises, and instructor supplements.

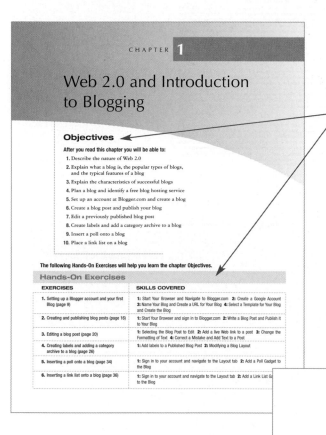

Each chapter opens with a list of numbered **Objectives**, clearly outlining what students will be able to accomplish after completing the chapter. The **Hands-On Exercises** are also outlined at the beginning of the chapter, letting students know what they will be doing in each chapter.

Learn-by-doing approach

Students learn how to use Web 2.0 technologies by completing a series of **Hands-On Exercises**. These Exercises are clearly distinguished from the explanatory text because the pages are shaded in green.

Question & Answer Format
Each section begins with a question, engaging students in a dialog with the authors and drawing them into the content.

Key terms are defined in the margins.

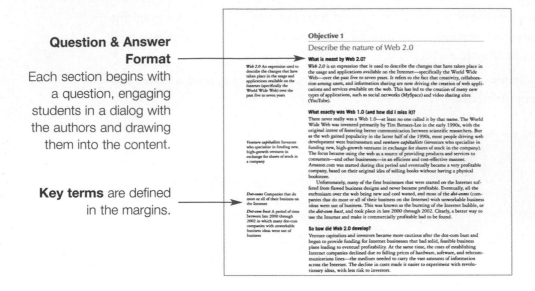

Objective 1
Describe the nature of Web 2.0

What is meant by Web 2.0?
Web 2.0 is an expression that is used to describe the changes that have taken place in the usage and applications available on the Internet—specifically the World Wide Web—over the past five to seven years. It refers to the fact that creativity, collaboration among users, and information sharing are now driving the creation of web applications and services available on the web. This has led to the creation of many new types of applications, such as social networks (MySpace) and video sharing sites (YouTube).

What exactly was Web 1.0 (and how did I miss it)?
There never really was a Web 1.0—at least no one called it by that name. The World Wide Web was invented primarily by Tim Berners-Lee in the early 1990s, with the original intent of fostering better communication between scientific researchers. But as the web gained popularity in the latter half of the 1990s, most people driving web development were businessmen and *venture capitalists* (investors who specialize in funding new, high-growth ventures in exchange for shares of stock in the company). The focus became using the web as a source of providing products and services to consumers—and other businesses—in an efficient and cost-effective manner. Amazon.com was started during this period and eventually became a very profitable company, based on their original idea of selling books without having a physical bookstore.

Unfortunately, many of the first businesses that were started on the Internet suffered from flawed business designs and never became profitable. Eventually, all the enthusiasm over the web being new and cool waned, and most of the *dot-coms* (companies that do most or all of their business on the Internet) with unworkable business ideas went out of business. This was known as the bursting of the Internet bubble, or the *dot-com bust*, and took place in late 2000 through 2002. Clearly, a better way to use the Internet and make it commercially profitable had to be found.

So how did Web 2.0 develop?
Venture capitalists and investors became more cautious after the dot-com bust and began to provide funding for Internet businesses that had solid, feasible business plans leading to eventual profitability. At the same time, the costs of establishing Internet companies declined due to falling prices of hardware, software, and telecommunications lines—the medium needed to carry the vast amounts of information across the Internet. The decline in costs made it easier to experiment with revolutionary ideas, with less risk to investors.

Alert boxes call attention to items that might cause students to get hung up.

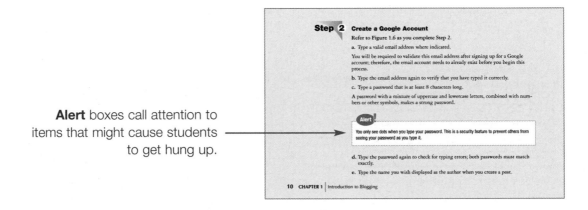

Step 2   Create a Google Account
Refer to Figure 1.6 as you complete Step 2.

a. Type a valid email address where indicated.

You will be required to validate this email address after signing up for a Google account; therefore, the email account needs to already exist before you begin this process.

b. Type the email address again to verify that you have typed it correctly.

c. Type a password that is at least 8 characters long.

A password with a mixture of uppercase and lowercase letters, combined with numbers or other symbols, makes a strong password.

> **Alert**
> You only see dots when you type your password. This is a security feature to prevent others from seeing your password as you type it.

d. Type the password again to check for typing errors; both passwords must match exactly.

e. Type the name you wish displayed as the author when you create a post.

10   CHAPTER 1 | Introduction to Blogging

Tip boxes provide students with useful tips and tricks.

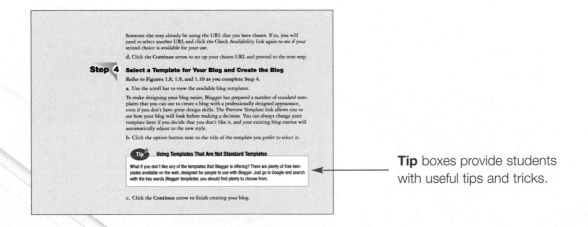

Someone else may already be using the URL that you have chosen. If so, you will need to select another URL and click the Check Availability link again to see if your second choice is available for your use.

d. Click the **Continue** arrow to set up your chosen URL and proceed to the next step.

Step 4   Select a Template for Your Blog and Create the Blog
Refer to Figures 1.8, 1.9, and 1.10 as you complete Step 4.

a. Use the scroll bar to view the available blog templates.

To make designing your blog easier, Blogger has prepared a number of standard templates that you can use to create a blog with a professionally designed appearance, even if you don't have great design skills. The Preview Template link allows you to see how your blog will look before making a decision. You can always change your template later if you decide that you don't like it, and your existing blog entries will automatically adjust to the new style.

b. Click the option button next to the title of the template you prefer to select it.

> **Tip   Using Templates That Are Not Standard Templates**
> What if you don't like any of the templates that Blogger is offering? There are plenty of free templates available on the web, designed for people to use with Blogger. Just go to Google and search with the key words *Blogger templates*; you should find plenty to choose from.

c. Click the **Continue** arrow to finish creating your blog.

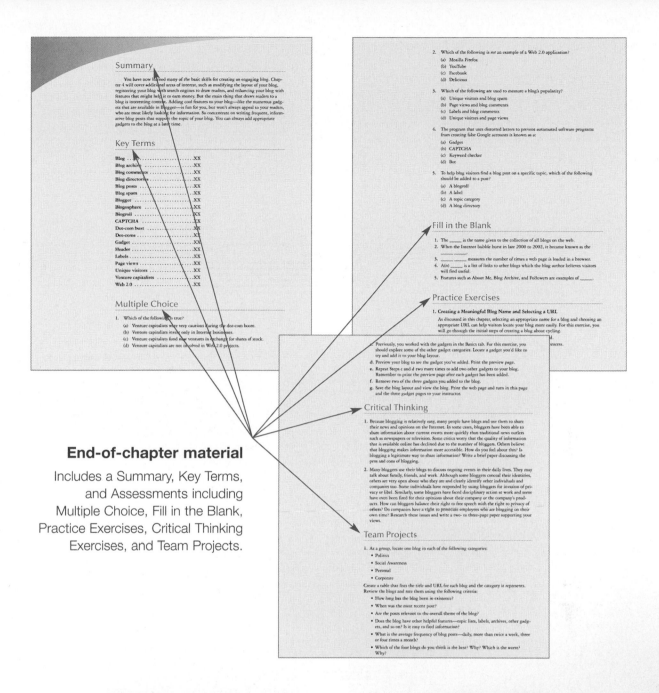

End-of-chapter material

Includes a Summary, Key Terms, and Assessments including Multiple Choice, Fill in the Blank, Practice Exercises, Critical Thinking Exercises, and Team Projects.

CHAPTER 1

Introduction to Blogging

Objectives

After you read this chapter, you will be able to:

1. Describe the nature of Web 2.0

2. Explain what a blog is, the popular types of blogs, and the typical features of a blog

3. Explain the characteristics of successful blogs

4. Plan a blog and identify a free blog hosting service

5. Set up an account at Blogger.com and create a blog

6. Create a blog post and publish your blog

7. Edit a previously published blog post

8. Create labels and add a category archive to a blog

9. Insert a poll onto a blog

10. Place a link list on a blog

11. Describe Internet resources that educate people about blogging

The following Hands-On Exercises will help you accomplish the chapter Objectives.

Hands-On Exercises

EXERCISES	SKILLS COVERED
1. Setting Up a Blogger Account and Your First Blog **(page 9)**	**Step 1:** Start Your Browser and Navigate to Blogger.com **Step 2:** Create a Google Account **Step 3:** Name Your Blog and Create a Uniform Resource Locator (URL) for Your Blog **Step 4:** Select a Template for Your Blog and Create the Blog
2. Creating and Publishing Blog Posts **(page 16)**	**Step 1:** Start Your Browser and Sign In to Blogger.com **Step 2:** Write a Blog Post and Publish It to Your Blog
3. Editing a Blog Post **(page 20)**	**Step 1:** Select the Blog Post to Edit **Step 2:** Add a Live Hyperlink to a Post **Step 3:** Change the Formatting of Text **Step 4:** Correct a Mistake and Add Text to a Post
4. Creating Labels and Adding a Category Archive to a Blog **(page 26)**	**Step 1:** Add Labels to a Published Blog Post **Step 2:** Modify a Blog Layout
5. Inserting a Poll onto a Blog **(page 34)**	**Step 1:** Sign In to Your Account and Navigate to the Layout Tab **Step 2:** Add a Poll Gadget to the Blog
6. Inserting a Link List onto a Blog **(page 36)**	**Step 1:** Sign In to Your Account and Navigate to the Layout Tab **Step 2:** Add a Link List Gadget to the Blog

Objective 1

Describe the nature of Web 2.0

What is meant by Web 2.0?

Web 2.0 is an expression that is used to describe the changes that have taken place in the usage and applications available on the Internet—specifically the World Wide Web—over the past five to seven years. It refers to the fact that creativity, collaboration among users, and information sharing are now driving the creation of web applications and services available on the web. This has led to the creation of many new types of applications, such as social networks (MySpace) and video sharing sites (YouTube).

What exactly was Web 1.0 (and how did I miss it)?

There never really was a Web 1.0—at least no one called it by that name. The World Wide Web was invented primarily by Tim Berners-Lee in the early 1990s, with the original intent of fostering better communication between scientific researchers. But as the web gained popularity in the latter half of the 1990s, most people driving web development were businessmen and *venture capitalists* (investors who specialize in funding new, high-growth ventures in exchange for shares of stock in the company). The focus became using the web as a source of providing products and services to consumers—and other businesses—in an efficient and cost-effective manner. Amazon.com was started during this period and eventually became a very profitable company, based on their original idea of selling books without having a physical bookstore.

Unfortunately, many of the first businesses that were started on the Internet suffered from flawed business designs and never became profitable. Eventually, all the enthusiasm over the web being new and cool waned, and most of the *dot-coms* (companies that do most or all of their business on the Internet) with unworkable business ideas went out of business. This was known as the bursting of the Internet bubble, or the *dot-com bust*, and took place in late 2000 through 2002. Clearly, a better way to use the Internet and make it commercially profitable had to be found.

So how did Web 2.0 develop?

Venture capitalists and investors became more cautious after the dot-com bust and began to provide funding for Internet businesses that had solid, feasible business plans leading to eventual profitability. At the same time, the costs of establishing Internet companies declined due to falling prices of hardware, software, and telecommunications lines—the medium needed to carry the vast amounts of information across the Internet. The decline in costs made it easier to experiment with revolutionary ideas, with less risk to investors.

What is the essence of a Web 2.0 application?

Web 2.0 sites get back to the original ideas of the World Wide Web: individuals sharing information with each other efficiently and effectively. Effective Web 2.0 ventures rely on user creativity to create and distribute an individual's intellectual property, such as videos or writing. Many successful Web 2.0 products include a social component that fosters interaction between individuals, either for the purpose of sharing information or just to chat and swap ideas or opinions. Social networking sites that encourage online communication between friends (like MySpace and Facebook), video sharing sites (such as YouTube), blogs (which are essentially online diaries), wikis that enable many people to collaborate and contribute to the development of a document (such as Wikipedia, shown in Figure 1.1), and folksonomy sites that use tags to manage and categorize web content (such as Delicious) are all examples of Web 2.0 applications.

Web 2.0 An expression used to describe the changes that have taken place in the usage and applications available on the Internet (specifically the World Wide Web) over the past five to seven years

Venture capitalists Investors who specialize in funding new, high-growth ventures in exchange for shares of stock in a company

Dot-coms Companies that do most or all of their business on the Internet

Dot-com bust A period of time between late 2000 through 2002 in which many dot-com companies with unworkable business ideas went out of business

---

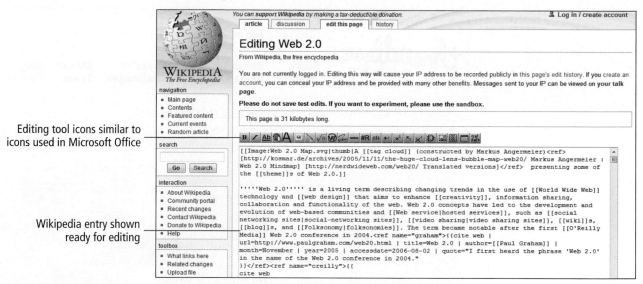

Editing tool icons similar to icons used in Microsoft Office

Wikipedia entry shown ready for editing

Figure 1.1 A Wikipedia page shown in editing mode. Anyone can create or edit a page in Wikipedia, which is a very efficient way to collaborate on creating an information document.

Are Web 2.0 companies more likely to survive and remain in business than earlier web ventures?

If the owners of Web 2.0 sites can figure out how to make money from user-generated content and social interaction, they will fare better than the early web companies that went bankrupt. Consider YouTube, the video sharing site. It is free to view videos on YouTube, and it costs nothing to establish an account and post a video you make on the site. So how does YouTube make money? So far, their main method of revenue generation is advertising. Millions of people visit YouTube every day to view videos, providing Google (the owner of YouTube) with a vast audience for advertising. You may have clicked on an ad you saw while on YouTube, which generated revenue for Google. Even if you've never clicked on an ad while viewing videos on YouTube, many other people are clicking, which allows YouTube to make money and survive.

Is advertising the only way for Web 2.0 companies to make money from their websites?

Advertising is by far the biggest source of revenue for most Web 2.0 sites, but some companies are finding other ways to convert user interaction and creativity into dollars. Threadless.com is a Web 2.0 company that has found a way to make money by selling tangible products (Figure 1.2). Threadless runs art contests on a regular basis. Anyone can submit a design to a Threadless contest. Threadless has built a vast online community of artists and people who appreciate clever design. The community votes on the art submitted to the contests to determine the winners. The winners receive $2,500 in cash and merchandise, and their designs are printed on t-shirts which Threadless then sells. Because the customers (the community) are essentially telling Threadless what they want to purchase by voting for designs, Threadless always has exceptionally strong demand for any products they produce.

In the rest of this book, we'll be exploring the major types of Web 2.0 applications, and, through hands-on exercises, we'll help you begin to explore Web 2.0 tools that you can use in your personal and business life to enhance productivity and communication. For the rest of this chapter, we'll focus on blogs.

Figure 1.2 T-shirts like "Some College Somewhere" sell well to the Threadless community, generating profits for both budding artists and the owners of Threadless.

Objective 2

Explain what a blog is, the popular types of blogs, and the typical features of a blog

What is a blog?

Blog Short for *web log*, a type of web page that features entries that provide a commentary on a single subject or a particular genre

Blogger A person who creates and maintains a blog

A *blog* (short for *web log*) is a type of web page that features entries that provide a commentary on a single subject (the benefits of recycling household garbage, for instance) or a particular genre (politics, religion, green living, fashion, and so on). A blog is essentially an online journal, often written by a single person. Postings to blogs are not necessarily in any particular order, but rather reflect what a *blogger* (a person who creates and maintains a blog) is thinking about at the time. Although today's blogs evolved from early Internet users maintaining personal online diaries that others could access and read, modern blogs often contain images and video. Blogging is quite popular, and there may be over 100 million bloggers actively maintaining their blogs; it is difficult to calculate an exact number.

Blogosphere The entire collection of all blogs on the web

Bloggers often enjoy reading other people's blogs and frequently write about their favorites in their own blogs. Therefore, many blogs contain references or hyperlinks to other blogs. The entire collection of all blogs on the web is known as the *blogosphere*.

What does a typical blog look like?

Whereas conventional websites have many pages, most of the action on a blog occurs on the blog's main web page, as shown in Figure 1.3. In addition to the main page, blog sites may include other pages that usually contain older blog entries. Features you will find on most blogs include:

Blog posts The text, images, and/or videos that provide information to blog readers; posts contain a title and the date they were posted to the blog site and are listed in reverse chronological order

- Posts – *Blog posts* are the text, images, and/or videos that provide information to blog readers. Posts contain a title and the date they were posted to the blog site. Blog posts are listed in reverse chronological order (i.e., the newest entries appear first).

Blog comments Written commentaries left by readers pertaining to a certain blog post

Blog archive A list of posts to the blog organized by date

Blogroll A list of hyperlinks to other blogs that the blog creator feels will be of interest to his or her readers

- Comments – **Blog comments** are written commentaries left by readers pertaining to a certain blog post. Not every blog permits readers to post comments. Comments are either displayed directly below a post or may be accessed from a link located next to or below the post.

- Archive – A **blog archive** is a list of posts to the blog, organized by date—usually organized by week or month. This provides readers the option of quickly finding recent posts to the blog.

- Blogroll – A **blogroll** is a list of hyperlinks to other blogs that the blog creator feels will be of interest to his or her readers.

- Topic list – In addition to an archive, many blogs now include a list of topics for the blog posts. This makes it easier for a reader to find relevant information on blogs that have a vast number of postings.

- Subscription links – Subscription links give readers an easy way to determine when a blog has been updated through the use of an RSS feed. An RSS feed is simply a web document that includes a list of the new content posted to a site, such as a blog, website, or wiki. The RSS feed is automatically updated as new content is added and notifies those readers who subscribe to the blog. We discuss RSS feeds in greater detail in Chapter 3.

What types of blogs are there?

Blogs may be written for many different purposes and are created and maintained by a wide variety of people and organizations. The most common categories are:

- Personal blogs – These are blogs created and maintained by a single individual and are by far the most common type of blog. They most often resemble a personal diary in which the creator shares their thoughts about a particular

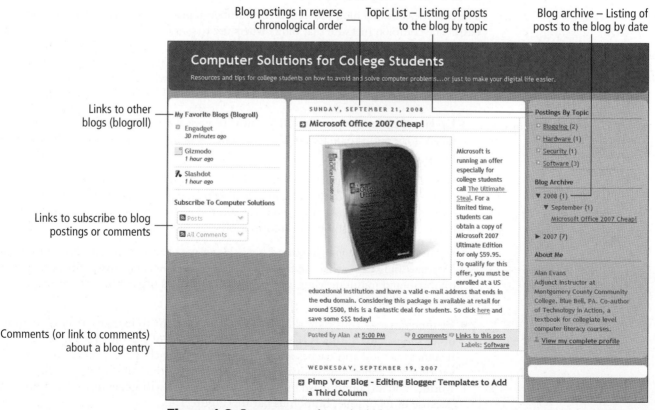

Figure 1.3 Components of a typical blog.

Explain what a blog is, the popular types of blogs, and the typical features of a blog   **5**

subject—or sometimes almost anything that comes to mind—in a running commentary. Personal blogs can have many purposes, such as:

- keeping friends and family informed of events in the blogger's life
- offering opinions on political and social issues
- informing others of a hobby about which the blogger is knowledgeable

■ Political blogs – Political candidates discovered the power of communicating through blogs during the campaigns preceding the 2004 presidential election, and political blogs continue to be influential today.

■ Social awareness blogs – Many nonprofit organizations or groups promoting social causes (such as recycling, gun control, and so on) use blogs to disseminate their message.

■ Media blogs – Many blogs (such as the Huffington Post at www.huffingtonpost .com) have become media outlets in their own right. Bloggers often report breaking news events before traditional media outlets (like televisions and newspapers) pick up on the stories. An interesting subcategory of media blogs is the expert or celebrity blog. Many journalists have their own blogs, apart from their regular news jobs. Similarly, quite a few celebrities of movie, TV, music, or sports fame have begun blogging too.

■ Corporate blogs – Businesses use blogs to reach their customers and inform them of new products and product enhancements. Small businesses especially like using blogs, because the cost is very reasonable, and may even be free, if you use the right blogging website.

Objective 3

Explain the characteristics of successful blogs

What makes a blog successful?

The best measure of a blog's success is the number of people that read it on a regular basis. The common measure that blog owners use to gauge their sites' popularity is how many *unique visitors* (different people that visit a website) and *page views* (each time a web page is loaded in a browser) their blogs generate each day. The ultimate goal for your blog is to keep readers returning by providing them with compelling information. To ensure readers will return on a regular basis, you should follow these guidelines:

■ Update the blog frequently – If a visitor to your blog comes back and there is no new information to be found, they are much less likely to visit your blog in the future.

■ Keep blog posts on topic – All blog posts should relate to the topic of your blog. If you are blogging about cool, new rock bands, don't suddenly start posting entries about the funny thing your cat did today. Irrelevant posts will make readers search for other sources of information.

■ Maintain a professional-looking blog – Having a clean, organized design for your blog and blog posts that are free of grammatical errors and misspellings helps to establish and maintain your credibility. Blog readers often equate sloppiness with inaccuracy.

■ Be innovative – Your blog should have a unique slant to it that sets it apart from other blogs. Often, this is the creative writing style of the blogger. In other instances, a blog approaches a topic in a unique way that other bloggers have not yet thought about. Cartoonist Dave Walker wrote "the dullest blog in the world," and although it isn't updated frequently, it still generates a lot of visitors because of its unique, humorous nature (Figure 1.4).

Unique visitors The number of different people who visit a website with a specific time period

Page views The number of times a web page is loaded in a browser

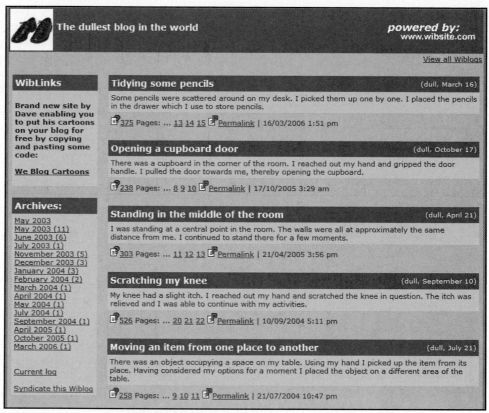

Figure 1.4 The dullest blog in the world is pretty unexciting, but it is a unique idea and generates a lot of visitors to the blog.

- Connect with others – Bloggers often permit readers to leave comments on a blog post to encourage interaction. The comments are visible to all readers of the blog. Successful bloggers also connect with other bloggers whom they admire or who maintain blogs which would be of interest to their readers. Links to these other sites are a common feature on blogs.

Blog directories Listings of blog sites, usually organized by topic

- Become indexed in search engines and blog directories – Your blog will only get visitors if people can find it. Having your blog indexed in search engines and *blog directories* (listings of blog sites usually organized by topic) will help people find your blog. If you are blogging about restoring your 1968 Mustang to original factory condition, you certainly want your site to appear in the results list when someone conducts a search for *restoring 1968 Mustangs*.

Objective 4

Plan a blog and identify a free blog hosting service

What steps should I take when planning my blog?

Although you may be eager to start generating posts for your blog, you should step back and think carefully about your blog before you begin. Addressing the following issues up front can save you a lot of time and perhaps prevent you from having to make extensive changes to your blog—or possibly even start over—in the future.

- What is your topic? – You obviously need a topic, and careful thought needs to go into the subject areas your blog will encompass. If your topic is too broad (i.e., saving energy), you may not attract much readership because people searching the web are often looking for specific information. Conversely, if your topic is too narrow (i.e., compact fluorescent lamps), you may quickly run out of things about which you can blog. A happy medium might be energy-saving tips for the home and office. After you hit all the basic tips (like installing automatic thermostats to control the temperature, putting adequate insulation in your attic, and so on), you should still have plenty to write about, because new energy-saving appliances and products are released all the time.

- What will you call your blog? – Selecting a title for a blog is important because it sets the tone for your blog. Additionally, because visitors often find a blog by using a search engine, the right title is critical for directing this search engine traffic to your blog. You should avoid using cutesy names or clever plays on words unless you are creating a personal blog. If you are developing a blog for commercial purposes, think about the key words someone would type into a search engine (such as Google), then work those key words into your blog title. Green Computing Tips would be a better title for a blog than Techno Green. Although Techno Green sounds cool, few people are likely to type that phrase in a search engine.

- What will you choose for your URL? – The Uniform Resource Locater (URL) is your blog's website address; it's what people will type into the browser's address box to reach your site. Ideally, your URL should be the same as, or similar to, your blog's title. However, it is best if the URL is concise and easy to remember. Your URL also needs to be unique—something that no one else has chosen. Key words can be helpful in this situation too. If you are using a blogging tool such as Blogger to host your blog, part of the address may also include the hosting site's domain name. Blogs created on Blogger typically include blogspot.com as the final part of the URL, so the full URL for your blog might be http://mythoughts.blogspot.com.

- How often will you post? – This is often determined by how much time you have to devote to your blog. If you are blogging only for personal fulfillment or to communicate with family and friends, the frequency of your posts is not that important. However, if you are trying to build a community and generate lots of visitors to your blog—perhaps in the hopes of making money from it—you need to be prepared to blog on a regular basis (several times per week or even daily).

- Will you accept comments? – When you set up your blog, you can select whether to allow readers to leave comments on posts. Some bloggers choose not to allow comments because managing comments can be time consuming. You need to review posts to delete inappropriate comments or offensive remarks (such as racist rhetoric or hate speech). You also will need to manage *blog spam*, which are comments that are posted to your blog by automated programs to specifically promote a product or website. If building a community is critical to the theme of your blog, you should probably allow comments. But you need to allow time to manage comments as well as create new posts.

Blog spam Comments that are posted to a blog by automated programs to specifically promote a product or website

- Will you accept posts written by others? – On a personal blog, you may want friends and family to be able to post entries. Corporate blogs may have several authors, each writing about a specific topic or area of interest. If you are trying to grow a blog into a major web destination, you may not be able to keep up with the demand for content. You may need to take on other blog authors to generate posts.

Where can I set up a blog?

There are numerous websites that provide free hosting for blogs, including Blogger (www.blogger.com), WordPress (www.wordpress.com), and LiveJournal (www.livejournal.com). Starting off your personal blog on a free site is usually a good idea. If you lose interest in your blog or lack the time to maintain it properly, you won't have invested any money in it. However, if you are considering launching a commercial blog site, you may want to locate a hosting service and register a domain name there instead of on one of the free sites. Having your own domain name makes your site appear more credible and professional. It also implies that you are serious about your topic and not just creating a blog on a whim. Hosting service fees vary depending upon the features you want to include in your plan, but many are quite affordable. The free hosting sites do impose some limitations on the features you can have on your blog, and you may not want these restrictions if your blog becomes very popular. Also, because free sites usually provide a URL that includes a common domain name, it is obvious to visitors that you are hosting on a free site, and that might detract from your blog's professional image.

In the next section, we'll use Blogger.com to set up an account and create your first blog.

Objective 5

Set up an account at Blogger.com and create a blog

Blogger.com is a site owned by Google where anyone can set up a blog for free. In the following hands-on exercises, you will set up your first blog and launch yourself into the blogosphere!

Hands-On Exercises

For purposes of the hands-on exercises in this chapter, we are assuming that Professor Schmeckendorf, a computer science professor at Ginormous State University (GSU), is setting up a blog for his computer literacy students to inform them about aspects of information technology that can make their lives easier.

1 | Setting Up a Blogger Account and Your First Blog

Steps: 1. Start Your Browser and Navigate to Blogger.com **2.** Create a Google Account **3.** Name Your Blog and Create a Uniform Resource Locator (URL) for Your Blog **4.** Select a Template for Your Blog and Create the Blog

Use Figures 1.5 through 1.11 as a guide in the exercise.

Start Your Browser and Navigate to Blogger.com

Refer to Figure 1.5 as you complete Step 1.

a. Turn on the computer.

b. Start your preferred browser, such as Internet Explorer, Firefox, or Safari. Type **www.blogger.com** in the address box of your browser.

c. If you are using a language other than English, select it from the drop-down menu.

Blogger supports over 40 languages.

d. If you already have a Google account, you may sign in to Blogger with your Google username (usually your email address) and password. Then click the **Sign In** button to enter the Blogger website. If you have never used Blogger before, you will be asked to define a username for yourself—for creating blog posts—and agree to Blogger's terms of service. Then you should proceed to Step 3.

e. If you do not already have a Google account, click the **Create Your Blog Now** arrow to begin the sign-up process for a Google account.

C – Select language here

D – Type existing Google Username and Password if you have them; then click Sign In

E – Click here to create a Google account if you don't have one

Figure 1.5 Hands-On Exercise 1, Step 1.

 Create a Google Account

Refer to Figure 1.6 as you complete Step 2.

a. Type a valid email address where indicated.

You will be required to validate this email address after signing up for a Google account; therefore, the email account needs to already exist before you begin this process.

b. Type the email address again to verify that you have typed it correctly.

c. Type a password that is at least 8 characters long.

A password with a mixture of uppercase and lowercase letters, combined with numbers or other symbols, makes a strong password.

You only see dots when you type your password. This is a security feature to prevent others from seeing your password as you type it.

d. Type the password again to check for typing errors; both passwords must match exactly.

e. Type the name you wish displayed as the author when you create a post.

This can be any name you choose—even a fictitious one. You may wish to avoid putting your real name here to help keep your identity private.

f. Type the distorted letters shown above the box into the text box.

The computer program being used here is known as a *CAPTCHA* (Completely Automated Public Turing test to tell Computers and Humans Apart). A CAPTCHA is a program that helps protect websites from having software programs (known as bots) execute procedures on the sites (in this case, signing up for a Google account). The CAPTCHA program generates a test that humans can pass but automated computer programs will fail. Humans are proficient at reading distorted text—shown here in blue. Computer programs cannot read the text and will not enter it accurately. Google does not want automated programs setting up thousands of Google accounts which could be used for nefarious operations such as spamming.

g. Click the link to the Terms of Service and read them. Click the checkbox to check it, indicating your agreement with the terms of service.

h. Click the **Continue** arrow to establish your Google account and proceed to the next step.

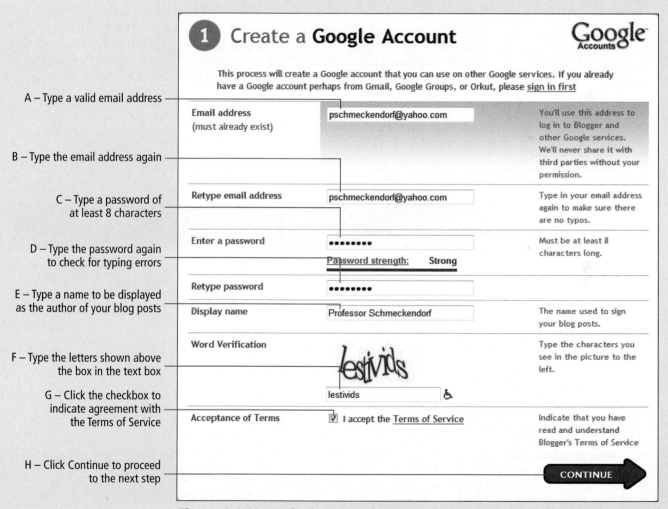

Figure 1.6 Hands-On Exercise 1, Step 2.

Step 3

Name Your Blog and Create a Uniform Resource Locator (URL) for Your Blog

Refer to Figure 1.7 as you complete Step 3.

a. Type a title for your blog.

The name of your blog should help define the topic of your blog. You can always change the name later if you decide something else would be more appropriate.

b. Type a URL for your blog.

The URL for your blog is very important because this is what people will type into their browser's address box to navigate to your blog. All blogs hosted by Blogger end in blogspot.com, but Blogger permits you to define the first part of the URL for your blog. Picking a URL that contains key words that someone would use in a search engine when looking for a blog on your chosen topic is highly recommended.

c. Click the **Check Availability** link to see if the URL you have chosen is available within the blogspot.com domain.

Figure 1.7 Hands-On Exercise 1, Step 3.

Someone else may already be using the URL that you have chosen. If so, you will need to select another URL and click the Check Availability link again to see if your second choice is available for your use.

d. Click the **Continue** arrow to set up your chosen URL and proceed to the next step.

Step 4 Select a Template for Your Blog and Create the Blog

Refer to Figures 1.8 through 1.10 as you complete Step 4.

a. Use the scroll bar to view the available blog templates.

To make designing your blog easier, Blogger has prepared a number of standard templates that you can use to create a blog with a professionally designed appearance, even if you don't have great design skills. The Preview Template link allows you to see how your blog will look before making a decision. You can always change your template later if you decide that you don't like it, and your existing blog entries will automatically adjust to the new style.

b. Click the option button next to the title of the template you prefer to select it.

> **Tip** ⭐ **Using Templates That Are Not Standard Templates**
>
> What if you don't like any of the templates that Blogger is offering? There are plenty of free templates available on the web, designed for people to use with Blogger. Just go to Google and search with the key words *Blogger templates*; you should find plenty to choose from.

c. Click the **Continue** arrow to finish creating your blog.

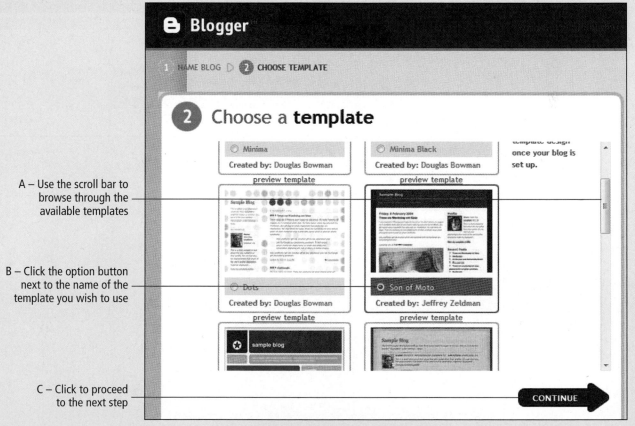

A – Use the scroll bar to browse through the available templates

B – Click the option button next to the name of the template you wish to use

C – Click to proceed to the next step

Figure 1.8 Hands-On Exercise 1, Steps 4a through 4c.

d. On the blog creation confirmation screen, click the **Start Blogging** arrow to proceed to the Create Post screen.

D – Click to proceed to the Create Post screen

Figure 1.9 Hands-On Exercise 1, Step 4d.

We'll cover creating blog entries in Hands-On Exercise 2. For now, we'll only view the blog we created.

e. On the Create Post screen, click the **View Blog** link to display the blog you just created.

E – Click the View Blog link to view the blog

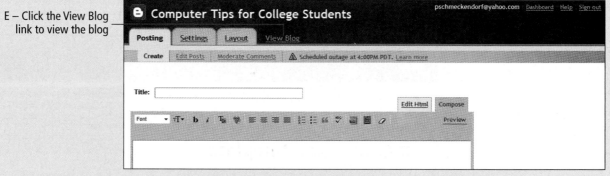

Figure 1.10 Hands-On Exercise 1, Step 4e.

The blog you created should look similar to what is shown in Figure 1.11. Your blog may look different because of the template you selected in Step 4b. Obviously, the information in the About Me section will reflect information about you and not Professor Schmeckendorf.

Figure 1.11 The blog you created should look similar to the one shown here. Your blog is now set up and ready for your first post.

You may now sign out of Blogger by clicking the Sign Out link in the upper right corner of the screen. You can also close your browser.

Objective 6

Create a blog post and publish your blog

Now that you have your blog set up, you are ready to write your first blog post. To generate effective blog posts, you should keep these guidelines in mind:

- Stay on topic – You should ensure that all blog posts are related to the theme of your blog. Professor Schmeckendorf's blog is designed to provide his students with helpful tips about computing; therefore, a good first post for his blog would be to direct students to a source of discounted software.

- Appropriate length – Given the vast amount of information available on the Internet and the limited time many web surfers have to find and use this information, you should try to keep your blog posts concise and to the point. A good target is 75 to 175 words, depending on the information being conveyed. Posts that direct someone to another site might be rather short. Sometimes you will need to have a longer post to convey a great deal of important information. But if your post is running longer than 300 words, you might want to consider breaking it up into several smaller posts.

- Links to other blogs and websites – Many posts reference information on other blogs or other websites. You should make sure to include clickable links in your blog post to make it easy for your readers to navigate to other relevant sites.

- Appropriate use of media – Many beginning bloggers get carried away with video and images in their posts. A blog conveys information primarily through the use of text. Don't overwhelm your audience by the use of gratuitous multimedia. Also, make sure you have permission to use the images and video you place on your blog. Most media is copyrighted and requires the permission of the copyright holder before you can use it. Don't just copy images you find on the web and post them on your blog site; this is often a copyright violation. Flickr (www.flickr.com) is a good site to find images because many Flickr posters—though not all—grant blanket permission to use their images. Morgue-File (www.morguefile.com) is another site that features free, high-resolution digital stock photography.

- Effective post title – The post title is extremely important because search engines index the titles of blog posts. Therefore, to drive traffic to your blog, use key words in your post titles that people might use to search for information on your post topic. A post titled My Summer Vacation might not generate much traffic, but one titled Hiking in the Grand Canyon – Bright Angel Trail is much more descriptive and uses more words that someone might enter into a search engine.

Hands-On Exercises

2 | Creating and Publishing Blog Posts

Steps: 1. Start Your Browser and Sign In to Blogger.com **2.** Write a Blog Post and Publish It to Your Blog

Use Figures 1.5 through 1.16 as a guide in the exercise.

 Step 1

Start Your Browser and Sign In to Blogger.com

Refer to Figures 1.12 and 1.13 as you complete Step 1.

a. Open a web browser and navigate to www.blogger.com.

b. Type the email address you used to sign up for your Blogger account in the Username box.

c. Type the password for your Blogger account in the Password box.

d. Click the **Sign In** button to access your Blogger account.

If you receive a message that your username and password do not match, you may have mistyped one of them. Also, check to ensure that the Caps Lock is not engaged on your keyboard, as username and passwords are case sensitive.

 Using the Remember Me Feature

If you are the only person using your computer, you may wish to select the checkbox next to the words Remember me? before clicking the Sign In button. This creates a cookie file on your computer that will automatically sign you in to the Blogger site when you return to the site. The cookie will be effective for two weeks, after which time you will need to sign in again. You should not select the Remember me? feature when you are using a public or shared computer, such as one in a computer lab at your school. If you do, any person using that same computer will have access to your blog.

The Remember me? checkbox should not be checked when using a public computer

D – Click to access your Blogger account

B – Type your email address in the Username box

C – Type your password in the Password box

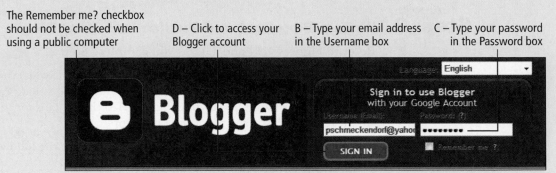

Figure 1.12 Hands-On Exercise 2, Steps 1b through 1d.

After you set up your account, the first screen you will see when you log in to Blogger is the Dashboard (Figure 1.13). The Dashboard is a summary screen where you can see and manage all the blogs in your account. You can create multiple blogs and manage them from a single Blogger account. You will also see system messages from Blogger administrators, indicated by a yellow triangle. These messages may or may not affect you. Click on the ones that interest you; ignore those that don't.

 Alert!

> If you see a message on your Dashboard that says you have not verified your email address, you should log in to the email account that you used when you created your Blogger account. There should be an email message from Blogger that contains a hyperlink for you to click to verify your email account. Blogger wants to know that your email account is a real, active account. If you can't find the email message, look in your spam (or junk mail) folder. If you never received the message, click the *Resend Verification Email* link on your Dashboard to receive a duplicate verification email.

e. Click the **New Post** button to navigate to the Create Post screen.

Click here to create a new blog

Pay attention to messages in this section

E – Click here to go to the Create Post screen

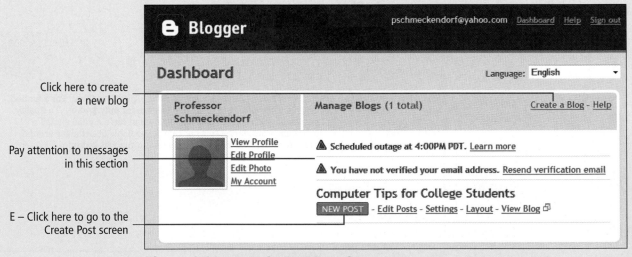

Figure 1.13 Hands-On Exercise 2, Step 1e.

Step 2 Write a Blog Post and Publish It to Your Blog

Refer to Figures 1.14 and 1.15 as you complete Step 2.

Blogger has three main screens (Postings, Settings, and Layout) that you access through navigation tabs. Each tab contains several subtabs that provide options for working on your blog. As shown in Figure 1.14, the subtabs for the Posting screen are Create, Edit Posts, and Moderate Comments.

a. Create a title for your blog post in the title box. Type the following text:

Microsoft Office 2007 for Students - Cheap!

b. Add the text for your post in the large text box in the center of the screen. Type the following text:

Microsoft is running an offer especially for college students call The Ultimate Steal. For a limited time, students can obtain a copy of Microsoft 2007 Ultimate Edition for only $59.95. To qualify for this offer, you must be enrolled at a US educational institution and have a valid e-mail address that ends in the edu domain. Considering this package is available at retail for around $500, this is a fantastic deal for students. So check it out and save some $$$ today!

c. Click the **Check Spelling** button to review the contents of your post for correct spelling. Click on any highlighted misspelled words to receive suggestions for the correct spellings. You can also delete a word and retype it correctly.

Although the spell-check tool in Blogger will find spelling errors, it does not check your entry for proper grammar. Make sure to review your post carefully for grammatical errors.

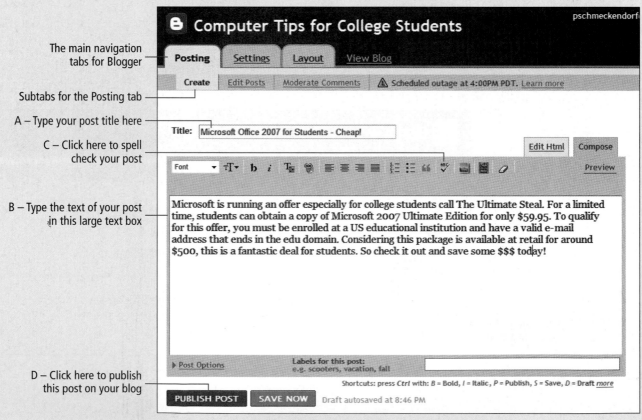

Figure 1.14 Hands-On Exercise 2, Steps 2a through 2d.

d. Click the **Publish Post** button to publish the entry to your blog and make it visible to readers. If you aren't yet ready to publish the post but wish to save the work you have done so far, click the **Save Now** button to save the post as a draft. Draft posts are not visible on your blog.

Figure 1.15 shows the message that is displayed on the Create screen directly after you have successfully published a blog entry. You should now view your blog and make sure that the entry looks the way you wish it to look on your blog.

e. Click either of the **View Blog** links to view your blog.

E – Click here to view your blog

Figure 1.15 Hands-On Exercise 2, Step 2e.

Figure 1.16 shows the blog with the first post. When you post an entry to a blog, the date and time you created it is assigned to the post, and the date is displayed on the blog post. Blogs display posts in reverse chronological order, so your most recent post will appear at the top of your blog. By default, Blogger includes a blog archive by month on your blog. Notice that the first post now appears in the blog archive.

You should now practice making posts to your blog. Click the New Post link at the top of the screen to navigate back to the Posting tab in Blogger. Repeat Steps 2a through 2d to create and publish at least two more posts to your blog before proceeding to Hands-On Exercise 3.

Click here to start your next post

Date you created the post

Post appears in blog archive

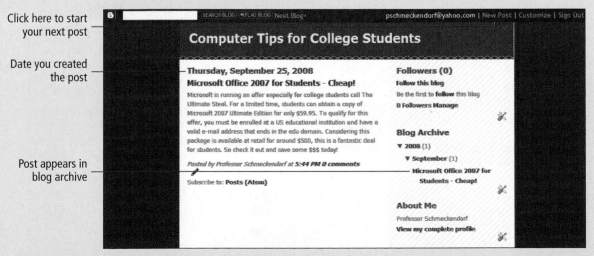

Figure 1.16 The first post on a blog.

Objective 7
Edit a previously published blog post

After publishing a post, you might think of additional information that you need to add. Or you might spot a spelling or grammar mistake in the post that you previously missed. Fortunately, Blogger provides you with an easy way to edit previously published blog posts.

Hands-On Exercises

3 | Editing a Blog Post

Steps: 1. Select the Blog Post to Edit **2.** Add a Live Hyperlink to a Post **3.** Change the Formatting of Text **4.** Correct a Mistake and Add Text to a Post

Use Figures 1.17 through 1.25 as a guide in the exercise.

Step 1 Select the Blog Post to Edit

Refer to Figures 1.17 and 1.18 as you complete Step 1.

a. Sign in to your Blogger account.

b. From the Dashboard screen, click the **Edit Posts** link to go to the Manage Posts page. The Edit Posts subtab will be active.

If you are already logged in to your Blogger account and are viewing your blog, you can click the New Post link displayed in the upper right corner of the screen (Figure 1.16). This will take you to the Create Post page. The Create subtab will be active. Click the **Edit Posts** subtab (Figure 1.14) to navigate to the Edit Posts page (Figure 1.18).

B – Click to navigate to the Edit Posts page

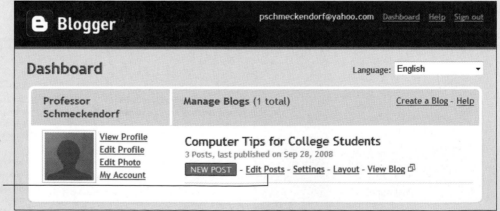

Figure 1.17 Hands-On Exercise 3, Step 1b.

The Edit Posts subtab lists all of the posts on your blog. As shown in Figure 1.18, there are currently three posts on our sample blog; your blog may have more or less, depending on how much you have done on your own. On this screen, you can manage your posts by viewing, editing, or deleting them.

c. Locate the *Microsoft Office 2007 for Students* post you created in Exercise 2. Click the **Edit** link next to the title to enter the editing mode.

C – Click the Edit link to revise the Microsoft Office 2007 for Students post

Figure 1.18 Hands-On Exercise 3, Step 1c.

 Add a Live Hyperlink to a Post

Refer to Figures 1.19 and 1.20 as you complete Step 2.

The Edit Posts screen looks almost identical to the Create Posts screen and it provides the same functionality. It would be helpful to add a hyperlink to our posting to direct students to the Microsoft site so that they can take advantage of the special offer. Your readers will appreciate links that make it easy for them to navigate to relevant pages. Therefore, we will now turn the phrase "The Ultimate Steal" into a live hyperlink.

a. Locate the phrase *The Ultimate Steal* in the first line of the blog post. Click directly to the left of the *T* in the phrase and, while holding the left mouse button down, move the cursor to the right to select (or highlight) the entire phrase *The Ultimate Steal*. Then release the left mouse button.

b. Click the **Link** button to display the Hyperlink dialog box.

B – Click the Link button to display the Hyperlink dialog box

A – Click and drag the mouse to highlight *The Ultimate Steal*

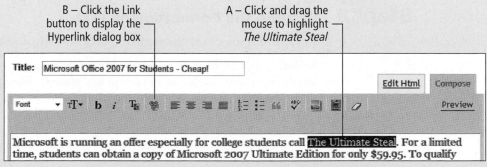

Figure 1.19 Hands-On Exercise 3, Steps 2a and 2b.

c. Type the URL of the website that you wish to use for the link in the URL text box of the Hyperlink dialog box. Type the following text:

http://theultimatesteal.com

Alert!

For your link to work, it must begin with **http://**. This text appears by default in the URL text box, so be sure not to delete it when you are typing your URL.

Copy a Long URL Name from Your Browser Address Window

If you are creating a link to a website that has a lengthy URL, open a new tab in your browser and browse to the website. Highlight the URL address in your browser's address window, then right-click to display the shortcut menu and select Copy. Return to your blog and perform Step 3c. Click in the URL box of the Hyperlink dialog box to select it. Be sure that the default text already in the URL box is selected, then right-click and select Paste from the shortcut menu options. This will ensure that you have entered the URL correctly and that you have not duplicated the http:// portion of the URL.

d. Click **OK** in the Hyperlink dialog box.

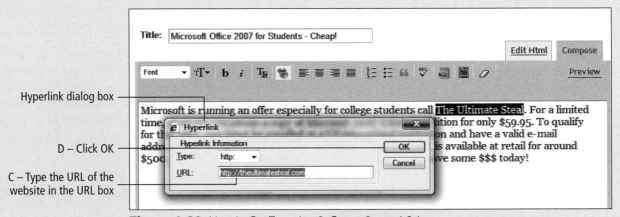

Hyperlink dialog box

D – Click OK

C – Type the URL of the website in the URL box

Figure 1.20 Hands-On Exercise 3, Steps 2c and 2d.

The text is now a clickable hyperlink, as shown in Figure 1.21.

Step 3 **Change the Formatting of Text**

Refer to Figures 1.21 through 1.23 as you complete Step 3.

Sometimes you will need to change the formatting of text in your post to add emphasis or draw attention to certain key phrases. Blogger provides you with some formatting options that should be familiar to you if you have used Microsoft Office before. Figure 1.21 identifies just a few of the options you can use to format text. You should use the formatting options carefully. Using too many colors, fonts, or other effects may actually be distracting for your viewers and make your blog appear amateurish.

Click to change the color
of the selected text

Text is now a
clickable hyperlink

Click the Font drop-down
arrow to select different fonts

Click to bold selected text

Click to italicize selected text

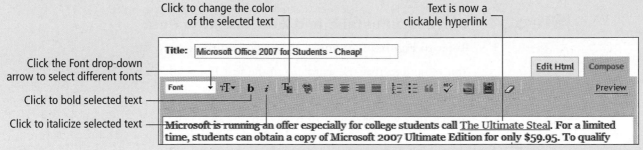

Figure 1.21 Hands-On Exercise 3, Step 3.

Before formatting text, the text must be selected. In the current post, it is important for students to know that they must have an email address that is in the edu domain. Therefore, it would be a good idea to format the phrase *edu domain* as bold text so that it stands out from the other text. And we can change the $$$ to a green font color to draw attention to the money-saving aspect of the offer.

a. Select the text *edu domain*.

b. Click **Bold** to change the text to bold.

B – Click to make the
selected text bold

A – Select the text
to be formatted

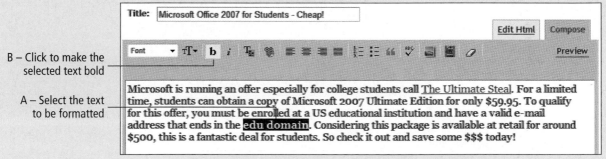

Figure 1.22 Hands-On Exercise 3, Steps 3a and 3b.

c. Select the text *$$$*.

d. Click the **Text Color** button to display the color choices grid.

e. Click one of the green squares from the color choices grid to change the selected text to green.

D – Click to display the
color choices grid

E – Click one of the green
squares to change the
selected text to green

C – Select the text
to be formatted

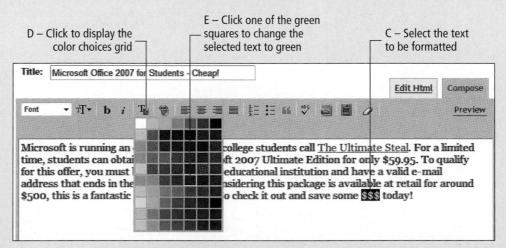

Figure 1.23 Hands-On Exercise 3, Steps 3c through 3e.

Step 4 **Correct a Mistake and Add Text to a Post**

Refer to Figures 1.24 and 1.25 as you complete Step 4.

You've noticed that the word *call* in the first line really should be *called*. And you remember that you need to remind students that although they can download the software from the website, they should consider purchasing the software on DVD so that they will have a backup copy in case they need it. You can edit the blog entry just like you would edit a Microsoft Word document by adding, changing, or deleting text.

a. Position your insertion point directly after the word *call* in the first line of the blog post. Type **ed** to make the correction.

b. Position your insertion point at the end of the blog post after *today!* Press **Enter** twice to start a new paragraph. Type the following text into the blog post window:

> **Even though you can download the software from the Web site, you should also consider purchasing (for an additional fee) the software on DVD. This will make reinstalling the software much easier in the future in case you have a problem (such as your hard drive fails).**

c. Now that all of your edits are finished, click the **Publish Post** button to post the revised entry.

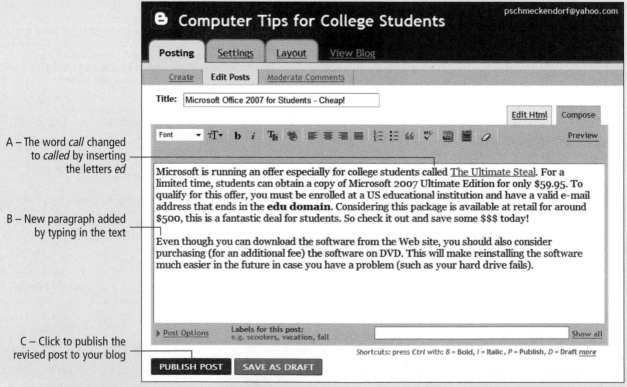

A – The word *call* changed to *called* by inserting the letters *ed*

B – New paragraph added by typing in the text

C – Click to publish the revised post to your blog

Figure 1.24 Hands-On Exercise 3, Steps 4a through 4c.

Click the link to view your blog with the revised blog entry (Figure 1.25). Notice that the date and time of the blog post does not change so that it will appear in the same sequence among blog entries as it did before you revised it.

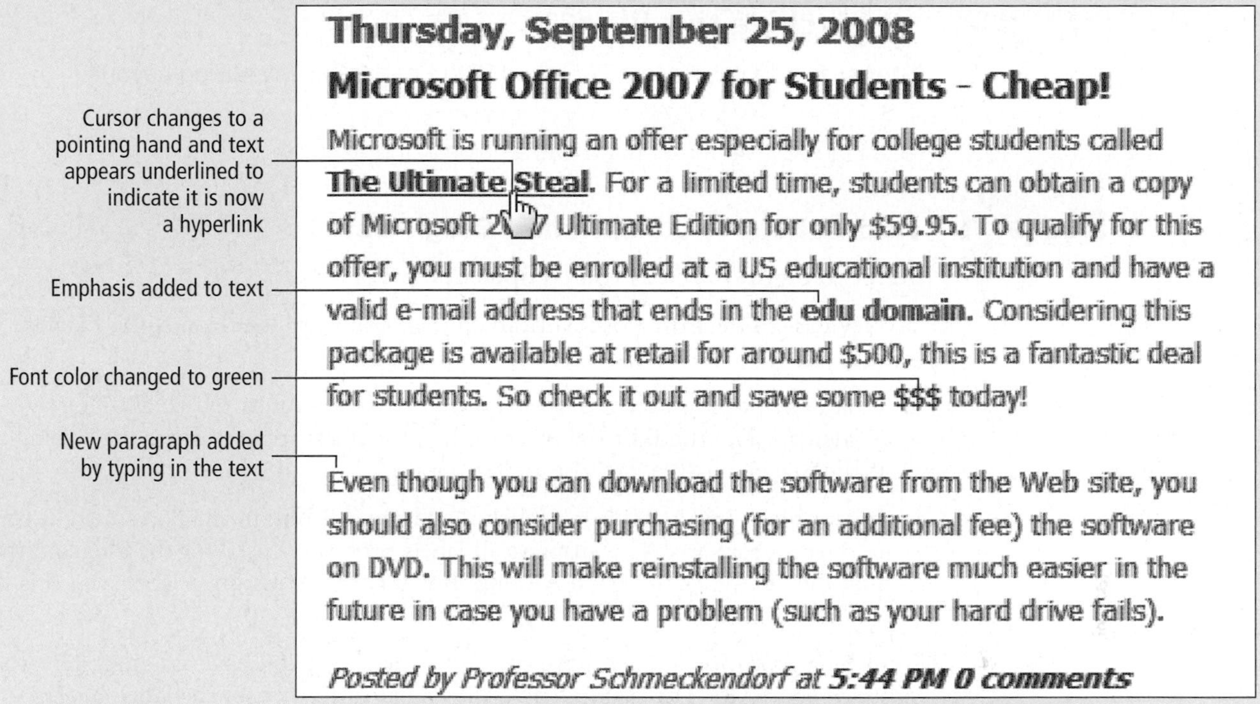

Cursor changes to a pointing hand and text appears underlined to indicate it is now a hyperlink

Emphasis added to text

Font color changed to green

New paragraph added by typing in the text

Thursday, September 25, 2008
Microsoft Office 2007 for Students - Cheap!

Microsoft is running an offer especially for college students called **The Ultimate Steal**. For a limited time, students can obtain a copy of Microsoft 2007 Ultimate Edition for only $59.95. To qualify for this offer, you must be enrolled at a US educational institution and have a valid e-mail address that ends in the **edu domain**. Considering this package is available at retail for around $500, this is a fantastic deal for students. So check it out and save some $$$ today!

Even though you can download the software from the Web site, you should also consider purchasing (for an additional fee) the software on DVD. This will make reinstalling the software much easier in the future in case you have a problem (such as your hard drive fails).

Posted by Professor Schmeckendorf at 5:44 PM 0 comments

Figure 1.25 Blog posting after edits.

Objective 8

Create labels and add a category archive to a blog

Although there is a blog archive of postings by date on the blog you created, readers often need a better way to find the material that they are interested in on your blog. Once a blog has many posts, it can be tedious to wade through date archives, reading blog post titles to sort out which entries are relevant. Organizing your posts by topic gives your readers a quick way to zero in on information relevant to them and makes your blog much more user-friendly.

Labels Topics or categories that are created by you to describe your blog posts

Blogger allows you to assign labels to your blog posts. *Labels* are topics or categories that are created by you to describe your blog posts. You can create as many different labels as you need to categorize your blog. You should assign labels to every blog entry. You can assign labels as you create the entries or you can edit entries that have already been published and add the labels then.

Hands-On Exercises

4 | Creating Labels and Adding a Category Archive to a Blog

Steps: 1. Add Labels to a Published Blog Post **2.** Modify a Blog Layout

Use Figures 1.26 through 1.34 as a guide in the exercise.

Step 1 Add Labels to a Published Blog Post

Refer to Figure 1.26a as you complete Step 1.

a. Navigate to the **Edit Posts subtab** on the Dashboard (see Hands-On Exercise 3, Step 1).

b. Locate the posting that you made previously on Microsoft Office 2007 for Students. Click the **Edit** link next to the title of that post to enter the editing mode (see Hands-On Exercise 3, Step 1).

c. If your blog already has labels, click the **Show All** link in the bottom right corner of the post text box. This displays all labels previously used for the blog and the link then becomes the **Hide All** link. If you have not assigned labels yet, this link will not be available and you may skip this step.

Your blog probably does not have any labels yet unless you have assigned some to posts on your own. The example blog shown here already uses the labels *Saving Money*, *Security*, and *Software*. You should think about whether a post falls into any of the previously defined label categories. Because this post is about software and saving money, both of those labels should be assigned to this post. You might also decide to create a new label called MS Office (short for Microsoft Office), because Professor Schmeckendorf anticipates providing his students with lots of tips on using Microsoft Office.

It is easy to create a new label on Blogger. Just type the new label in the Labels for This Post box for a blog post. Once the post is published, the new label is applied and will be available for use on other posts.

d. In the Labels for This Post text box, type the labels **Saving Money**, **Software**, and **MS Office** for this post. When adding multiple labels, separate them by adding a comma and a space after each one in the list. You don't need to add a comma after the last label.

e. Click the **Publish Post** button to republish the post with the labels assigned to it.

Repeat Steps 1b through 1e to assign labels to all posts on your blog. Figure 1.26b shows an example of how a blog entry looks on a blog once labels have been assigned to it. Now that you have assigned labels to your blog, it is time to modify the layout by adding a category archive to the blog.

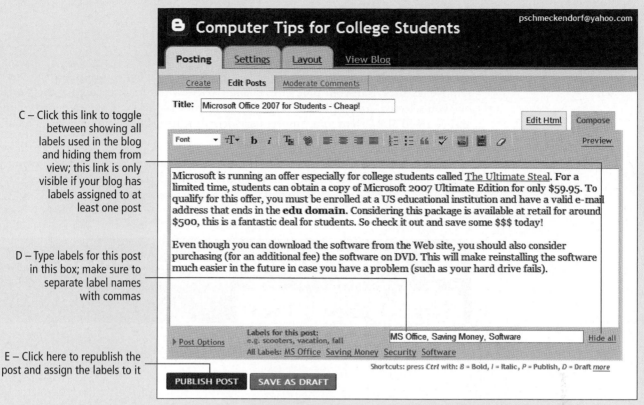

C – Click this link to toggle between showing all labels used in the blog and hiding them from view; this link is only visible if your blog has labels assigned to at least one post
D – Type labels for this post in this box; make sure to separate label names with commas
E – Click here to republish the post and assign the labels to it
Computer Tips for College Students
pschmeckendorf@yahoo.com
Posting
Settings
Layout
View Blog
Create
Edit Posts
Moderate Comments
Title:
Microsoft Office 2007 for Students - Cheap!
Edit Html
Compose
Font
Preview
Microsoft is running an offer especially for college students called The Ultimate Steal. For a limited time, students can obtain a copy of Microsoft 2007 Ultimate Edition for only $59.95. To qualify for this offer, you must be enrolled at a US educational institution and have a valid e-mail address that ends in the edu domain. Considering this package is available at retail for around $500, this is a fantastic deal for students. So check it out and save some $$$ today!
Even though you can download the software from the Web site, you should also consider purchasing (for an additional fee) the software on DVD. This will make reinstalling the software much easier in the future in case you have a problem (such as your hard drive fails).
Post Options
Labels for this post:
e.g. scooters, vacation, fall
MS Office, Saving Money, Software
Hide all
All Labels: MS Office Saving Money Security Software
Shortcuts: press Ctrl with: B = Bold, I = Italic, P = Publish, D = Draft more
PUBLISH POST
SAVE AS DRAFT

Figure 1.26a Hands-On Exercise 4, Steps 1c through 1e.

Thursday, September 25, 2008
Microsoft Office 2007 for Students - Cheap!
Microsoft is running an offer especially for college students called The Ultimate Steal. For a limited time, students can obtain a copy of Microsoft 2007 Ultimate Edition for only $59.95. To qualify for this offer, you must be enrolled at a US educational institution and have a valid e-mail address that ends in the edu domain. Considering this package is available at retail for around $500, this is a fantastic deal for students. So check it out and save some $$$ today!
Even though you can download the software from the Web site, you should also consider purchasing (for an additional fee) the software on DVD. This will make reinstalling the software much easier in the future in case you have a problem (such as your hard drive fails).
Posted by Professor Schmeckendorf at 5:44 PM 0 comments
Labels: MS Office, Saving Money, Software

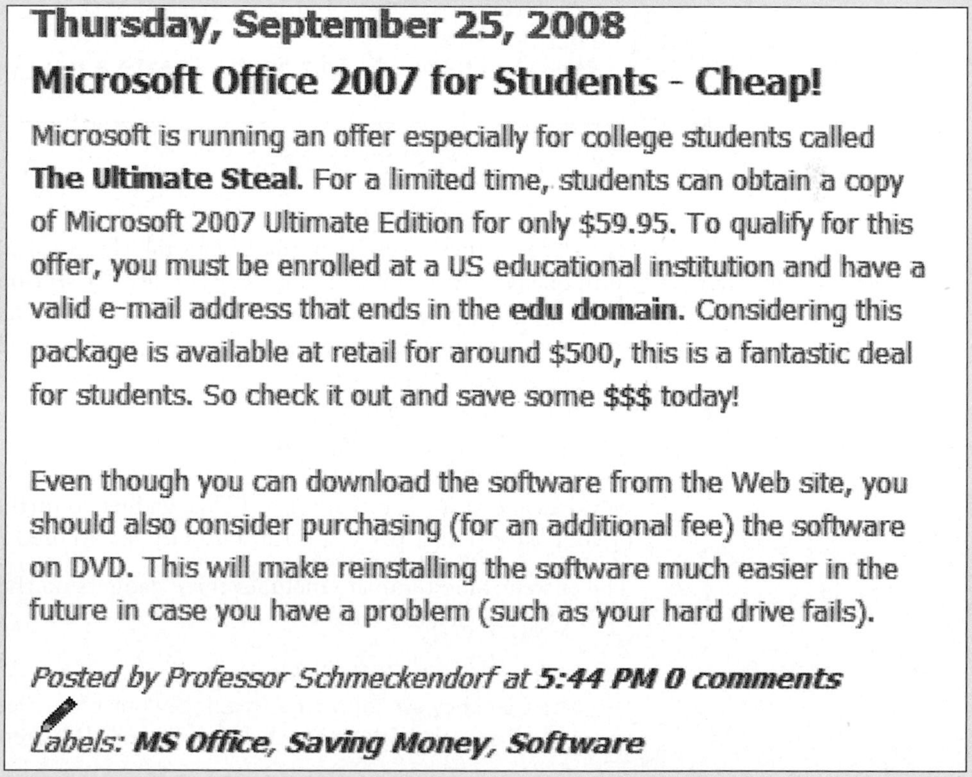

Figure 1.26b Labels assigned to a blog post appear underneath the post.

Step 2 Modify a Blog Layout

Refer to Figures 1.27 through 1.34 as you complete Step 2.

The blog layout controls what is visible on a blog. The layout tab is used to add or remove features from your blog or to change to a new template if you get tired of the one you selected. You will modify the layout of your blog to add the category archive and you will also delete some unnecessary default features that Blogger places on all blogs.

a. From the blog publishing confirmation screen—or anyplace else on the Posting tab screen—click the **Layout** tab to go to the Edit Layout page. If necessary, click the **Page Elements** subtab to make it the active tab.

A – Click here to go to the Edit Layout page

Figure 1.27 Hands-On Exercise 4, Step 2a.

Header Section of a blog that contains the title of your blog and can contain a subtitle in certain templates

Gadget A section of your blog that contains code that results in some type of functionality for your blog

The Page Elements subtab of the Layout tab (Figure 1.28) shows where the main components of your blog are located. The *header* section contains the title of your blog and can contain a subtitle in certain templates. The Blog Posts section is where your posts are located on the blog. The Gadgets sections contain the features of your blog. A *gadget* is a section of your blog that contains code that results in some type of functionality for your blog. Blog archives, clocks, calendars, and even virtual pets can be added using a gadget. Blogger provides some premade gadgets that you can easily insert into the blog layout. You can also obtain HTML code from third-party websites and place it in a special HTML gadget to further enhance the functionality of your blog. Third-party applications will be explored in Chapter 3.

The current blog template includes three gadgets on the right side that are assigned by Blogger as default gadgets:

- Followers – The Followers gadget allows registered users to click a link and indicate that they are following (reading) your blog. Because Professor Schmeckendorf doesn't wish to use this gadget, it will be removed from the blog.

- Blog Archive – The Blog Archive gadget provides a list of blog postings, grouped by month. Because this gadget is useful to many blog readers, it will remain on the blog.

- About Me – The About Me gadget shows information about the blog author that is drawn from your Blogger profile. You can add more information to your Blogger profile whenever you wish. If you don't want to be identified as the author of your blog, you should remove the About Me gadget.

Blog posts section

Header section

Gadget sections

B – Click here to display the Configure Followers List dialog box

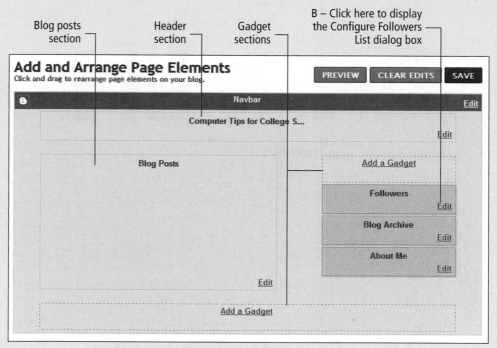

Figure 1.28 The Page Elements subtab. Hands-On Exercise 4, Step 2b.

If your blog layout screen doesn't look like the one pictured in the book, you may have chosen a different standard Blogger template than the one used in the example. Your layout should have the same sections as the one shown in the book, but those sections might be located in different places on the screen. You should be able to follow along with the rest of this section; your gadgets will have the same names as the ones in the book.

b. Click the **Edit** link in the Followers gadget box to display the Configure Followers List dialog box.

c. In the **Configure Followers List** dialog box, click **Remove**.

d. Click **OK** in the browser dialog box to confirm deletion of the Followers gadget.

Notice that the Followers gadget has now been removed from the layout screen, and a yellow box appears above the layout detailing the changes you made to the page elements (see Figure 1.30). Using a gadget to track followers of a blog is not that helpful. Other website statistics, such as unique visitors and page views, are more useful in analyzing the traffic generated by a blog.

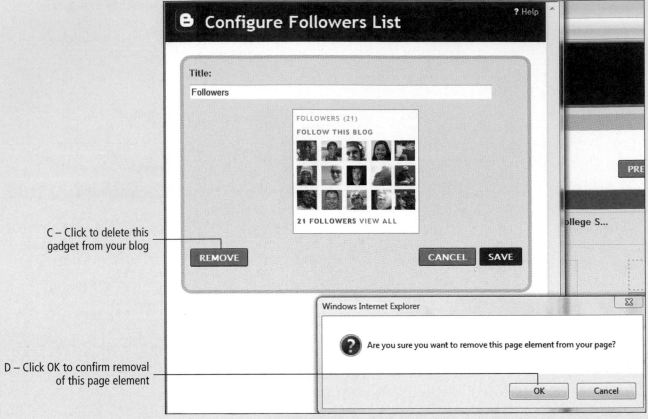

C – Click to delete this gadget from your blog

D – Click OK to confirm removal of this page element

Figure 1.29 Hands-On Exercise 4, Steps 2c and 2d.

e. Click the **Add a Gadget** link to display a list of gadgets that can be added to your blog.

f. There are many categories of gadgets. Make sure the Basics list is highlighted and displayed (Figure 1.31). If it is not, click the **Basics** link to display it.

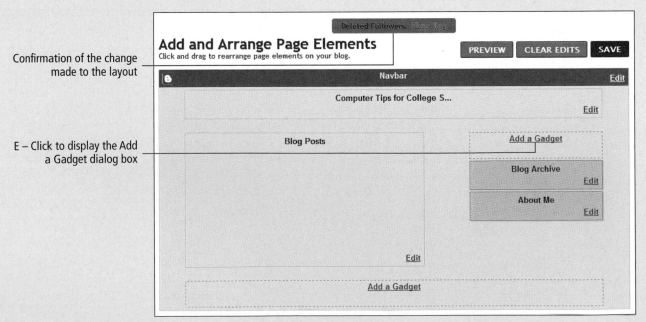

Confirmation of the change made to the layout

E – Click to display the Add a Gadget dialog box

Figure 1.30 Hands-On Exercise 4, Step 2e.

g. Use the scroll bar to scroll through the Basics list until you find the Labels gadget.

h. Click the **Add** button, which appears as a plus symbol, to display the Configure Labels dialog box.

F – Ensure that the Basics list is highlighted; if it is not, click here to display the list

G – Scroll down until you find the Labels gadget shown below

H – Click the Add button to display the Configure Labels dialog box

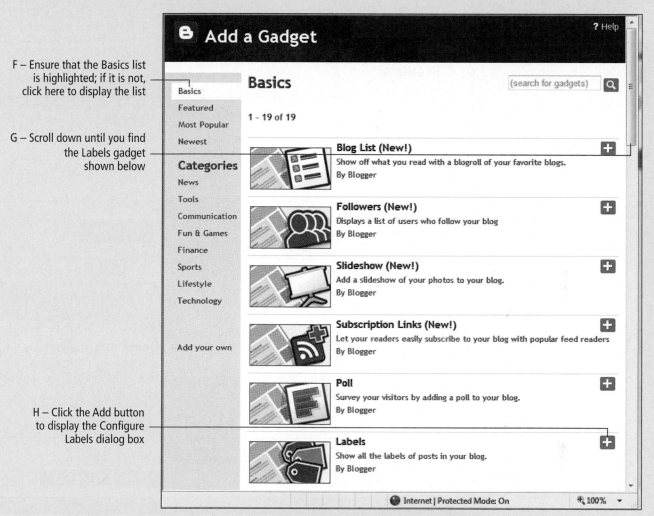

Figure 1.31 Hands-On Exercise 4, Steps 2f through 2h.

i. Type a title for your list of labels in the **Title** box. You should choose something other than labels (the default); that is probably not descriptive enough for your readers.

j. Click the appropriate option button to sort the labels alphabetically or by frequency. Frequency is determined by the number of blog posts that use each label. Sorting labels alphabetically usually makes the most sense for your readers, as it is easier to find a topic you are looking for in an alphabetical list.

k. Click the **Save** button to add the label archive to your blog.

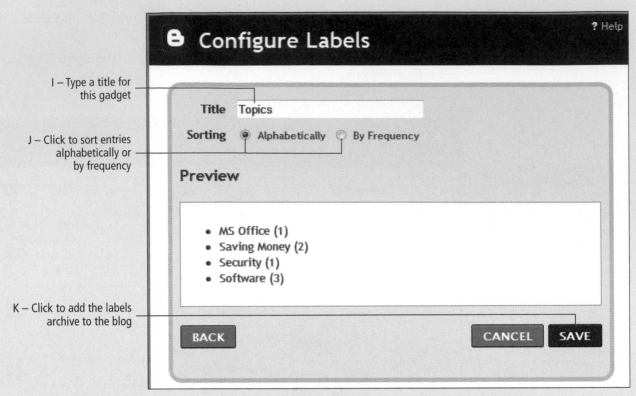

I – Type a title for this gadget

J – Click to sort entries alphabetically or by frequency

K – Click to add the labels archive to the blog

Figure 1.32 Hands-On Exercise 4, Steps 2i through 2k.

You will see that the label archive (titled *Topics*) has been added to the blog layout (Figure 1.33). At this point, the changes you have made are not yet permanently saved to your blog. You should preview the changes to ensure that your blog looks the way you intend before making the changes permanent.

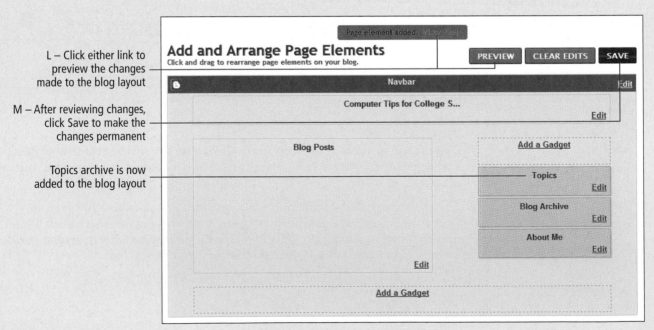

L – Click either link to preview the changes made to the blog layout

M – After reviewing changes, click Save to make the changes permanent

Topics archive is now added to the blog layout

Figure 1.33 Hands-On Exercise 4, Steps 2l and 2m.

l.   Click the **Preview** button or the **View Blog** link to display your blog (Figure 1.34). The blog will open in a new browser window. Review the blog to ensure that the changes you made appear as you expected.

The Topics archive is now displayed

The Followers gadget has been deleted

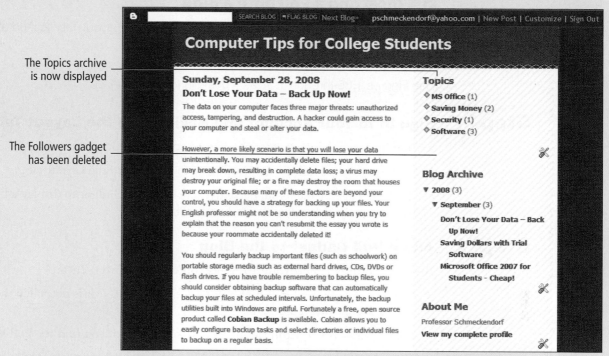

Figure 1.34 Preview of the blog after making layout changes.

m.   If the changes are correct, close the blog preview window and return to the Layout screen. Click **Save** to make the changes permanent and republish your blog. The blog should now look the way it did when you previewed it. If you do not want to save the changes you made to the blog, click the **Clear Edits** button.

The preview shows how the blog will appear to readers after the changes have been made. Notice that the Topics archive displaying the list of labels has been added, while the Followers gadget has been deleted.

Objective 9

Insert a poll onto a blog

Web users, including the readers of your blog, like the web to be interactive. Allowing users to leave comments about your blog posts is one way of encouraging interactivity and developing a sense of community. Another way is by deploying polls on your blog. The polls should pertain to the topic of your blog and should cover an issue that you think will be of interest to your readers.

Hands-On Exercises

5 | Inserting a Poll onto a Blog

Steps: 1. Sign In to Your Account and Navigate to the Layout Tab **2.** Add a Poll Gadget to the Blog

Use Figures 1.35 through 1.37 as a guide in the exercise.

Step **1** ### Sign In to Your Account and Navigate to the Layout Tab

a. Sign in to your Blogger account, if necessary.

b. Click the **Layout** link on the Dashboard to navigate to the Layout tab.

c. With the Page Elements subtab active, click **Add a Gadget** to display a list of available gadgets (see Hands-On Exercise 4, Step 2e).

Step **2** ### Add a Poll Gadget to the Blog

Refer to Figures 1.35 through 1.37 as you complete Step 2.

a. Make sure the Basics list is highlighted and displayed. If it is not, click the **Basics** link to display it (Figure 1.31).

b. Use the scroll bar to scroll through the Basics list until you find the Poll gadget.

c. Click the **Add** button—which looks like a plus symbol—next to the Poll gadget to launch the Create a Poll dialog box.

C – Click to configure your poll

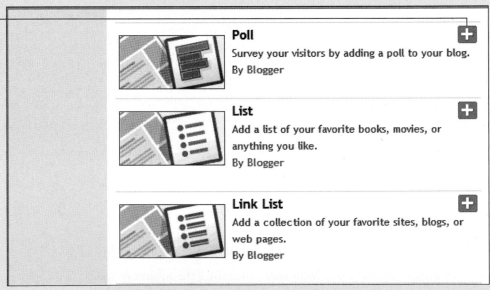

Figure 1.35 Hands-On Exercise 5, Step 2c.

d. Type your poll question in the **Question** text box.

e. Type the possible answers to the poll question in the Answers text boxes provided. If you have more boxes than you need, use the **Remove** link to delete the ones you don't want. If you need more answer boxes, click the **Add Another Answer** link to create more answer boxes.

f. Click **Save** to place the poll on your blog.

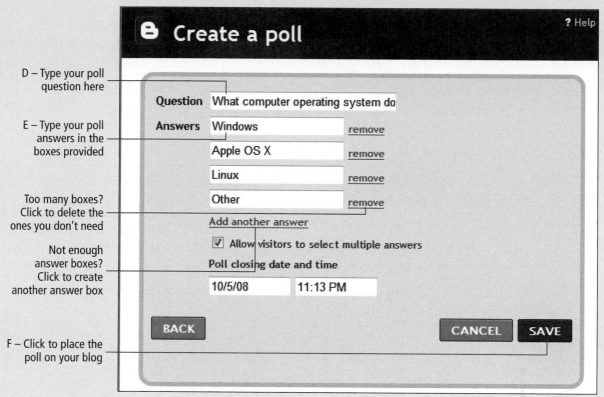

D – Type your poll question here

E – Type your poll answers in the boxes provided

Too many boxes? Click to delete the ones you don't need

Not enough answer boxes? Click to create another answer box

F – Click to place the poll on your blog

Figure 1.36 Hands-On Exercise 5, Steps 2d through 2f.

g. Click **Save** on the Page Elements subtab to save the changes to the blog layout.

h. Click any **View Blog** link to display the blog with the poll posted to it.

Your readers now merely have to select their answer from the available choices and click the Vote button to participate in the poll. Clicking the Show Results link allows readers to see the results of the voting.

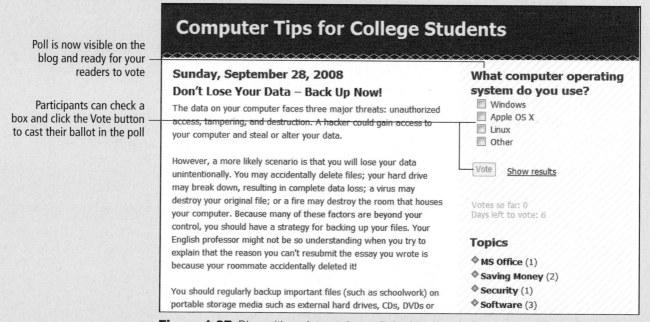

Poll is now visible on the blog and ready for your readers to vote

Participants can check a box and click the Vote button to cast their ballot in the poll

Figure 1.37 Blog with an interactive poll deployed on it.

Polls are open for voting for a limited amount of time, which you define (the default is a week). After that, the results are still shown on your blog, but visitors can no longer vote. Putting new polls up from time to time is another way to generate interest in your blog.

Objective 10

Place a link list on a blog

Regardless of the topic of your blog, you are going to find other blogs and websites that would be of interest to your readers. You can make it convenient for your blog visitors to find important websites you recommend by placing a list of hyperlinks to these sites on your blog. This list can be easily updated as you find other sites to recommend to your audience.

Hands-On Exercises

6 | Inserting a Link List onto a Blog

Steps: 1. Sign In to Your Account and Navigate to the Layout Tab **2.** Add a Link List Gadget to the Blog

Use Figures 1.38 through 1.41 as a guide in the exercise.

 Sign In to Your Account and Navigate to the Layout Tab

a. Sign in to your Blogger account, if necessary.

b. Click the **Layout** link on the Dashboard to navigate to the Layout tab.

c. With the Page Elements subtab active, click **Add a Gadget** to display a list of available gadgets (see Hands-On Exercise 4, Step 2e).

 Add a Link List Gadget to the Blog

Refer to Figures 1.38 through 1.41 as you complete Step 2.

a. Make sure the Basics list is highlighted and displayed. If it is not, click the **Basics** link to display it (Figure 1.31).

b. Use the scroll bar to scroll through the Basics list until you find the Link List gadget.

c. Click the **Add** button next to the Link List gadget to launch the Configure Link List dialog box.

C – Click to configure
your Link List

Figure 1.38 Hands-On Exercise 6, Step 2c.

Hint: Before you start configuring your Link List, you should have gathered the URLs and the titles of the websites you wish to include in your Link List.

d. Type a title for your Link List in the Title box. You should use a descriptive title that lets your blog readers know what the list is designed to do.

e. Click the **Sorting** drop-down arrow to view the available sorting options. Sort Alphabetically is probably the most useful choice for your blog visitors; it is easier to find information you are looking for in an alphabetic list.

f. In the New Site URL text box, type the URL for the first website that you wish to add to your list.

g. In the New Site Name text box, type the name of the website.

h. Click the **Add Link** button to add this site to your list and to prepare the Configure Link List dialog box to accept the next website for your list.

i. Repeat Steps 2f through 2h as many times as necessary to add all the links you have identified to your list.

j. After you have added the last link, click the Save button to deploy the Link List on your blog.

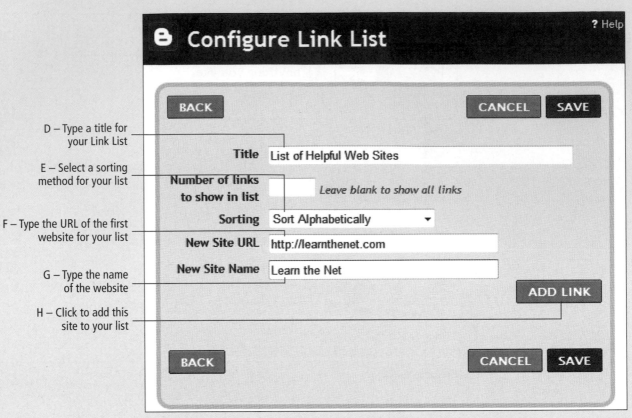

D – Type a title for your Link List

E – Select a sorting method for your list

F – Type the URL of the first website for your list

G – Type the name of the website

H – Click to add this site to your list

Configure Link List

? Help

BACK   CANCEL   SAVE

Title   List of Helpful Web Sites

Number of links to show in list   _Leave blank to show all links_

Sorting   Sort Alphabetically ▼

New Site URL   http://learnthenet.com

New Site Name   Learn the Net

ADD LINK

BACK   CANCEL   SAVE

Figure 1.39 Hands-On Exercise 6, Steps 2d through 2h.

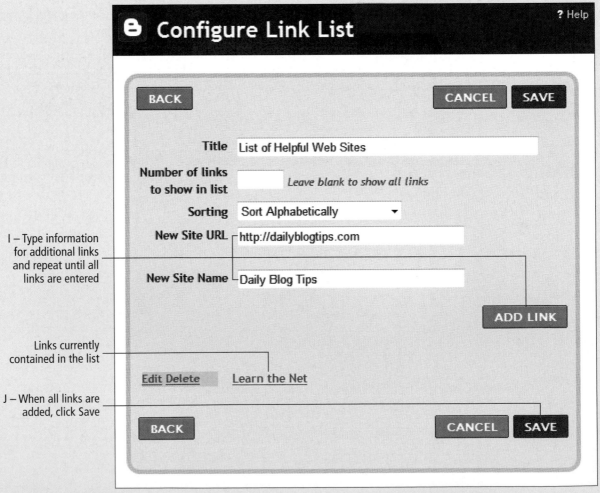

I – Type information for additional links and repeat until all links are entered

Links currently contained in the list

J – When all links are added, click Save

Configure Link List

? Help

BACK   CANCEL   SAVE

Title   List of Helpful Web Sites

Number of links to show in list   _Leave blank to show all links_

Sorting   Sort Alphabetically ▼

New Site URL   http://dailyblogtips.com

New Site Name   Daily Blog Tips

ADD LINK

Edit Delete   Learn the Net

BACK   CANCEL   SAVE

Figure 1.40 Hands-On Exercise 6, Steps 2i and 2j.

k. Click **Save** on the Page Elements subtab to save the changes to the blog layout.

l. Click any **View Blog** link to display the blog with the Link List posted to it.

m. Click the **Sign Out** link in the upper right corner of the blog to exit.

Link List is now displayed on the blog

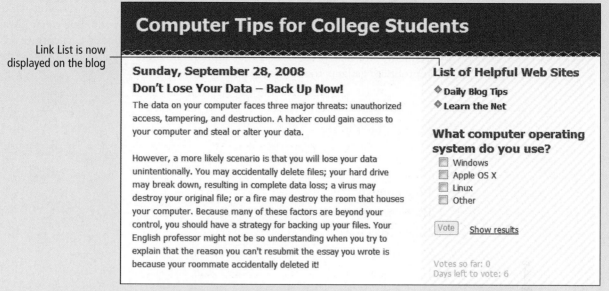

Figure 1.41 A blog after adding a Link List gadget.

Objective 11

Describe Internet resources that educate people about blogging

Because blogging has become quite popular, there is a wealth of information on the Internet that can help you learn more about creating effective blogs. In fact, there are many blogs created solely for the purpose of teaching people how to blog. Here are some resources you may want to explore:

- Daily Blog Tips (www.dailyblogtips.com) – A well-written blog by Daniel Scocco, author of several successful blogs. This blog allows Daniel to share the lessons he has learned while blogging. It offers great advice for novice and experienced bloggers in straightforward language.

- Tips for New Bloggers (www.tips-for-new-bloggers.blogspot.com) – This site is specifically designed for novice bloggers who are using the Blogger site. It's even hosted on Blogger! Although it hasn't been updated for a while, it still contains valuable information, especially on changing or modifying Blogger templates.

- Blogging Tips (www.bloggingtips.com) – Another well-crafted blog that provides advice for novice and experienced bloggers. They have an entire category of tips just for people using Blogger.

- YouTube Blogger Help (www.youtube.com/user/BloggerHelp) – Videos created by the people at Blogger to help you get started blogging. Make sure to search YouTube for other useful blogging videos. Try searching terms that involve the information you are seeking, such as *Blogger templates*.

Summary

You have now learned many of the basic skills for creating an engaging blog. Chapter 3 will cover additional areas of interest, such as modifying the layout of your blog, registering your blog with search engines to draw readers, and enhancing your blog with features that might help it to earn money. But the main thing that draws readers to a blog is interesting content. Adding cool features to your blog—like the numerous gadgets that are available in Blogger—is fun for you, but won't always appeal to your readers, who are most likely looking for information. So concentrate on writing frequent, informative blog posts that support the topic of your blog. You can always add appropriate gadgets to the blog at a later time.

Key Terms

Multiple Choice

1. Which of the following is true?

    (a) Venture capitalists were very cautious during the dot-com boom.

    (b) Venture capitalists invest only in Internet businesses.

    (c) Venture capitalists fund new ventures in exchange for shares of stock.

    (d) Venture capitalists are not involved in Web 2.0 projects.

2. Which of the following is *not* an example of a Web 2.0 application?

(a) Mozilla Firefox

(b) YouTube

(c) Facebook

(d) Delicious

3. Which of the following are used to measure a blog's popularity?

(a) Unique visitors and blog spam

(b) Page views and blog comments

(c) Labels and blog comments

(d) Unique visitors and page views

4. The program that uses distorted letters to prevent automated software programs from creating false Google accounts is known as a:

(a) Gadget

(b) CAPTCHA

(c) Keyword checker

(d) Bot

5. To help blog visitors find a blog post on a specific topic, which of the following should be added to a post?

(a) A blogroll

(b) A label

(c) A topic category

(d) A blog directory

Fill in the Blank

1. The _____ is the name given to the collection of all blogs on the web.
2. When the Internet bubble burst in late 2000 to 2002, it became known as the _____ _____.
3. _____ _____ measures the number of times a web page is loaded in a browser.
4. A(n) _____ is a list of links to other blogs which the blog author believes visitors will find useful.
5. Features such as About Me, Blog Archive, and Followers are examples of _____.

Practice Exercises

1. Creating a Meaningful Blog Name and Selecting a URL

As discussed in this chapter, selecting an appropriate name for a blog and choosing an appropriate URL can help visitors locate your blog more easily. For this exercise, you will go through the initial steps of creating a blog about cycling.

a. Sign in to your Blogger account and go to the Dashboard.

b. Click the **Create a Blog** link to begin the blog creation process.

c. Select a meaningful blog title and type it into the **Title** text box.

d. Select an appropriate URL and use the **Check Availability** link to check the URL's availability. Once you've found an available URL, print out the web page.

e. Repeat Steps c and d two more times, remembering to print out the results each time.

f. Because you do not need to create this blog, close the browser window to end the blog creation process. Log out of your Blogger account. Turn in the three pages showing the title and URL to your instructor.

2. **Creating and Revising Blog Posts**

Well-respected blogs usually consist of frequent posts that are well-written and contain useful or entertaining information. In this exercise, you will create new posts for your blog and revise them to include several formatting styles.

a. Sign in to Blogger and return to the blog you created in this chapter.

b. Create three new blog posts. Each post should be about a different aspect of information technology.

c. Be sure that each post has a meaningful title relating to the post's content.

d. Insert at least one live hyperlink in each post.

e. Publish each post as you complete it.

f. View your blog and print out the page showing your new posts. You will turn in this page to your instructor.

g. After you have published the posts, return to one of them and edit it. Select a key word or phrase and change the font color. Apply bold formatting to another selection and apply italic formatting to a third selection.

h. Publish the revised post and view the blog. Print out this page and the page showing your original posts, and then turn them in to your instructor. Log out of your Blogger account.

3. **Creating and Using Labels**

Labels help blog visitors locate information contained in your blog. Blog posts that have one or more meaningful labels are easier to find. In this exercise, you will practice creating and applying labels to existing blog entries.

a. Sign in to your Blogger account and return to the blog you updated in Practice Exercise 2. You will need to create and apply labels to the new posts you've added to the blog.

b. Click the **Show All** link as you work with each of the three new blog posts to view the existing labels.

c. If a label already exists for the blog post topic, add it to the *Labels for this post* text box.

d. Create a new label if an appropriate label doesn't exist.

e. If more than one label applies to a blog post, apply any that match the post's content.

f. Publish each post as it is completed. Once all the labels have been applied, view the blog. Print the blog page and give it to your instructor or send your instructor an email with the blog's URL. Log out of your Blogger account.

4. **Inserting and Removing a Gadget**

Gadgets may be used to provide helpful items on a blog or to provide visual interest. In this exercise, you will practice adding and removing gadgets.

a. Sign in to your Blogger account and return to the blog you created in this chapter.

b. Navigate to the Page Elements subtab to work with the gadgets.

c. Previously, you worked with the gadgets in the Basics tab. For this exercise, you should explore some of the other gadget categories. Locate a gadget you'd like to try and add it to your blog layout.

d. Preview your blog to see the gadget you've added. Print the preview page.

e. Repeat Steps c and d two more times to add two other gadgets to your blog. Remember to print the preview page after each gadget has been added.

f. Remove two of the three gadgets you added to the blog.

g. Save the blog layout and view the blog. Print the web page and turn in this page and the three gadget pages to your instructor.

Critical Thinking

1. Because blogging is relatively easy, many people have blogs and use them to share their news and opinions on the Internet. In some cases, bloggers have been able to share information about current events more quickly than traditional news outlets such as newspapers or television. Some critics worry that the quality of information that is available online has declined due to the number of bloggers. Others believe that blogging makes information more accessible. How do you feel about this? Is blogging a legitimate way to share information? Write a brief paper discussing the pros and cons of blogging.

2. Many bloggers use their blogs to discuss ongoing events in their daily lives. They may talk about family, friends, and work. Although some bloggers conceal their identities, others are very open about who they are and clearly identify other individuals and companies too. Some individuals have responded by suing bloggers for invasion of privacy or libel. Similarly, some bloggers have faced disciplinary action at work and some have even been fired for their opinions about their company or the company's products. How can bloggers balance their right to free speech with the right to privacy of others? Do companies have a right to prosecute employees who are blogging on their own time? Research these issues and write a two- to three-page paper supporting your views.

Team Projects

1. As a group, locate one blog in each of the following categories:
   • Politics
   • Social Awareness
   • Personal
   • Corporate

Create a table that lists the title and URL for each blog and the category it represents. Review the blogs and rate them using the following criteria:
   • How long has the blog been in existence?
   • When was the most recent post?
   • Are the posts relevant to the overall theme of the blog?
   • Does the blog have other helpful features—topic lists, labels, archives, other gadgets, and so on? Is it easy to find information?
   • What is the average frequency of blog posts—daily, more than twice a week, three or four times a month?
   • Which of the four blogs do you think is the best? Why? Which is the worst? Why?

Include your findings on the table and turn it in to your instructor.

2. You used Blogger to create blogs in this chapter. Split your team into two groups and explore the WordPress (www.wordpress.com) and LiveJournal (www.livejournal.com) free blogging tools. Compare and contrast each of the three tools (WordPress, LiveJournal, and Blogger). How easy is it to set up an account at each site? Can you add labels to your blog posts? What types of templates are available? Are other features available? Put together a brief presentation and share your findings with the class.

CHAPTER 2

Podcasting

Objectives

After you read this chapter, you will be able to:

1. Explain what a podcast is, what podcasts are used for, and where to find podcasts

2. Describe the software and hardware needed to listen to or view podcasts

3. Describe the software and hardware needed to create podcasts

4. Explain the characteristics of quality podcasts and the preparation needed to create your own podcasts

5. Download and install Audacity software

6. Record an audio podcast

7. Import video to your computer

8. Create a video podcast using Windows Movie Maker

9. Upload a podcast to the Internet

10. Describe Internet resources that educate people about podcasting

The following Hands-On Exercises will help you accomplish the chapter Objectives.

Hands-On Exercises

EXERCISES	SKILLS COVERED
1. Download and install Audacity software (page 54)	**Step 1:** Start Your Browser and Navigate to the Audacity Download Page **Step 2:** Download and Install the Audacity Software **Step 3:** Download and Install the LAME MP3 Encoder
2. Record an audio podcast (page 65)	**Step 1:** Ensure That Your Recording and Playback Devices Are Configured **Step 2:** Start Audacity and Set Preferences **Step 3:** Record a Podcast **Step 4:** Export a Podcast to an MP3 File
3. Produce a video podcast (page 79)	**Step 1:** Download the Media Files to Your Computer **Step 2:** Start Windows Movie Maker and Import the Media Files **Step 3:** Assemble the Components of the Podcast on the Storyboard **Step 4:** Add Transitions and Titles to the Podcast **Step 5:** Export Your Podcast to an AVI file
4. Upload a podcast to the Internet (page 90)	**Step 1:** Create an Account at Podbean.com **Step 2:** Upload Podcast Files to Podbean.com

Objective 1

Explain what a podcast is, what podcasts are used for, and where to find podcasts

What is a podcast?

Podcast A group of audio or video files, usually issued in a series or sequence, that can be subscribed to and downloaded from the Internet

Vidcast or Vodcast A video podcast

A *podcast* is a group of audio or video files, usually issued in a series or sequence, that can be subscribed to and downloaded from the Internet. The word *podcast* originated from a combination of two words: *iPod* and *broadcast*. One of the first and most popular personal media players (PMPs) is the Apple iPod, and therefore its name was co-opted into the name of this media. While audio podcasts are usually referred to only as podcasts, video podcasts are sometimes called *vidcasts* or *vodcasts*. Many people listen to audio podcasts or watch video podcasts every day on their computers or PMPs.

When I download an episode of my favorite television show, am I watching a podcast?

Downloading one episode of a TV show to your iPod or watching the episode online in a streaming format on your computer probably does not fall into the definition of a podcast. However, if you purchase an entire season of a television show and new episodes are downloaded to your computer or PMP when they become available, then you are participating in a podcast.

Web feed A data format for a web page that enables it to provide information when the page's content is updated

A key component of podcasts is that they can be subscribed to, and followers of a podcast are alerted when new "episodes" are available. This is accomplished by the use of web feeds. A *web feed* is a data format for a web page that enables it to provide information when the page's content is updated. RSS is a popular type of web feed that is used to syndicate content on the Internet. We'll explain more about RSS feeds in Chapter 3. For now, just be aware that web feeds like RSS help notify people when new content is available for podcasts.

Why do people create podcasts?

Podcasts are used mostly to inform or entertain. Podcasts are easy and inexpensive to create and can provide individuals with an outlet for their opinions or creativity. In the past, you needed to be on a broadcast radio or television station to reach a large audience. With podcasting and the Internet, you can reach a wide-ranging audience from the comfort of your own home. Many podcasts are like mini radio or television shows that talk about politics or current events or feature comedy skits.

Other podcasts, like Coffee Break Spanish (www.coffeebreakspanish.com), are a series of how-to instructions that teach a skill—in this case, how to speak Spanish. Technical podcasts that provide commentaries on technology, such as This Week in Tech (http://twit.tv), shown in Figure 2.1, are popular with people in technology-related industries. Podcasts that demystify technology for novice users or educate consumers on technical areas, such as the HDTV and Home Theater Podcast (www.htguys.com), are quite common. If you look hard enough, you can probably find a podcast on almost any area of interest.

Figure 2.1 Well-known technology experts comment on technology-related events in the This Week in Tech podcast.

Where can I find podcasts that interest me?

There are many good podcast directories that make it easy to find podcasts with content that interests you, including Apple iTunes (www.apple.com/itunes), Podcast Alley (http://podcastalley.com/podcast_genres.php), and Podcast.com (www.podcast.com). On sites such as Podcast.com (Figure 2.2a), you can often search for specific topics by using the site's search tool. Many podcast directories contain

Enter key words here to search for a specific type of podcast

Figure 2.2a Podcast.com features a vast array of interesting podcasts.

sections on podcasts that are organized by topic, and often the podcasts you will find there are free. Poscast.com organizes podcasts by channel and also provides staff recommendations and a list of featured publishers (Figure 2.2b). You can also use a search to find even more useful content. Simply enter key words such as *Windows tips* followed by the word *podcast* and check out the results.

Podcasts are organized by channel (topic)

You can also select a podcast by featured channel, staff pick, publisher, or topic

Figure 2.2b Podcast.com offers over 85,000 different podcasts on a variety of topics. Select a channel to find podcasts on the topic of your choice.

Objective 2

Describe the software and hardware needed to listen to or view podcasts

Do I need an iPod (or other PMP) to listen to or view podcasts?

You do not need an iPod or any other type of PMP to take part in podcasting. Any software designed to play audio and video files—such as Windows Media Player, iTunes, or RealPlayer—allows you to view or listen to podcasts. Although you don't need a PMP, you will need a computer and a connection to the Internet to download podcasts. And, obviously, you'll need either speakers or headphones to listen to the audio tracks from podcasts.

To subscribe to podcasts, you need software that is specially designed to go out and check the Internet for new episodes of the podcasts to which you subscribe. Software of this type is known as a *podcatcher* or an *aggregator*. Podcatcher software

Podcatcher or Aggregator
Software that is specially designed to go out and check the Internet for new episodes of the podcasts to which you subscribe

can either be installed on your computer like iTunes or can be web-based software like Google Reader (Figure 2.3). When you subscribe to a podcast, your podcatcher software checks the web feed for that podcast whenever you launch—or log into—your software to see if there are any new episodes available. Then you can easily see if there are new episodes that interest you.

Click to play this episode

List of podcasts to which you are subscribed; click the title to view available episodes

Figure 2.3 Google Reader makes it easy to subscribe to podcasts and listen to current episodes.

Where are the podcast files stored?

With web-based solutions such as Google Reader, the podcast files you listen to remain stored on the Internet at the websites that contain the podcasts. In the case of software such as iTunes, which is installed on your computer, the podcasts are downloaded from the Internet and stored on your computer. The podcasts can then be downloaded to your PMP the next time you *sync,* or connect, your PMP to your computer.

Sync The process of connecting your PMP to your computer to update its contents

Objective 3

Describe the software and hardware needed to create podcasts

What hardware do I need to create my own podcasts?

You may already own all the hardware you need to create your own podcasts. The following is a list of the essential equipment:

- Computer with Internet access – You'll need a computer to run the software required to record and edit your podcasts. You'll also need the computer to be connected to the Internet so that you can distribute your podcasts online. This should be a broadband connection (such as cable or DSL) and not a dial-up connection. Video podcast files can be huge, and even audio podcast files can be rather large. Uploading your content with a dial-up connection would be frustrating at best.

- Sound card – All modern computers include a sound card, because the expectation is that users will want a multimedia experience. The sound card should have a microphone input jack and a headphone output jack. If you are using an older desktop computer that does not have a built-in sound card, you can purchase a sound card at your local computer retailer and easily install it.

- Microphone – For recording sound, you need a microphone to input the sound of your voice into the computer. If you own a notebook computer, it may already have a microphone installed in it which may be sufficient for creating podcasts. You can also purchase an external microphone that will plug into a jack on your computer that is connected to the computer's sound card.

- Headphones or speakers – You will need to listen to the playback of podcasts you create, so speakers or headphones are essential. You might even consider purchasing a headset, which is a device that includes both headphones and a microphone (Figure 2.4). An adjustable microphone on a headset allows you to find a microphone position that is optimal for your recording needs and allows you to keep your hands free for working on the computer while you speak.

Figure 2.4 Headsets combine headphones and microphones in one device. The Plantronics Audio 355 Multimedia Headset includes an adjustable microphone for optimal recording results.

Pop filter A mesh screen that is placed directly in front of a microphone to disrupt the fast flow of air as it speeds towards the microphone

- Pop filter (optional) – Microphones don't react well to the human voice when sounds like the letter *p* are pronounced. The rush of air accompanying these sounds causes popping noises to occur on the recording. To prevent this, you need to use a pop filter. A *pop filter* is a mesh screen that is placed directly in front of a microphone to disrupt the fast flow of air as it speeds towards the microphone. You can buy pop filters from music supply stores or make a home-made one—like the one shown in Figure 2.5—from a wooden embroidery hoop and a pair of pantyhose. Because pops can be quite annoying to listeners, you really should use a pop filter if you want to be taken seriously as a podcaster.

Figure 2.5 Even a homemade pop filter like the one shown here will improve the quality of your podcasts.

- Video camera or camcorder – For recording video, you'll need a camera that can capture video (perhaps a cell phone) or a video camera (camcorder). Although most video cameras come with built-in microphones, the sound quality may not be optimal for producing a high-quality video podcast. Most video cameras have a port into which you can plug an external microphone, so a microphone might be a good investment if you are doing serious video podcasting.

- Tripod – Watching a shaky, wobbly video is not fun for anyone. A tripod is a stand that is designed to hold a video camera steady to ensure better-quality video. Tripods are not expensive and will go a long way towards making your videos look more professional.

What software do I need to create my own podcasts?

There are many software packages available that enable you to produce high-quality audio and video podcasts. This software may be purchased, but there are also shareware and freeware options. To start out, free software—or software included with Windows—allows you to begin producing quality podcasts at little or no cost. Consider these options:

- Sound Recorder – Sound Recorder is a basic sound recording program that is included with Windows. Click the Start button, then All Programs, and then the Accessories folder to locate this program. Although it doesn't have many features, you can use it to record simple audio podcasts.

- Audacity (http://audacity.sourceforge.net) – This full-featured sound recording package is available for free. Audacity is an open source software package that provides you with many options for recording and editing audio, such as using multiple sound tracks (like music and voice) and adding special effects to recordings. It is available for Windows, Mac OS X, and Linux and is used by many podcasters.

- Windows Movie Maker – This video software tool allows you to import video to your computer from video capture devices and combine video with still photographs and sound tracks to produce very high-quality video podcasts. The software is easy to use and is included as part of the Windows operating system. Although it doesn't have quite as many features as some high-end video production software suites, it will still allow you to begin producing video podcasts quickly and easily.

- CamStudio (http://camstudio.org) – Sometimes you may want to record video that captures what is happening on your computer screen. This is often useful if you are producing a tutorial to show people how to use a software package or how to navigate around a complex website. CamStudio is a free open source software package that enables you to record all on-screen and audio activity occurring on your computer and export it to video files that can be used as part of a podcast. In combination with a microphone, this software allows you to produce high-quality, narrated tutorials very quickly.

Objective 4

Explain the characteristics of quality podcasts and the preparation needed to create your own podcasts

What makes a podcast high quality?

Exceptional podcasts are entertaining as well as informative. They stick to their topic, and the information they present is well organized. New episodes of the podcast are produced on a regular basis, because listeners appreciate and expect fresh content.

What steps should I take when planning a podcast?

Planning is critical to establishing a successful podcast and accomplishing your objectives, whether they be informing, marketing, or entertaining. Well-designed podcasts are usually more engaging than ones that are haphazardly thrown together. Consider these four basic steps:

1. **Determine a topic for your podcast.** Successful podcasts are created by people who are passionate about their topics. Carefully consider your personal interests. Do you have a hobby that you would like to share with others? If you love seeking out new Indie rock bands that your friends haven't heard about yet, a podcast promoting new bands you have heard could be very engaging. What are your areas of expertise? If you are an avid long-distance bicyclist, your experience and knowledge in selecting appropriate cycling gear could be valuable to others. What topics could you discuss for hours on end? If you love spending time playing fantasy football and discussing key moves that improve your fantasy team, you will probably find others who could benefit from your insights.

   Perhaps you live in an area where there are a lot of leisure activities. You could create a podcast that informs people about what there is to do when they visit your community. The possibilities for topics are endless, but you should pick one and make sure that your podcasts all relate to the core topic so as not to confuse or alienate your loyal listeners.

2. **Pick an appropriate format for your podcast.** Radio and television shows usually have a set format, and podcasts can benefit from a set format too. Shows are usually divided into segments. Consider the *Late Show with David Letterman*. David does a monologue (segment 1), comedy bits either at his desk or in the audience (segment 2), the Top Ten List (segment 3), an interview with a guest (segment 4), an interview with a second guest (segment 5), a musical performance (segment 6), and then the show ends. Viewers feel more comfortable when they know what to expect at certain points during a show.

If you were considering doing a podcast about leisure activities in your area, your format might be as follows: Introduction, perhaps with theme music (segment 1), spotlight on the featured location for the week (segment 2), upcoming activities in the local area (segment 3), interview with a special guest (segment 4), and a wrap-up that includes a preview of the next show (segment 5).

You also need to consider whether an audio or a video format is appropriate for your podcast. Audio takes up much less space than video and is much quicker to download from the web. And audio is a great format for many types of podcasts, such as political commentaries and humor. But if the topic of your podcast needs visual images to support its message (such as demonstrating proper water-skiing techniques), video may be the best format for your podcast.

3. **Consider the optimal length for your podcast.** Your podcast needs to be long enough to get your information out to listeners but not so long that you bore them. When in doubt, keep a podcast short (generally under 20 minutes). If you have a particularly long topic to cover, consider breaking the podcast into smaller chunks and creating two or three podcasts that cover all the issues for one topic.

4. **Develop a schedule for new episodes of your podcast.** Regular contact with your listeners is important. They will forget about you and your podcast if new episodes are not released on a regular basis. Many podcasts feature new episodes on a weekly basis. If you don't have the time to produce new episodes regularly, you should really think long and hard about whether podcasting is something that you want to pursue.

Should I write a script for my podcast?

Very few people can produce engaging content spontaneously. Most people benefit from scripting out their ideas ahead of time, which helps determine proper sequencing of ideas. Having a script or an outline also ensures that you will cover all pertinent information and that you don't leave out any critical pieces of data. But if you are using a script, don't read the script word for word as you record the podcast. This usually results in a recording that sounds very mechanical or monotonous. Use the script as a guideline for what you are going to say. And don't worry if you make mistakes—you can always erase your file and start again.

Where should I record my podcast?

You need a quiet room, free of distractions and extraneous noise. Microphones are sensitive and can pick up all sorts of background noise, such as fans, air conditioners, televisions, ringing phones, roommates, family members, etc. So make sure that there is nothing in the room where you are recording that is generating sound besides you. If you are recording outdoors, you should be aware that your microphone—even one on a camcorder—will probably pick up many extraneous sounds, such as wind noise, street traffic, or birds. You may find that the soundtrack for a video that you filmed in less than optimal sound conditions might need to be rerecorded in a nice, quiet room in your home.

Objective 5

Download and install Audacity software

You are going to need software to record your audio podcast episodes. Although you could use Sound Recorder—which is included with Windows—you probably want a program that includes more advanced features.

Hands-On Exercises

For purposes of the hands-on exercises in this chapter, we are assuming that Professor Schmeckendorf, a computer science professor at Ginormous State University (GSU), is recording podcasts for his computer literacy students to inform them about aspects of information technology that can make their lives easier.

1 | Download and Install Audacity Software

Steps: 1. Start Your Browser and Navigate to the Audacity Download Page
2. Download and Install the Audacity Software **3.** Download and Install the LAME MP3 Encoder

Use Figures 2.6 through 2.19 as a guide in the exercise.

 Step 1

Start Your Browser and Navigate to the Audacity Download Page

Refer to Figures 2.6 and 2.7 as you complete Step 1.

a. Turn on the computer.

b. Start your preferred browser (Internet Explorer, Firefox, Safari, etc.). Type **http://audacity.sourceforge.net/download** in the address box of your browser and press **Enter**.

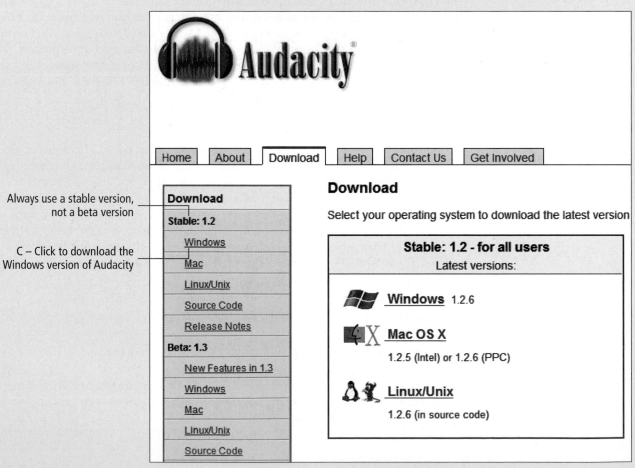

Figure 2.6 Hands-On Exercise 1, Steps 1a through 1c.

Sometimes a *beta version* of the Audacity software will be available for download. Beta software is a computer program that is still being tested and evaluated; therefore, it may not work as expected. Unless you are an extremely experienced computer user, you should not download the beta version; you should select a stable version of the software instead.

c. You should now click the appropriate link for the operating system you are using. We are assuming that Windows is the OS for the rest of this example, so click the **Windows** link.

d. Click the **Audacity Installer** link to download the installation file.

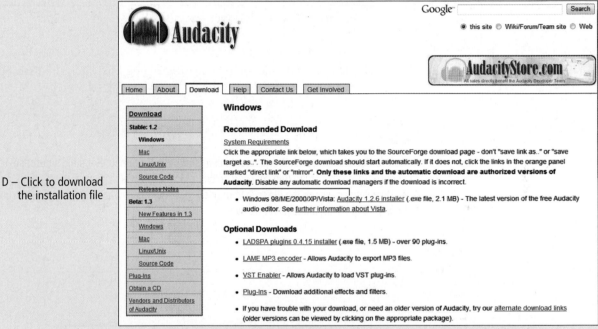

D – Click to download the installation file

Figure 2.7 Hands-On Exercise 1, Step 1d.

 Download and Install the Audacity Software

Refer to Figures 2.8 through 2.14 as you complete Step 2.

Depending upon the browser you are using, you might receive a message that—for your protection—your browser has blocked the file from downloading. The following example shows you how to proceed using Internet Explorer 7. You may experience slight differences if you are using another browser. Check with your instructor for additional instructions.

a. Click the **message bar** at the top of the browser to display the drop-down menu.

b. Click **Download File** from the drop-down menu. This action will reload the web page and start the file download process.

A – Click the message bar to display the drop-down menu

B – Click Download File to begin the download

Figure 2.8 Hands-On Exercise 1, Steps 2a and 2b.

c. In the **File Download – Security Warning** dialog box, click the **Run** button to download and run the installation file for the Audacity software.

If you are downloading a file from an unknown source, or are unsure of a file's purpose, it is best to choose Save rather than Run. You can select a location in which to save the file and, once it has been downloaded, check the file with your antivirus and antispyware software prior to running it, to be sure it does not contain any malware.

C – Click Run to launch the Audacity installation file

Figure 2.9 Hands-On Exercise 1, Step 2c.

Depending upon the version of Internet Explorer and the version of Windows that you are running, a security warning box may display on your screen. The Audacity installation file is safe to download and install, so you can bypass this warning.

d. In the **Security Warning** dialog box, click the **Run** button to begin the Audacity installation process.

D – Click Run to bypass the security warning and begin the installation

Figure 2.10 Hands-On Exercise 1, Step 2d.

If you are running Windows Vista, the **User Account Control** dialog box may appear. This is an additional warning mechanism in Windows Vista to prevent unauthorized software from being installed on your computer. Click the **Allow** option to proceed with the installation.

e. The **Audacity Setup Wizard** dialog box should now be displayed on your screen. Click the **Next** button to continue the installation process.

The next screen in the installation dialog box is the License Agreement screen. You should review the license to ensure that you agree with the terms of the agreement before proceeding with the installation.

f. Click the **I Accept the Agreement** option to select it and make the Next button active.

g. Click the **Next** button to continue the installation process and display an information screen.

h. Review the contents of the information screen, then click the **Next** button to continue the installation process.

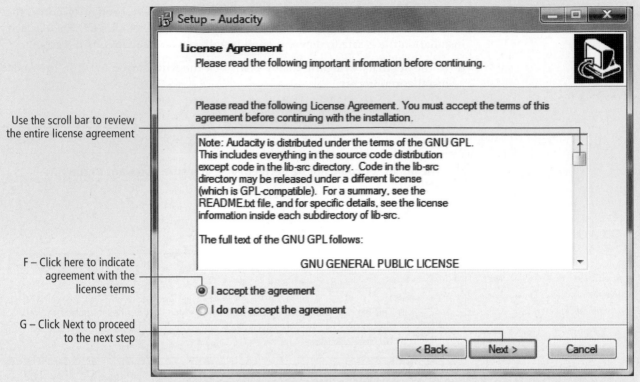

Use the scroll bar to review the entire license agreement

F – Click here to indicate agreement with the license terms

G – Click Next to proceed to the next step

Figure 2.11 Hands-On Exercise 1, Steps 2f and 2g.

i. Accept the default folder location for installed files (C:\Program Files\Audacity) or browse to find a different folder to hold the Audacity files. If you are performing this exercise in a computer lab, check with your instructor for the correct location.

j. Click the **Next** button to proceed to the Select Additional Tasks screen.

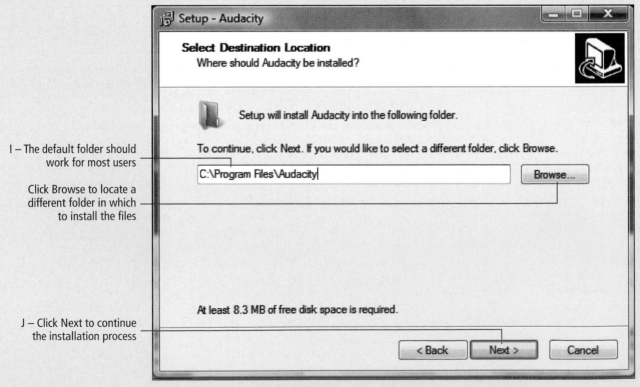

I – The default folder should work for most users

Click Browse to locate a different folder in which to install the files

J – Click Next to continue the installation process

Figure 2.12 Hands-On Exercise 1, Steps 2i and 2j.

k. Confirm that the checkboxes next to **Create a Desktop Icon** and **Associate Audacity Project Files** are both checked. This will ensure the creation of an icon on the desktop to start Audacity and will also ensure that Audacity is automatically started when Audacity project files are opened.

l. Click the **Next** button to proceed to the **Ready to Install** dialog box.

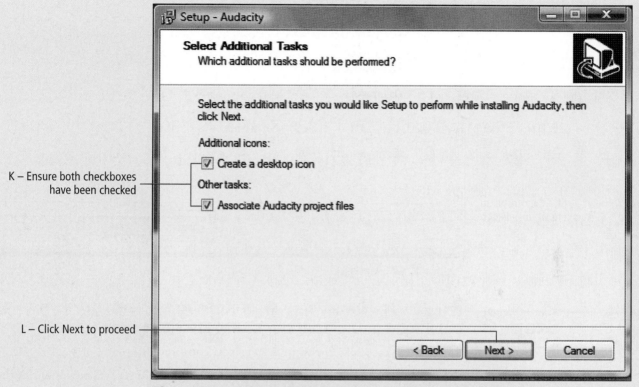

K – Ensure both checkboxes have been checked

L – Click Next to proceed

Figure 2.13 Hands-On Exercise 1, Steps 2k and 2l.

m. In the **Ready to Install** dialog box, click the **Install** button to complete the installation of Audacity.

n. When the installation is complete, you will see a **Completing the Audacity Setup Wizard** dialog box. Uncheck the **Launch Audacity** checkbox and click **Finish** to complete the installation. You will launch Audacity in a separate exercise. Leave your browser open for the next step.

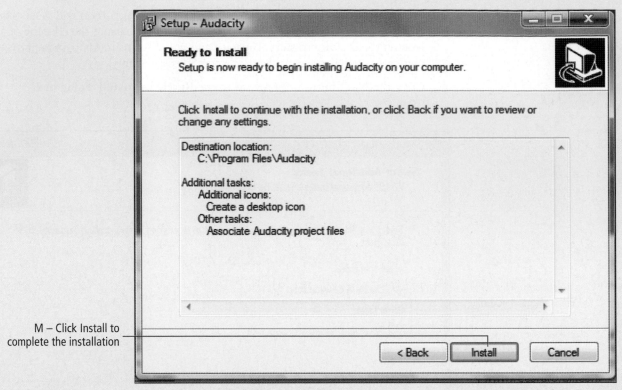

M – Click Install to complete the installation

Figure 2.14 Hands-On Exercise 1, Step 2m.

Step 3 Download and Install the LAME MP3 Encoder

Refer to Figures 2.15 through 2.19 as you complete Step 3.

You will most likely want to create MP3 files for your podcasts, as this is one of the most popular audio filetypes on the Internet. When you record a file in Audacity, it uses a proprietary file format called *Audacity Project Files*. An Audacity project consists of a project file (the file extension is .aup) and a project data folder. The project data folder has the same name as the project file but includes **_data** at the end of the folder name. It is important that the file and the folder remain together; if they become separated, the Audacity file will not work. Exporting an Audacity file to an MP3 format eliminates this problem. Audacity needs an additional file to allow it to export files to an MP3 format. Fortunately, this file is also free; it is known as the *LAME MP3 Encoder*.

a. Type **http://lame.buanzo.com.ar** in the address box of your browser and press **Enter** to proceed to the LAME MP3 Encoder Binaries page.

b. Scroll down the page until you see the **For Audacity on Windows** section. Click the **libmp3lame-win-3.98.2.zip** link to download the zipped file.

Zipped folders (or zipped files) Groups of files that have been compressed using special file compression software to condense the files so that they are smaller in size and can be downloaded quickly

Extracted Files which have been unzipped, or restored, to their original size

 Using Zipped Folders

Zipped folders (or **zipped files**) are groups of files that have been compressed using special file compression software to condense the files so that they are smaller in size and can be downloaded quickly. Zipped folders must be **extracted**, or unzipped, to restore the files to their original size before they can be used. Windows XP and Windows Vista include file compression utility software. If you have a version of Windows that does not include unzipping software, you can download a free file compression program at www.camunzip.com.

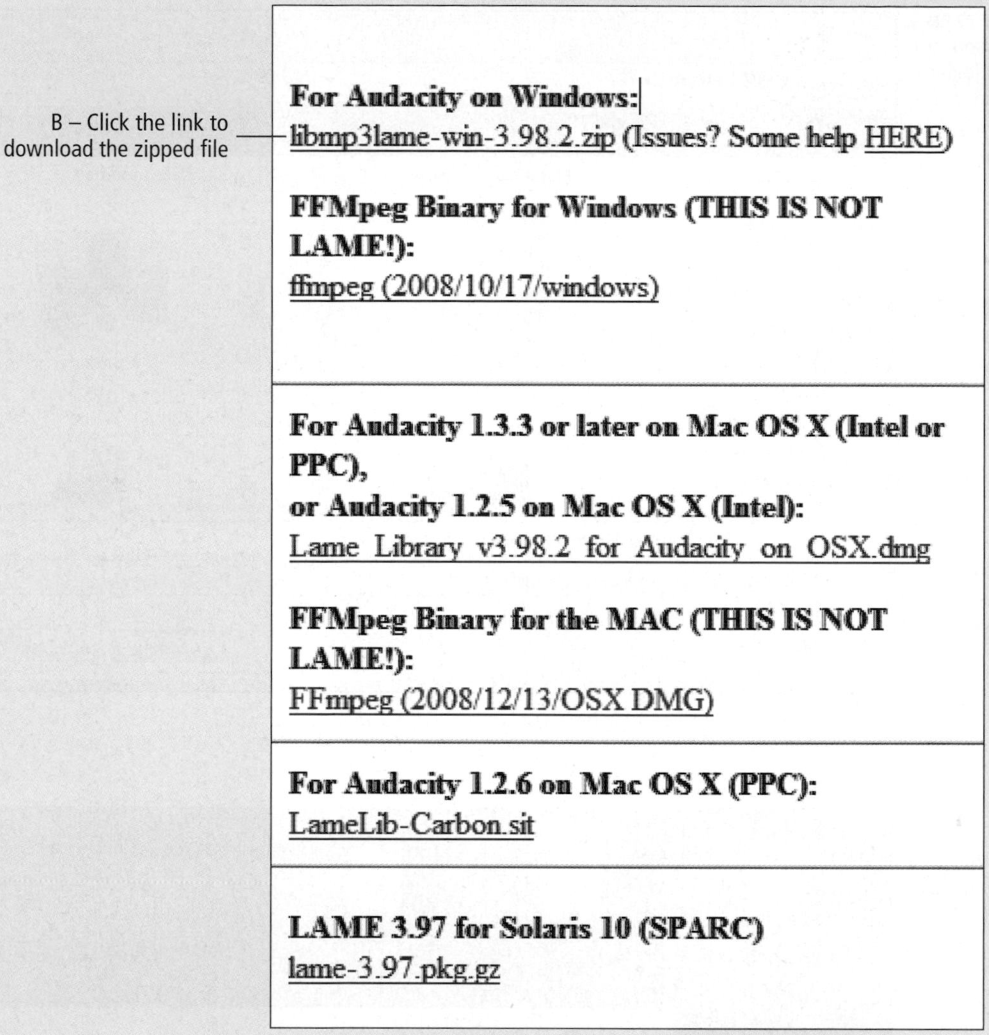

B – Click the link to download the zipped file

For Audacity on Windows:
libmp3lame-win-3.98.2.zip (Issues? Some help HERE)

FFMpeg Binary for Windows (THIS IS NOT LAME!):
ffmpeg (2008/10/17/windows)

For Audacity 1.3.3 or later on Mac OS X (Intel or PPC),
or Audacity 1.2.5 on Mac OS X (Intel):
Lame Library v3.98.2 for Audacity on OSX.dmg

FFMpeg Binary for the MAC (THIS IS NOT LAME!):
FFmpeg (2008/12/13/OSX DMG)

For Audacity 1.2.6 on Mac OS X (PPC):
LameLib-Carbon.sit

LAME 3.97 for Solaris 10 (SPARC)
lame-3.97.pkg.gz

Figure 2.15 Hands-On Exercise 1, Step 3b.

c. When the **File Download** dialog box appears, click the **Save** button to display the **Save As** dialog box.

d. In the **Save As** dialog box, navigate to an appropriate place on your hard drive in which to save the zipped folder you are downloading. Your desktop is probably a convenient place.

e. Click the **Save** button to download and save the folder in the specified location. Once the download is complete, a **Download Complete** dialog box may appear. If necessary, click **Close** to dismiss this dialog box.

f. Locate the zipped folder on your desktop (or in the location where you saved it). The folder name is libmp3lame-win-3.98.2.

g. Right-click the zipped folder and select **Extract All** from the shortcut menu.

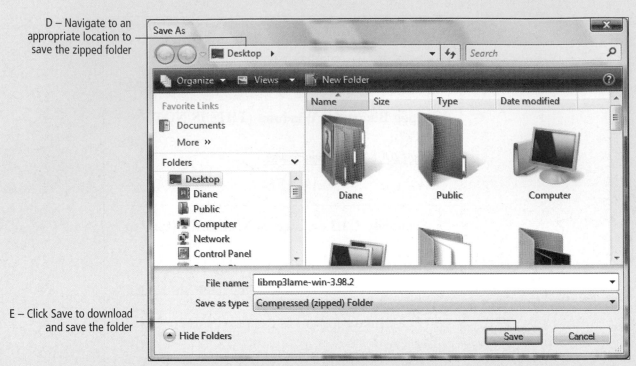

D – Navigate to an appropriate location to save the zipped folder

E – Click Save to download and save the folder

Figure 2.16 Hands-On Exercise 1, Steps 3d and 3e.

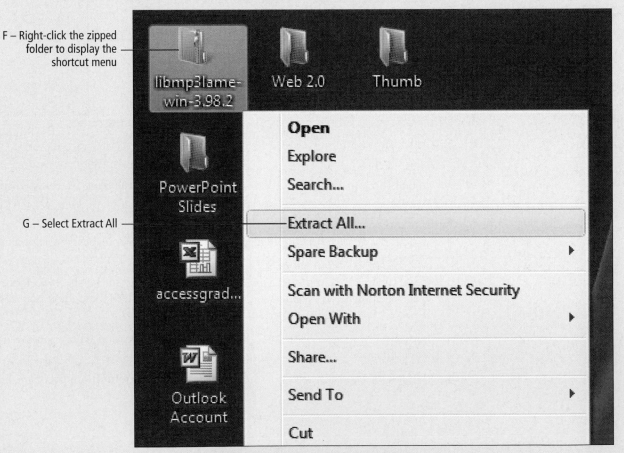

F – Right-click the zipped folder to display the shortcut menu

G – Select Extract All

Figure 2.17 Hands-On Exercise 1, Steps 3f and 3g.

h. In the **Extract Compressed (Zipped) Folders** dialog box, click the **Browse** button to display the **Select a Destination** dialog box.

i. In the **Select a Destination** dialog box, navigate to the folder where you installed the Audacity files (such as C:\Program Files\Audacity). Click the **OK** button to return to the **Extract Compressed (Zipped) Folders** dialog box. This also inserts the file location into the **Files Will Be Extracted to This Folder** text box.

j. If necessary, click the **Show Extracted Files When Complete** checkbox to place a check there. Click the **Extract** button to decompress the files and install them in the folder specified in the previous step.

Windows Vista users may see a **Destination Folder Access Denied** dialog box. If you have administrator rights, click the **Continue** button to continue installing the files. If you do not have administrator rights, see your professor for instructions on how to proceed. You may also see the **User Account Control** dialog box. If necessary, click the **Allow** option to proceed.

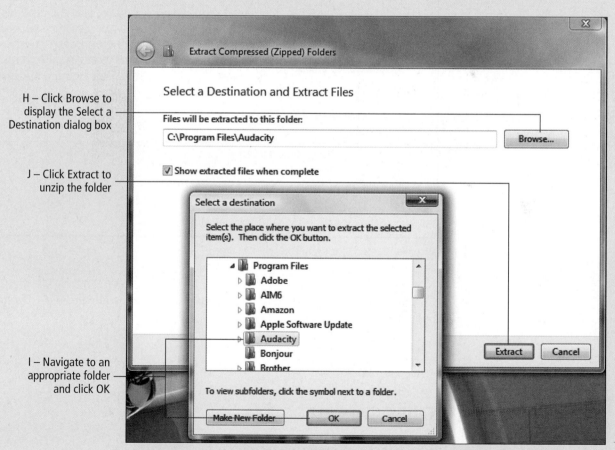

H – Click Browse to display the Select a Destination dialog box

J – Click Extract to unzip the folder

I – Navigate to an appropriate folder and click OK

Figure 2.18 Hands-On Exercise 1, Steps 3h through 3j.

k. Right-click the **Windows Start** button and select **Explore** from the shortcut menu to start Windows Explorer.

l. Navigate to the location where you extracted the zipped folder (known as the destination folder) and locate the folder named libmp3lame-3.98.2.

Remember where you placed this folder. You will need to tell Audacity where to find the files contained in it the first time you wish to export a sound file to an MP3 format.

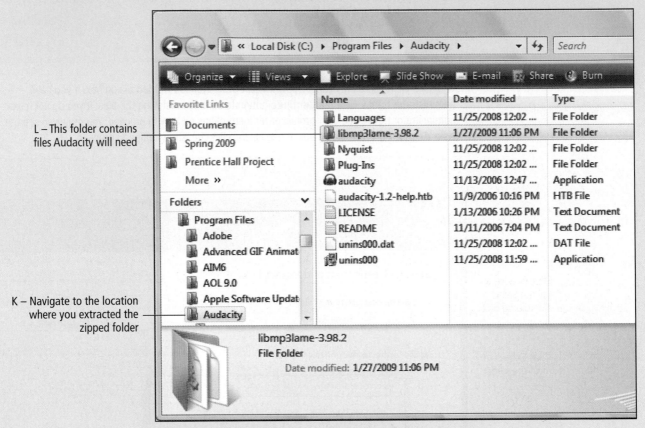

Figure 2.19 Hands-On Exercise 1, Steps 3k and 3l.

Congratulations! You now have the necessary software installed to record your first podcast.

Objective 6

Record an audio podcast

Now that you have installed the Audacity software, you are ready to record your first podcast. You may use a script of your own or you can follow the example which follows of Professor Schmeckendorf's first podcast to his students.

For Professor Schmeckendorf's first podcast, he has decided to direct students to the Microsoft Office 2007 Ultimate Steal website in case they wish to purchase a discounted version of the Office 2007 software. For the podcast, he develops the following script:

Microsoft is running an offer especially for college students called The Ultimate Steal. Students can obtain a copy of Microsoft Office 2007 Ultimate Edition for only $59.95. To qualify for this offer, you must be enrolled at a U.S. educational institution and have a valid email address that ends in the edu domain. Since GSU does provide you with an email address in an edu domain, you all should be eligible. Considering this package is available at retail for around $500, this is a fantastic deal for students. So go to theultimatesteal.com to check it out and save some money today!

Hands-On Exercises

2 | Record an Audio Podcast

Steps: 1. Ensure That Your Recording and Playback Devices Are Configured **2.** Start Audacity and Set Preferences **3.** Record a Podcast **4.** Export a Podcast to an MP3 File

Use Figures 2.20 through 2.33 as a guide in the exercise.

Step 1 Ensure That Your Recording and Playback Devices Are Configured

Refer to Figures 2.20 and 2.21 as you complete Step 1.

a. Connect your microphone to your computer if you are using an external microphone. Turn on any external speakers that are connected to your computer or plug your headphones into the computer.

b. Click the Windows **Start** button and select **Control Panel** from the menu options.

c. In the Control Panel, click the **Sound** icon (for Windows Vista) or the **Sounds and Audio Devices** icon (for Windows XP). This will display the **Sound** dialog box.

The rest of this example will provide directions for configuring sound devices in Windows Vista, but Windows XP sound devices are configured in a similar manner.

d. In the **Sound** dialog box, click the **Playback** tab if necessary. If you are currently playing music—or other audio—on your computer, the sound level bar should show green, indicating that the speakers or headphones are working. And, of course, you should hear sound coming out of the speakers!

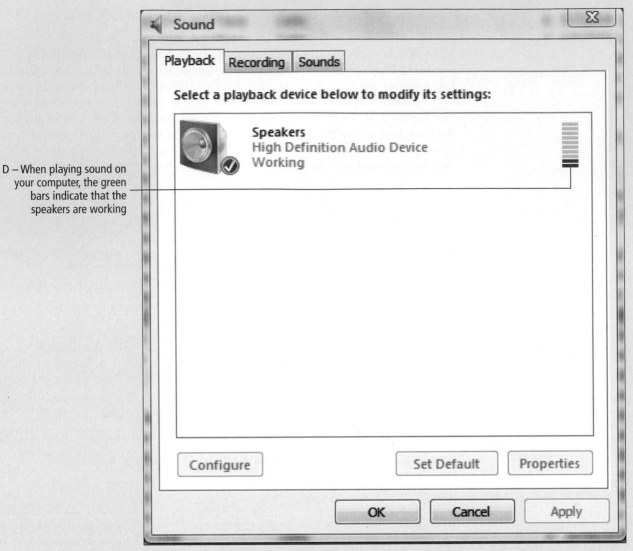

D – When playing sound on your computer, the green bars indicate that the speakers are working

Figure 2.20 Hands-On Exercise 2, Step 1d.

e. First, turn off any music or other sounds that you are currently playing through your computer. In the **Sound** dialog box, click the **Recording** tab. Speak into the microphone. The sound level bar should show green, indicating that the microphone is working properly.

f. After you've ensured that the recording and playback devices are working properly, click **Cancel** to close the **Sound** dialog box.

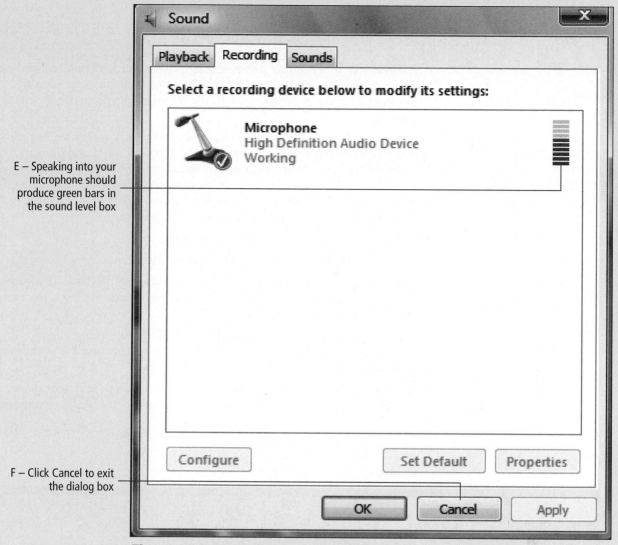

E – Speaking into your microphone should produce green bars in the sound level box

F – Click Cancel to exit the dialog box

Figure 2.21 Hands-On Exercise 2, Steps 1e and 1f.

 Alert!

If your speakers or your microphone are not working properly, you may have a problem with the sound card in your computer, or the Windows sound drivers (special software that allows computer programs to communicate with hardware devices) may be improperly installed. Consult with your professor or a computer technician to resolve the problem.

 Step 2

Start Audacity and Set Preferences

Refer to Figures 2.22 through 2.25 as you complete Step 2.

a. Click the **Start** button, select **All Programs**, then select **Audacity** from the list of programs (or double-click the Audacity icon on your desktop) to start the Audacity software.

Figure 2.22 shows what the Audacity software should look like when the program is first launched. Your screen may look different if another student has changed the preferences on the computer on which you are working, but the functionality of the program should be the same. Some key features of the Audacity interface are as follows:

- Selection tool – When this icon is selected, the cursor will look like an I-beam when you are working in a sound file. Select this tool when you want to highlight a certain portion of a sound file to change its properties (such as deleting it).

- Zoom tool – When this icon is selected, the cursor will look like a magnifying glass when you are working in a sound file. Clicking the sound file will zoom in on the file and spread out the time line so that there is a smaller portion of the sound file on the screen. This makes it easier to edit the file (such as cutting out pauses). Right-clicking while this tool is selected will zoom out on the time line to display more of the audio file on the screen at one time.

- Play button – Click to play back a sound file.

- Record button – Click to record a new sound file.

- Pause button – Click to temporarily stop recording or playback. Clicking the Pause button a second time will resume the playback or the recording exactly where you left off.

- Stop button – Click to stop playback or recording. Resuming playback or recording after the Stop button is clicked will start the playback at the beginning of the file or begin recording a new audio file.

- Time line – Shows (in seconds) how long the audio file is and what point in time you are at in the recording file. This is important when editing sound files.

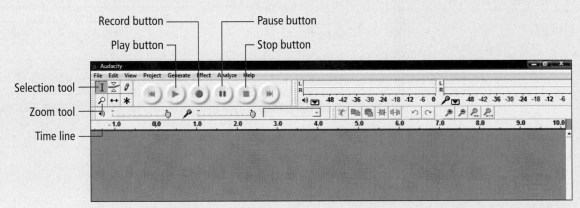

Figure 2.22 Hands-On Exercise 2, Step 2a.

b. From the **Edit** menu, select **Preferences** to display the **Audacity Preferences** dialog box. Click the **Audio I/O** tab if necessary.

Your default playback and recording devices should be showing in the device text boxes if they are properly configured and turned on. If they are not showing, click the drop-down arrows next to the device boxes and select from the list of devices available. For Windows Vista, the Microsoft Sound Mappers should be the default devices.

Ensure that Mono is selected as the format for channels. Mono means that only one channel of audio is recorded instead of two (the stereo setting). One channel is sufficient for voice recording and generates a smaller-size audio file. Your listeners should appreciate smaller files because they will take up less space on their personal media players when they download your podcast.

Now you need to set the preferences for exporting the audio files you will record to an MP3 format. You need to tell Audacity where to locate the LAME encoder file that you downloaded in Hands-On Exercise 1, Step 3.

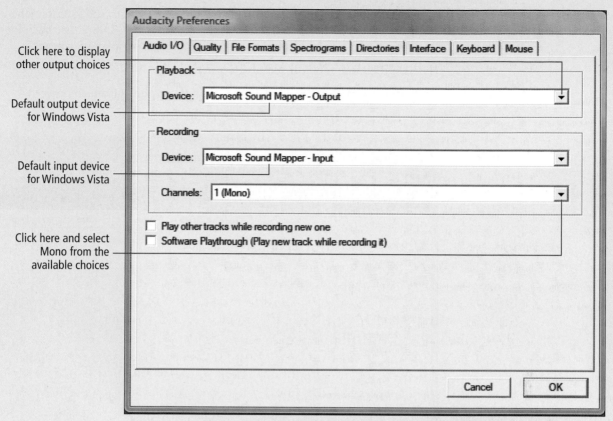

Click here to display other output choices

Default output device for Windows Vista

Default input device for Windows Vista

Click here and select Mono from the available choices

Figure 2.23 Hands-On Exercise 2, Step 2b.

c. In the **Audacity Preferences** dialog box, click the **File Formats** tab.

d. Under the section entitled *MP3 Export Setup*, click the **Find Library** button to display the **Export MP3** dialog box. Click the **Yes** button in this dialog box to display the **Where Is lame_enc.dll?** dialog box.

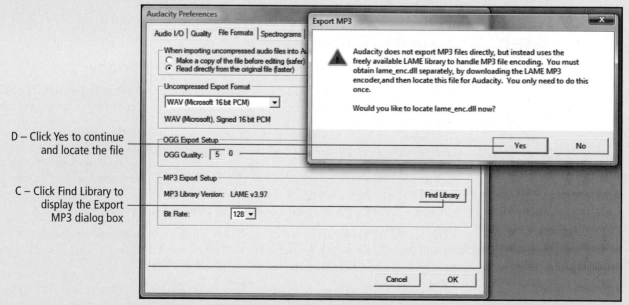

D – Click Yes to continue and locate the file

C – Click Find Library to display the Export MP3 dialog box

Figure 2.24 Hands-On Exercise 2, Steps 2c and 2d.

e. In the **Where Is lame_enc.dll?** dialog box, navigate to the location where you unzipped the LAME encoder files folder, libmp3lame-3.98.2. In the Folders pane on the left, click the **libmp3lame-3.98.2** folder to display its contents.

f. Click the **lame_enc.dll** file to select it.

g. With the lame_enc.dll file selected, click the **Open** button to proceed.

F – Click the lame_enc.dll file to select it

E – Navigate to the place where you stored the folder containing the LAME encoder files

G – Click Open to proceed

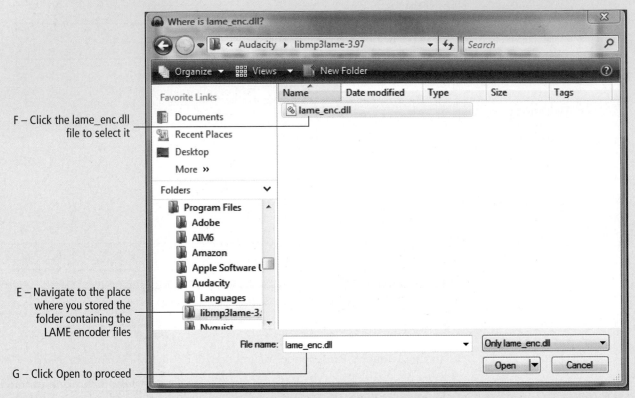

Figure 2.25 Hands-On Exercise 2, Steps 2e through 2g.

h. In the **Audacity Preferences** dialog box, click the **OK** button to save your preferences.

 Step 3   Record a Podcast

Refer to Figures 2.26 through 2.31 as you complete Step 3.

You are now ready to record your podcast. There are two main issues which you must be concerned with while recording an audio file: 1) the recording sound level and 2) dealing with mistakes.

Sound level Your podcast will be hard to understand if the sound recording levels are too high, as your voice will be distorted. Therefore, it is a good idea to test the levels at the beginning of your recording. The easiest way to vary the levels is to move closer to or farther away from the microphone or to speak in a softer or louder voice. Figure 2.26 shows a sample test recording to establish sound levels.

The recording level meter can be used as a guide for recording levels. It is only active while you are recording an audio track. The farther to the right that the level meter goes, the more likely that the sound will be distorted.

The audio track window also gives you a clear indication of the suitability of your audio levels. The blue wavy lines represent the audio in the recording. When the blue lines bump up against the top or bottom edge of the audio track window, the recording levels are too high and the sound is most likely distorted. In Figure 2.26, the section of the recording shown outlined in the yellow box indicates recording levels that should be acceptable.

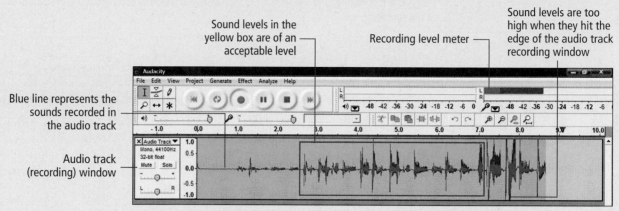

Figure 2.26 Sample test recording with sound levels displayed.

You should test the levels each time you begin to record to get the microphone positioned at an appropriate distance from your mouth. Remember to speak at the same general volume level throughout the recording. You can test the levels at the beginning of a podcast file and edit out the sound test later on. There is no need to create a separate file just for the sound test.

Mistakes While Recording Even with a detailed script to follow, you are likely to make some mistakes while you are recording. Because you can easily edit a sound file, there is no need to stop the recording and start the entire file over again. Just pause, gather your thoughts, and go back to the sentence in your script that comes before you made the mistake. Repeat that sentence and continue recording. You can always edit out the mistake later on.

a. If you have not already done so, start the **Audacity** program.

b. Click the **Record** button and do a sound level check.

c. Record your podcast by speaking at a moderate pace (not too fast or too slow). If you are using Professor Schmeckendorf's script from earlier in the chapter, your podcast may look something like Figure 2.27 after you record it.

d. When you are done recording, click the **Stop** button.

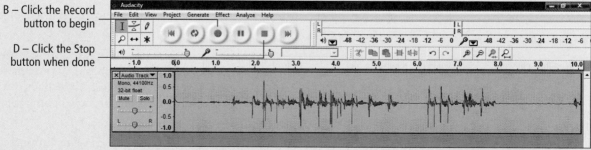

Figure 2.27 Hands-On Exercise 2, Steps 3b and 3d.

> **Alert !**
>
> Your recording won't look exactly like Figure 2.27. The differences result from different sound levels (voice levels), different lengths of sound level checks at the beginning of the recording, how fast you are speaking, and the number of mistakes you made which resulted in repeating portions of the recording.

You should play back your recording (by clicking the Play button) and see if it is of acceptable quality. If it isn't, just record it again using different sound levels. If the sound is acceptable, then determine which portions of the recording you need to delete (such as the sound check and any mistakes you fixed).

In this particular recording, there was almost 10 seconds of sound check at the beginning which needs to be deleted. A mistake was made 37 seconds into the recording and the correction began at 41.5 seconds, so you also need to delete the portion with the mistake (from 37 to 41.5 seconds).

e. Use the scroll bar at the bottom of the Audacity screen to return to the beginning of the audio file.

f. Click the **Selection Tool** to select it.

g. Click at the beginning of the area to be selected (in this case, the beginning of the recording).

h. While holding down the left mouse button, drag to select the appropriate area representing the sound check (in this case, the first 10 seconds of the recording).

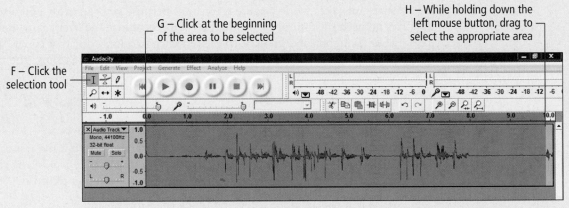

Figure 2.28 Hands-On Exercise 2, Steps 3f through 3h.

i. With the appropriate area selected, click the **Edit** menu and select **Delete** to remove the selected portion of the recording.

As you make changes to the sound file, the time line adjusts to display the new running time. Originally, the next portion to be deleted began approximately 37 seconds into the recording. Because you have cut almost 10 seconds out of the recording by deleting the sound check, the second portion now begins approximately 27 seconds into the recording.

j. Play back the recording to locate the mistake that needs to be eliminated. Use the scroll bars to move to the appropriate portion of the time line.

k. Click at the beginning of the area to be selected and, while holding down the left mouse button, drag to select the appropriate area.

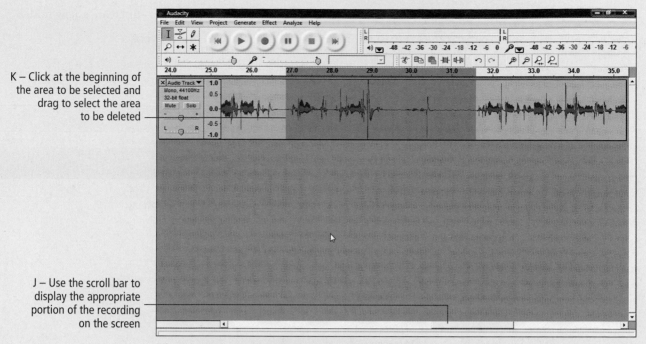

K – Click at the beginning of the area to be selected and drag to select the area to be deleted

J – Use the scroll bar to display the appropriate portion of the recording on the screen

Figure 2.29 Hands-On Exercise 2, Steps 3j and 3k.

l. With the appropriate area selected, click the **Edit** menu and select **Delete** to remove the selected portion of the recording.

m. Play back the recording a final time to ensure that all appropriate edits have been made and that you are happy with the final quality of the recording.

n. From the **File** menu, select **Save Project As** to display the **Save Project As** dialog box.

A Warning box might be displayed, explaining that you will be saving the project in an Audacity file format (.aup file extension) and that this file format can't be played back by most other software. Click **OK** to proceed. You will export a file to an MP3 format in the next section.

o. Click the **Browse Folders** arrow to display the expanded **Save Project As** dialog box.

O – Click to display expanded dialog box

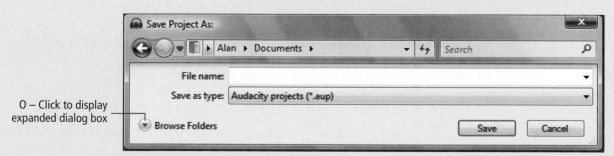

Figure 2.30 Hands-On Exercise 2, Step 3o.

p. Navigate to the folder where you wish to save the file—or create a new folder.

q. Type **Podcast_1_Your_Name** in the File Name text box.

r. Click the **Save** button to save the file.

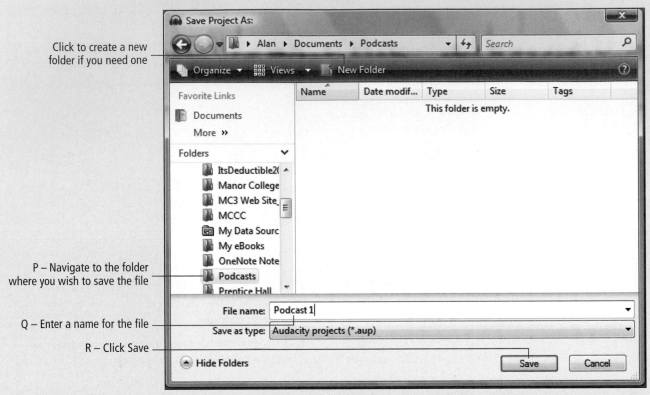

Figure 2.31 Hands-On Exercise 2, Steps 3p through 3r.

Step 4 Export a Podcast to an MP3 File

Refer to Figures 2.32 and 2.33 as you complete Step 4.

The most common format for audio podcasts is an MP3 file. MP3 files are used because most multimedia software and portable media players can play them back. Also, the MP3 format produces very efficient files that take up less space than many other formats. Therefore, you should distribute your podcasts in MP3 format.

a. If the audio file you wish to export is not open, from the **File** menu, select **Open.** Browse to the folder where you saved the podcast file and select it to open it in Audacity.

b. Click **File** and select **Export as MP3** to display the **Save MP3 File As** dialog box.

c. Navigate to the folder in which you wish to save the MP3 file.

d. Type **Podcast Volume 1-1_Your_Name** in the File Name text box.

e. Click the **Save** button to display the **Edit the ID3 Tags for the MP3 File** dialog box.

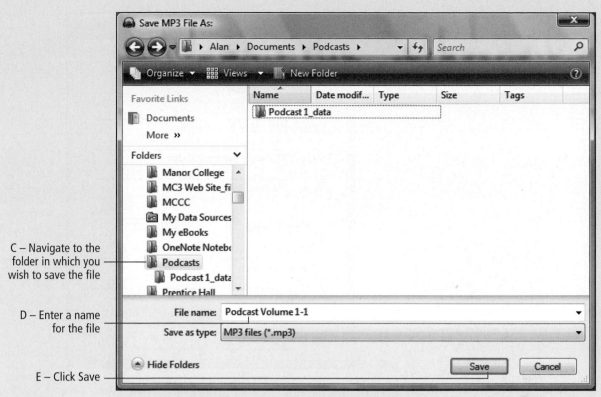

C – Navigate to the folder in which you wish to save the file

D – Enter a name for the file

E – Click Save

Figure 2.32 Hands-On Exercise 2, Steps 4c through 4e.

ID3 tags Pieces of information that are attached to MP3 audio files

ID3 tags are pieces of information that are attached to MP3 audio files. They display on the screen when the files are played back in software programs or on personal media players. You should fill in tags with descriptive information so that people who listen to your podcast know where it came from and who recorded it.

f. Fill in the appropriate information in each of the boxes in the **Edit the ID3 tags for the MP3 file** dialog box. Some suggestions are:

- Title – A descriptive title that informs the listener about the topic of this particular podcast.

- Artist – The name of the person (or organization) that distributes the podcast.

- Album – The podcast series numbers (volume and episode numbers).

- Track Number and Year – The volume and episode numbers again.

- Genre – *Podcast* would be optimal here. But because Audacity doesn't offer that as an option, *Speech* is also descriptive of the type of audio file.

- Comments – Consider including the URL where people can find your podcasts.

g. Click the **OK** button to export the Audacity project file to an MP3 file.

h. Play back the MP3 file using Windows Media Player or the media player of your choice to ensure that the file sounds the way you intended.

i. Close the media player; then close Audacity.

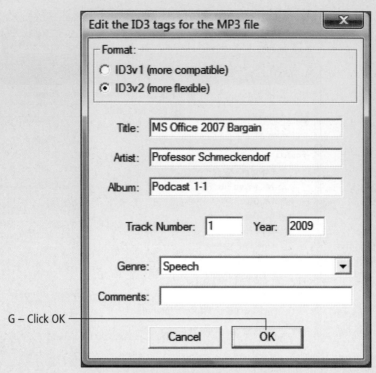

Edit the ID3 tags for the MP3 file   X

Format:
- ○ ID3v1 (more compatible)
- ● ID3v2 (more flexible)

Title: MS Office 2007 Bargain

Artist: Professor Schmeckendorf

Album: Podcast 1-1

Track Number: 1   Year: 2009

Genre: Speech ▼

Comments:

G – Click OK

Cancel   OK

Figure 2.33 Hands-On Exercise 2, Steps 4f and 4g.

Objective 7

Import video to your computer

If you are recording video with a camcorder or other video capture device, you will need to transfer the video to your computer at some point so that you can use it to produce your podcast. This will require connecting your video capture device to your computer. Although some devices can connect to your computer wirelessly, most use a cable that connects to a USB or FireWire port.

Windows will recognize video devices as soon as you connect them to your computer and turn them on. You may have installed software that came with your video device to import video to your computer, or you can use the Windows video capture protocols. Capturing video works differently depending upon the video device used. In the examples that follow, we'll show you how to import video from a Canon digital camera that is also capable of recording video. This process may vary slightly for your video device but should be similar enough for you to follow. Consult the manuals that came with your video device for complete instructions.

When you connect a video device to your Windows computer and turn it on, Windows Vista or XP displays the AutoPlay dialog box, which should look similar to the one shown in Figure 2.34. You have the following options:

- Import pictures (video) using Windows – This option will start a wizard (a programmed set of software steps) which will allow you to import video or pictures to your computer. Wizards usually require following rigid steps, so they may be cumbersome to use when importing large quantities of video clips or pictures. With a camcorder connected to the computer, selecting this option presents you with a wizard that has on-screen controls that mimic the controls on your camcorder for playback of video (play, stop, pause, fast forward, etc.), making it easy to capture the exact pieces of a video recording that you wish to download.

- Download using other software – Various programs can appear here, depending upon what software was installed that came with your video capture device. For the Canon camera we are using for this example, the Canon CameraWindow software has been installed and would be a good option for importing our media.

- Open device to view files using Windows Explorer – With cameras and cell phones, the video (or still images) are usually stored on flash memory cards. When viewed with Windows Explorer, the memory card appears as a new drive containing folders and files. This is a good option to select for downloading video from digital cameras or cell phones that can also record video, because the video is stored in discrete files as opposed to continuous segments on camcorders. We'll select this option for importing our video in this example.

Alert

If the **AutoPlay** dialog box does not appear, you can open Windows Explorer by right-clicking the **Start** button and selecting **Explore** from the shortcut menu.

Name of digital device connected to the computer

Select this option to use a wizard to import your media

If proprietary software is installed on your computer, it will appear here as an option for downloading

For digital cameras and phones, using Windows Explorer to search the device for media to download is a good option

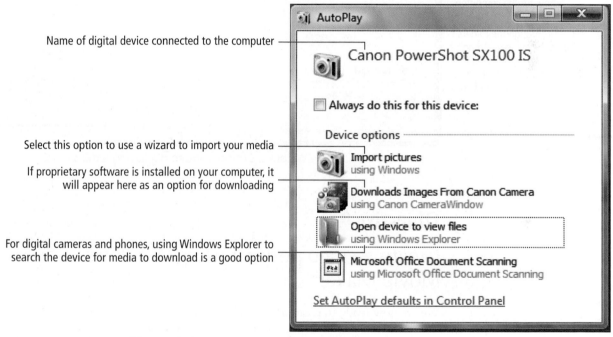

Figure 2.34 A sample AutoPlay dialog box.

When you select the option **Open Device to View Files Using Windows Explorer,** an Explorer window should open that looks similar to Figure 2.35. The digital device you are using should appear as a device connected to your computer (usually listed below the other devices on your computer, such as the hard drive or DVD drive). The digital device is assigned a drive letter such as *F:* or *G:*—the actual letter will vary depending upon the number of devices connected to your computer. Once you've located your digital device, you can browse through the storage media folders to find the folder that contains the video (or other digital media) that you wish to download to your computer. You can then copy the files to an appropriate directory on your computer's hard drive.

Again, these steps are for illustrative purposes only and will vary depending upon the type of digital device you are using. But once you have your digital video files downloaded to the computer, you are ready to begin producing your video podcast.

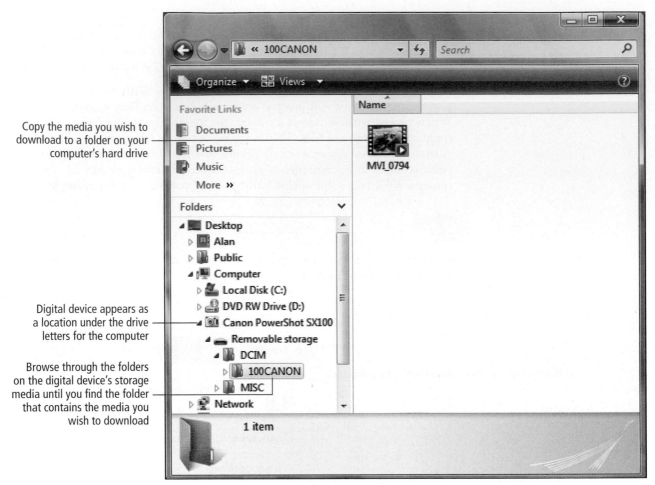

Copy the media you wish to download to a folder on your computer's hard drive

Digital device appears as a location under the drive letters for the computer

Browse through the folders on the digital device's storage media until you find the folder that contains the media you wish to download

Figure 2.35 A sample Windows Explorer screen displaying a media file.

Objective 8

Create a video podcast using Windows Movie Maker

We are now ready to create Professor Schmeckendorf's first video podcast about war driving. All we need are the video clips that will comprise the podcast.

 Alert!

In the hands-on exercise that follows, you will need two video clips and a picture file (jpg) that have been prepared for you. The first step of the hands-on exercise will detail how to download these files from the Internet. However, your instructor may have already downloaded these files and placed them on your school's network for your convenience. So check with your instructor before proceeding with Step 1.

Hands-On Exercises

3 | Produce a Video Podcast

Steps: 1. Download the Media Files to Your Computer **2.** Start Windows Movie Maker and Import the Media Files **3.** Assemble the Components of the Podcast on the Storyboard **4.** Add Transitions and Titles to the Podcast **5.** Export Your Podcast to an AVI file

Use Figures 2.36 through 2.49 as a guide in the exercise.

Step **Download the Media Files to Your Computer**

a. Open your web browser and type **www.pearsonhighered.com/nextseries** in the browser address box. Press **Enter**.

b. From the list of books provided, point to the title of this book and click. This will take you to the companion website for the book.

You will need to download two zipped files that contain the student files for this chapter.

c. Click the **Student Data Files** link.

d. Click the **Chapter 2 Part** 1 link to begin downloading the file to your computer. The **File Download** dialog box will appear.

e. In the **File Download** dialog box, click the **Save** button to display the **Save As** dialog box.

f. Browse through the folders (or create a new folder) on your computer's hard drive or your flash drive to find an appropriate place to save the file.

g. Click the **Save** button to download the file and save it to your computer.

h. Repeat steps d through g to download the Chapter 2 Part 2 student data file and save it to the same location as the Part 1 file.

i. Refer to Hands-On Exercise 1, Step 3 earlier in this chapter for guidelines for unzipping and extracting the files.

j. After the files have been downloaded, close your browser.

 Alert!

Depending on the browser you are using, the file names may differ slightly from those shown here. An underscore symbol may replace a space between words.

Step **Start Windows Movie Maker and Import the Media Files**

Refer to Figures 2.36 through 2.38 as you complete Step 2.

Professor Schmeckendorf is creating a video podcast to explain to his students how war driving works. War driving is an activity in which an individual drives around trying to locate a wireless network signal to connect a computer to for free. We'll use the media you just downloaded to create this podcast with Windows Movie Maker.

a. Click the **Start** button and select **All Programs**. Find Windows Movie Maker in the list of available programs and click it to launch the program.

b. If necessary, click the **Show or Hide Tasks** icon to display the Tasks list on the left side of the Movie Maker main window.

c. In the **Import** group, click **Videos** to display the **Import Media Items** dialog box.

B – If necessary, click to display the Tasks list

C – Click the Videos link to import the media you just downloaded

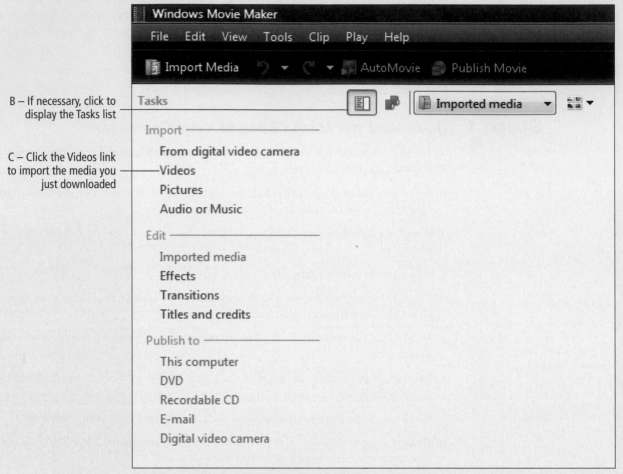

Figure 2.36 Hands-On Exercise 3, Steps 2b and 2c.

d. Browse to the folder where you saved the student data files for Chapter 2 that you downloaded in Step 1 of this hands-on exercise and locate More Information on War Driving.jpg, War Driver Signal Acquisition.avi, and War Driver Surfing.avi. If you do not see the files, change the Type of Files option to **All Files.**

e. Ctrl-click the three media files to select them all.

f. Click the **Import** button to import the selected files into Windows Movie Maker.

The imported media should now appear in the Movie Maker window. Clicking on one of the imported media clips will cause that media to be displayed in the preview window.

The bottom section of the Movie Maker window can display a time line or a storyboard. If the time line is displayed, click the **Timeline** drop-down arrow and select **Storyboard.**

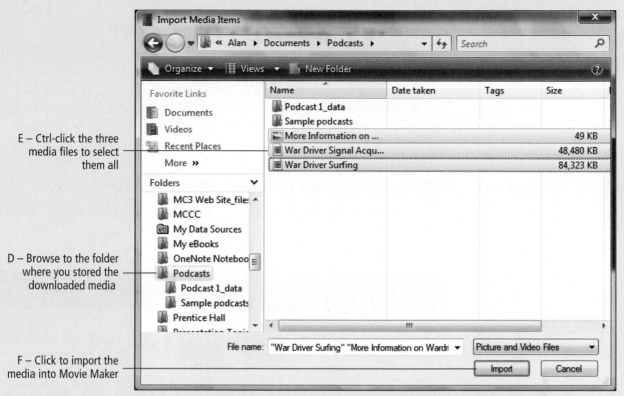

E – Ctrl-click the three media files to select them all

D – Browse to the folder where you stored the downloaded media

F – Click to import the media into Movie Maker

Figure 2.37 Hands-On Exercise 3, Steps 2d through 2f.

Storyboard A panel, or series of panels, arranged in sequence to portray the action or events that will occur in a video

Transitions Effects that take place in between media clips

The storyboard is where you construct your movie (video). A *storyboard* is a panel, or series of panels, arranged in sequence to portray the action or events that will occur in the video. You can click imported media and drag it into the media boxes on the storyboard line. *Transitions,* effects that take place in between media clips, can be placed in the small transition boxes between the media boxes.

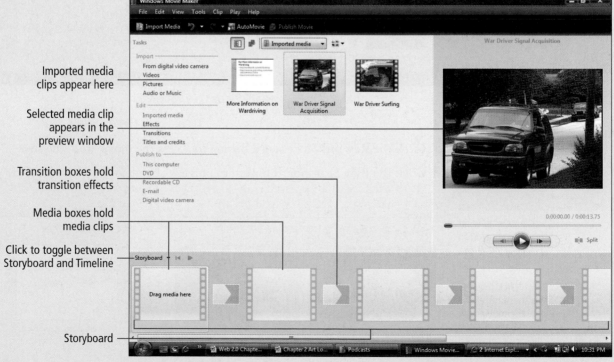

Imported media clips appear here

Selected media clip appears in the preview window

Transition boxes hold transition effects

Media boxes hold media clips

Click to toggle between Storyboard and Timeline

Storyboard

Figure 2.38 Windows Movie Maker screen displaying imported media clips.

Step 3 Assemble the Components of the Podcast on the Storyboard

Refer to Figures 2.39 and 2.40 as you complete Step 3.

The clips should be laid out on the storyboard line in the order in which they should appear. The War Driver Signal Acquisition clip should come first, then the War Driver Surfing clip, and finally, the More Information on War Driving image.

a. Click and drag the **War Driver Signal Acquisition** clip to the first media box on the storyboard line.

b. Click and drag the **War Driver Surfing** clip to the second media box.

c. Click and drag the **More Information on War Driving** image to the third media box.

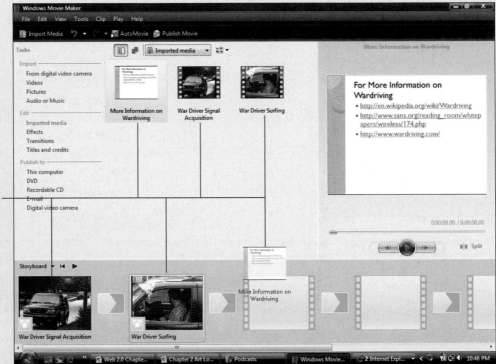

Click and drag the imported media clips to the storyboard line

Figure 2.39 Hands-On Exercise 3, Steps 3a through 3c.

d. Click the **Rewind Storyboard** button to access the movie from the start.

e. Click the **Play Storyboard** button to preview the movie you have created.

D – Click the Rewind Storyboard button to access the movie from the start

E – Click the Play Storyboard button to preview the movie that you have created

Figure 2.40 Hands-On Exercise 3, Steps 3d and 3e.

Step 4 Add Transitions and Titles to the Podcast

Refer to Figures 2.41 through 2.45 as you complete Step 4.

Transitions are effects that take place when moving from one media clip to the next. These can help make the movement from clip to clip less jarring to the eye.

a. In the **Tasks** menu on the left side of the Movie Maker main window, under the **Edit** group, click **Transitions** to display the available transition effects.

b. Click and drag the **Diagonal, Box Out** transition effect to the transition box located between the first two media clips.

c. Repeat Step b to add the same transition effect between the second and third clips.

d. Click the **Rewind Storyboard** button and then the **Play Storyboard** button to view the movie with the transition effects included.

A – Click to display the available transitions effects

D – Use the Rewind and Play buttons to view the movie with the transitions included

B & C – Click and drag the Diagonal, Box Out effect to the first two transition boxes

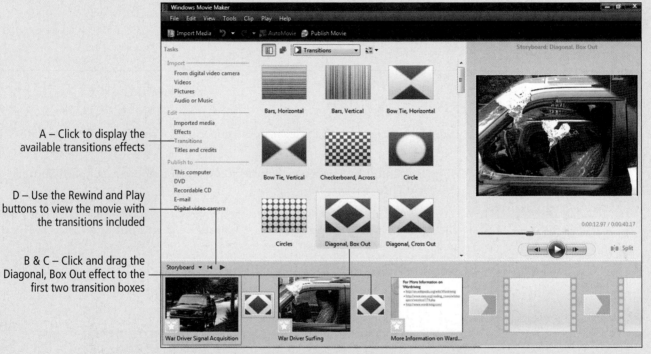

Figure 2.41 Hands-On Exercise 3, Steps 4a through 4d.

Title slides are useful for introducing your podcast and adding credits to the end of your podcast. Title slides can also be inserted before any media clip or can be overlaid (displayed on screen while the media clip is playing) on any clip. Professor Schmeckendorf has determined that it would be good for this podcast to have a title at the beginning and credits at the end.

e. In the **Tasks** menu on the left side of the Movie Maker main window, under the **Edit** group, click **Titles and Credits** to display the available options.

f. From the list of options, click the **Title at the Beginning** link to generate a title slide.

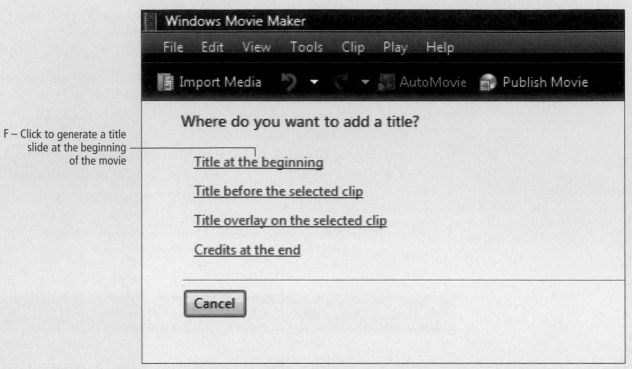

F – Click to generate a title slide at the beginning of the movie

Figure 2.42 Hands-On Exercise 3, Step 4f.

g. Type **War Driving 101 Podcast** in the upper half of the **Enter Text for Title** text box.

h. Type **Presented by Professor Schmeckendorf** in the lower half of the **Enter Text for Title** text box.

i. The text will automatically appear in the preview window so that you can review the slide. To make changes, click the **Change the Text Font and Color** link and make any changes you deem necessary.

j. Click the **Add Title** button to add the title slide you created to the beginning of your movie.

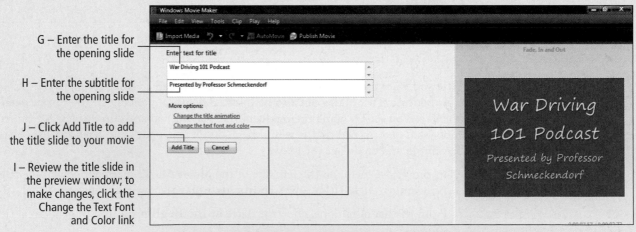

G – Enter the title for the opening slide

H – Enter the subtitle for the opening slide

J – Click Add Title to add the title slide to your movie

I – Review the title slide in the preview window; to make changes, click the Change the Text Font and Color link

Figure 2.43 Hands-On Exercise 3, Steps 4g through 4j.

k. In the **Tasks** menu on the left side of the Movie Maker main window, click **Titles and Credits** under the **Edit** group to display the available options.

l. From the list of options, click the **Credits at the End** link to generate an ending credits slide.

m. Type the following credits in the appropriate boxes as shown in Figure 2.44:

War Driving 101 Podcast
Presented by Professor Schmeckendorf
Ginormous State University (GSU)
For more podcasts go to:
http://pschmeckendorf.podbean.com

n. Review the credits in the preview window. Click the **Change the Title Animation** or **Change the Text Font and Color** links to make any changes.

o. Click the **Add Title** button to add the credits to the end of the movie.

M – Enter the text for the credits in the appropriate boxes

N – Review the credits in the preview window; click the Change the Title Animation or Change the Text Font and Color links to make any changes

O – Click Add Title to add the credits to the end of the movie

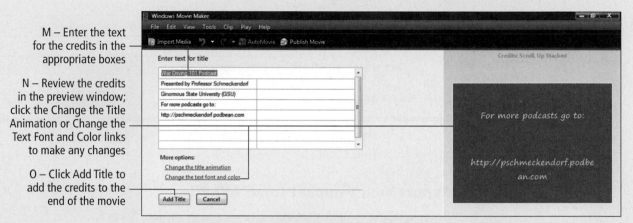

Figure 2.44 Hands-On Exercise 3, Steps 4m through 4o.

Now that the movie is in final form (with titles and credits), you should save the file to avoid losing your work. You will be saving the movie file in the Windows Movie Maker Project file format, which is not a format that can be universally viewed by most media players. In the next step of the hands-on exercise, you'll convert the file to a format that is more useful to your viewers.

p. Click **File** and select **Save Project As** to display the **Save Project As** dialog box.

q. If necessary, click the **Browse Folders** drop-down arrow. Browse through the folders on your computer to find an appropriate place to save the file.

r. Type **War Driving 101 Movie Maker Format** in the **File name** text box.

s. Click the **Save** button to save the file.

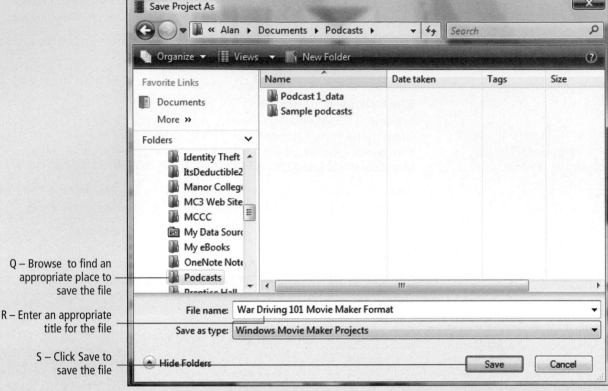

Q – Browse to find an appropriate place to save the file

R – Enter an appropriate title for the file

S – Click Save to save the file

Figure 2.45 Hands-On Exercise 3, Steps 4q through 4s.

Step 5 Export Your Podcast to an AVI File

Refer to Figures 2.46 through 2.49 as you complete Step 5.

To make it easy for subscribers to your podcast to view the file, you need to convert the movie you just made to a common video file format such as AVI. Fortunately, this is easy to accomplish in Windows Movie Maker.

a. In the main window in Movie Maker, click the **Publish Movie** icon on the toolbar to display the first **Publish Movie** dialog box.

b. The Publish Movie dialog box provides a list of locations to which you can publish the movie. Click **This Computer** to store the file on your computer until it is uploaded to the Internet.

c. Click the **Next** button to move to the second **Publish Movie** dialog box.

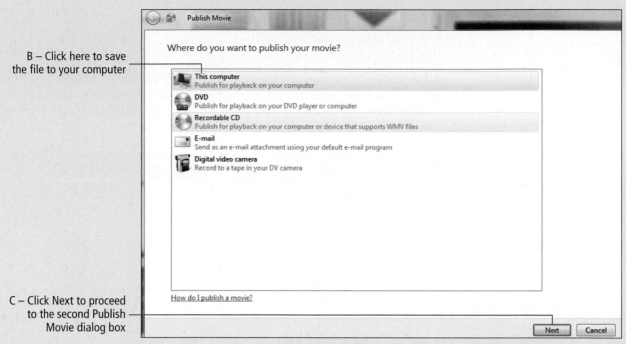

B – Click here to save the file to your computer

C – Click Next to proceed to the second Publish Movie dialog box

Figure 2.46 Hands-On Exercise 3, Steps 5b and 5c.

d. Type **War Driving 101 Podcast** in the **File name** text box.

e. Click the **Browse** button to search your hard drive for an appropriate folder in which to save the file.

f. Click the **Next** button to move to the third **Publish Movie** dialog box.

D – Enter a name for the file

E – Click to browse your hard drive for an appropriate folder in which to save the file

F – Click Next to move to the third Publish Movie dialog box

Figure 2.47 Hands-On Exercise 3, Steps 5d through 5f.

g. Click the **More settings** option to select it.

h. Click the **drop-down arrow** to display the list of available filetypes. Select the **DV-AVI (NTSC)** filetype.

i. Click the **Publish** button to convert the file to AVI format and save it to the hard drive. Depending upon the size of the file, you may experience a slight delay while the file is being converted. The final **Publish Movie** dialog box will open.

G – Click the More settings option

H – Click the drop-down arrow and select the DV-AVI (NTSC) filetype

I – Click Publish to convert the file to AVI format and save it

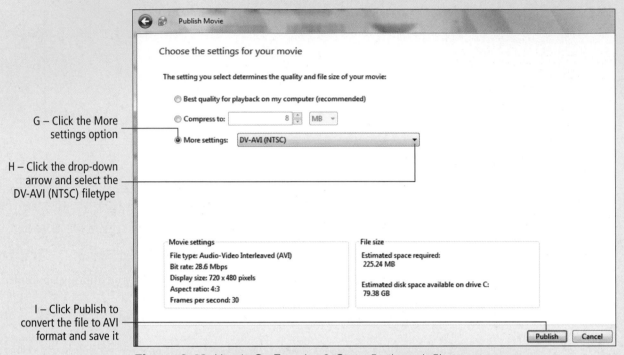

Figure 2.48 Hands-On Exercise 3, Steps 5g through 5i.

j. If necessary, click the **Play Movie When I Click Finish** checkbox to place a check mark there.

k. Click **Finish** to complete the Publish Movie process. Windows Media Player will open and play the movie. Close Windows Media Player.

J – Click the checkbox to view the movie when you are done

K – Click Finish

Figure 2.49 Hands-On Exercise 3, Steps 5j and 5k.

l. Return to Windows Movie Maker and, from the **File** menu, select **Exit** to close the program. If you are prompted to save changes, click **No**.

Congratulations! You now have a video podcast that is ready for posting on the Internet.

Objective 9

Upload a podcast to the Internet

Once you start creating podcasts, you need a way to distribute them to your audience. There are many podcast hosting services on the Internet, but a good one to start with is Podbean.com. They offer free accounts to get new podcasters started so that you can make sure their services work for you before you commit any money. Podbean can handle audio and video podcasts.

Hands-On Exercises

4 | Upload a Podcast to the Internet

Steps: 1. Create an Account at Podbean.com **2.** Upload Podcast Files to Podbean.com

Use Figures 2.50 through 2.57 as a guide in the exercise.

 Step 1 **Create an Account at Podbean.com**

Refer to Figures 2.50 through 2.52 as you complete Step 1.

a. Open your web browser and navigate to **www.podbean.com**.

b. Locate the Podcast Publishers section and click the **Free Sign Up Now** link to begin the Podbean Basic Account creation process.

B – Click to create an account

Figure 2.50 Hands-On Exercise 4, Step 1b.

c. Ensure that the free **Podbean Basic Account** option is selected. Scroll down to the next section.

d. Type a member name for your account in the **Member Name** text box. This becomes part of the URL for your podcast site, so choose carefully.

e. Type your email address in the **E-mail** text box. You must use a valid email address because Podbean will send your initial password to this email account. You won't be able to access your Podbean account until you have retrieved the password.

f. Enter your personal information as required in the appropriate boxes.

g. Click the **Terms of Service** link. Podbean's Terms of Service will open in a new browser window. Review the terms and close the window when you are done. If necessary, click the **Service** checkbox to insert a check and agree to the terms of service for your Podbean account.

h. In the **Verification** section, type the text shown in the CAPTCHA box above. This text will be different than the text shown in Figure 2.51.

i. If you do not wish to receive the Podbean newsletter, click the **Yes, Email Me Podbean Newsletter** checkbox to uncheck the box.

j. Click the **Sign Up Now** button to create your account.

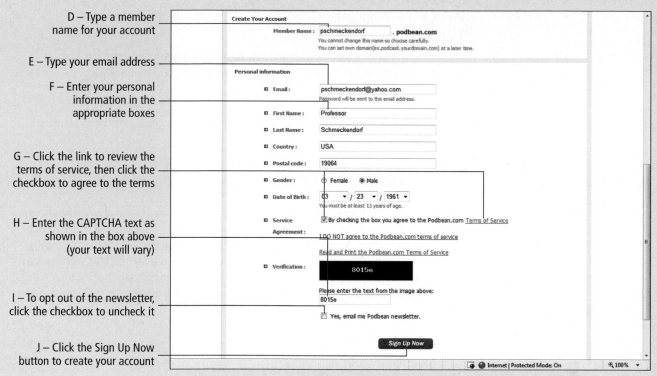

D – Type a member name for your account

E – Type your email address

F – Enter your personal information in the appropriate boxes

G – Click the link to review the terms of service, then click the checkbox to agree to the terms

H – Enter the CAPTCHA text as shown in the box above (your text will vary)

I – To opt out of the newsletter, click the checkbox to uncheck it

J – Click the Sign Up Now button to create your account

Figure 2.51 Hands-On Exercise 4, Steps 1d through 1j.

Alert!

If you receive an error message, check to be sure that you have entered all of the required information. You will need to re-enter the CAPTCHA text because it will have changed. You may also need to uncheck the newsletter checkbox again.

In five to ten minutes, Podbean will send an email to the address you provided. The email will contain the password for your Podbean account. Retrieve your password and return to www.podbean.com.

k. Click the **Log In** link at the top right corner of the site to display the login screen.

l. Type your username and password in the boxes provided.

m. Click the **Login** button to access your account. Uncheck the checkbox next to **Remember Me** if you are working on a public or shared computer.

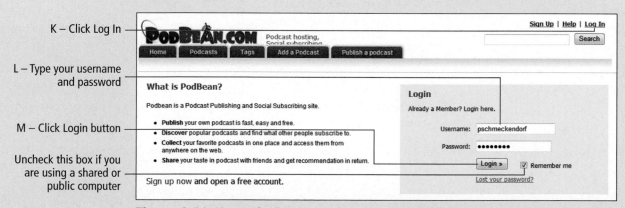

K – Click Log In

L – Type your username and password

M – Click Login button

Uncheck this box if you are using a shared or public computer

Figure 2.52 Hands-On Exercise 4, Steps 1k through 1m.

Alert!

The first time you login to your account, you may be asked to upload a podcast logo (picture) to associate with your podcast. You can ignore this by clicking the **Skip for Now** link.

n. Click the **Publish a Podcast** tab at the top of the page to go to the Dashboard page. This is the control center for your podcast site.

Tip **Changing Your Password**

When you first accessed your Podbean account, you used a password provided by Podbean. You should change this password to something that you will be able to remember but that will not be easily guessed by others. To change your password, click the **Profile** link at the top of the page, then click the **Change Password** link. In the **Update Your Password** section, type your new password. You must retype your password to ensure that it was entered correctly the first time. Click the **Update Account** button, then click the **My Podcast** link at the top of the page to return to the Dashboard.

Step 2 **Upload Podcast Files to Podbean.com**

Refer to Figures 2.53 through 2.57 as you complete Step 2.

You should have two files that you can upload immediately: the audio podcast you created in Exercise 2 and the video podcast you created for Professor Schmeckendorf in Exercise 3.

a. On the **Dashboard** screen, click the **Upload** link to begin the uploading process.

A – Click to begin uploading files

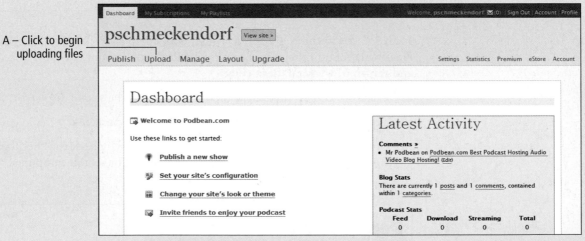

Figure 2.53 Hands-On Exercise 4, Step 2a.

b. On the **Media Manager** screen, click the **Upload** icon to proceed to the next screen.

B – Click here to proceed to the next screen

Figure 2.54 Hands-On Exercise 4, Step 2b.

The video podcast created in Exercise 3 may be too large to post to the free Podbean account. Because the MP3 audio podcast created in Exercise 2 is smaller, you will post this one to the account.

c. Click the **Browse** button to locate **Podcast Volume 1-1,** the audio podcast file created in Exercise 2. Click the file and click the **Open** button to display the file in the **Upload Files to Your Account** list.

d. Click the **Upload** button to transfer the audio file to your Podbean account. When the upload is complete, the file name will appear in the Current Media files list.

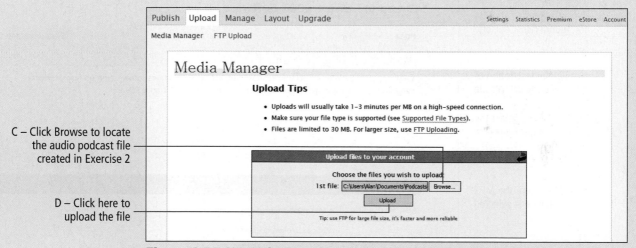

C – Click Browse to locate the audio podcast file created in Exercise 2

D – Click here to upload the file

Figure 2.55 Hands-On Exercise 4, Steps 2c and 2d.

Your Podbean account has many features that are similar to a blog. One feature allows you to publish an entry similar to a blog post that describes the podcast episode you just uploaded.

e. Click the **Publish** link at the top of the Dashboard to proceed to the **Write Post/Episode** screen.

f. Just as with blogs, you can create tags for your podcasts. You must create at least one tag consisting of two or more characters for the podcast. Type **Office 2007** in the **Tags** text box.

g. You also need to provide a title for your podcast. Type **Cheap MS Office 2007 Software** in the **Title** text box.

h. Similarly, it is helpful for your audience to know what your podcast is about before they attempt to download it. Type the following description in the **Post** text box:

Volume 1 of the Professor Schmeckendorf podcast series contains information on how students can purchase the Ultimate edition of Microsoft Office 2007 for only $59.95!

i. In this step, you will associate the audio file you have already uploaded with the post you are creating. In the **Podcasting** section, click the **Select From Account** drop-down arrow and select **PodcastVolume1-1.mp3**. This is the file that you already uploaded to the Podbean site.

j. Because there is a wide variety of filetypes that you can upload to Podbean, you also need to identify the filetype. If necessary, click the **File Type** drop-down arrow and select **MP3 - Standard Audio (iPod Compliant)**.

k. Click the **Auto Detect** button in the **Duration** section to compute the duration of the podcast file.

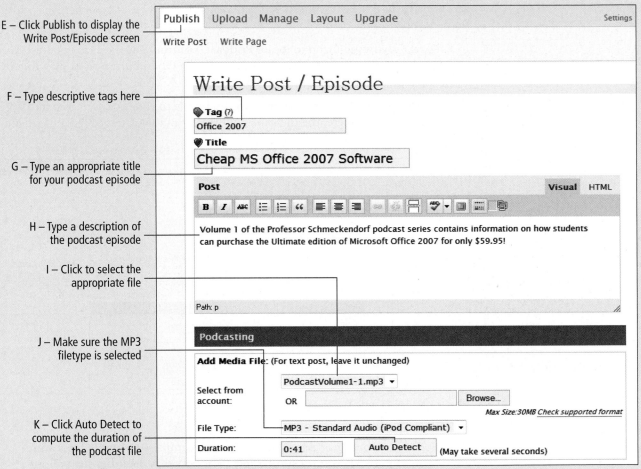

E – Click Publish to display the Write Post/Episode screen

F – Type descriptive tags here

G – Type an appropriate title for your podcast episode

H – Type a description of the podcast episode

I – Click to select the appropriate file

J – Make sure the MP3 filetype is selected

K – Click Auto Detect to compute the duration of the podcast file

Figure 2.56 Hands-On Exercise 4, Steps 2e through 2k.

l. At the bottom of the **Write Post/Episode** screen, click the **Publish** button to publish your episode on your Podbean site.

m. At the top of the **Dashboard** screen, click the **View Site** button to see what your podcast site looks like with your first episode posted (Figure 2.57).

There is a lot more you should do to enhance your Podbean site if you are planning to host regular podcasts. You should definitely provide a page on the site that describes your podcast and its theme. The About page option works well for this. You might even want to tell listeners a bit about yourself. So explore the options in Podbean and enhance your site. You might quickly develop a very loyal following if you are producing quality podcasts.

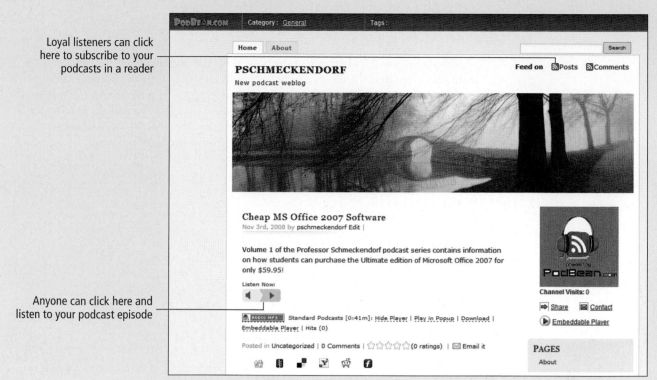

Loyal listeners can click here to subscribe to your podcasts in a reader

Anyone can click here and listen to your podcast episode

Figure 2.57 Hands-On Exercise 4, Step 2m.

Objective 10

Describe Internet resources that educate people about podcasting

Because podcasting has become quite popular, there is a wealth of information on the Internet that can help you learn more about creating effective audio and video podcasts. Here are some resources you may want to explore:

- How to Podcast (www.how-to-podcast-tutorial.com) – A well-written tutorial by Jason Van Orden who generates a number of his own podcasts. Jason takes the reader step by step through podcast planning and recording. He even has video files that demonstrate how to use Audacity.

- How to Create Your Own Podcast (http://computer.howstuffworks.com/how-to-podcast.htm) – This is another tutorial from the excellent How Stuff Works site. This tutorial covers the basics of podcasting and has links to additional technical articles for more in-depth information about how podcasts work.

- The Podcasting Underground (http://podcastingunderground.com) – A blog that provides tips for becoming a successful podcaster. Also includes news stories on podcasting.

- Making a Podcast (www.apple.com/itunes/whatson/podcasts/specs.html) – Important information from the folks at Apple to help you understand how to create a podcast, as well as the process for submitting your podcast to Apple and getting it indexed in iTunes. You definitely want your podcast available in iTunes because it will help you build an audience quickly.

Summary

You have now learned many of the basic skills for creating engaging podcasts. The main thing that draws listeners to a podcast is interesting, original content. Adding cool features to your podcast like theme music, sound effects, and other gimmicks might be fun for you but won't always appeal to your listeners, who are most likely looking for information or entertainment. So concentrate on generating well-produced podcast episodes on a regular schedule that support the general theme of your podcast, and you should be well on your way to building a loyal audience.

Key Terms

Multiple Choice

1. The software designed to check the Internet for new podcast episodes is known as a:

    (a) vodcast.

    (b) podcatcher.

    (c) synchronizer.

    (d) pop filter.

2. To have data about a podcast appear on a PMP or on screen, the information should be added as a(n):

    (a) ID3 tag.

    (b) Screen tip.

    (c) MP3 encoder.

    (d) aggregator.

3. Which of the following statements is true about transitions?

    (a) Transitions are a series of panels arranged to portray action or events.

    (b) Transitions provide information about a podcast.

    (c) Transitions cannot be previewed in Windows Movie Maker.

    (d) Transitions are effects that take place between media clips.

4. Which of the following statements is *not* true about zipped folders?

    (a) Zipped folders can only be used in Windows Vista.

    (b) Zipped folders must be extracted before they can be used.

    (c) Zipped folders are created with file compression software.

    (d) Zipped folders enable files to download quickly.

5. Which term describes software that is still in the testing stage and may not work as expected?

    (a) Compressed file

    (b) Zipped file

    (c) Beta version

    (d) Aggregator software

6. Which of the following statements is *not* true about pop filters?

    (a) A pop filter helps to prevent popping sounds on a recording.

    (b) A pop filter is used to eliminate high-frequency feedback.

    (c) A pop filter is a mesh screen placed in front of a microphone.

    (d) A pop filter can help make your recordings sound more professional.

7. In order to use the files contained in a zipped folder, they must first be:

    (a) compacted.

    (b) downloaded.

    (c) debugged.

    (d) extracted.

8. When planning a podcast, which of the following is *not* a step that needs to be considered?

    (a) Decide on an aggregator.

    (b) Determine a topic.

    (c) Consider the optimal length for the podcast.

    (d) Develop a schedule.

9. Which of the following statements is *not* true about podcasts?

    (a) A podcast is a group of audio or video media files.

    (b) To listen to or view a podcast, an iPod is required.

    (c) You can use a podcatcher to subscribe to a podcast.

    (d) A vidcast is a video podcast.

10. Which of the following is *not* an example of hardware that can be used when creating a podcast?

    (a) Sound card

    (b) Speakers

    (c) Audacity

    (d) Camcorder

Fill in the Blank

1. A _____ is a panel, or series of panels, arranged to portray the action or events in a video.
2. To download a podcast to a PMP, you must connect, or _____, it to your computer.
3. A(n) _____ _____ is an optional piece of equipment placed in front of a microphone to improve sound quality.
4. A(n) _____, also known as a *vodcast*, is a podcast that includes audio and video components.
5. _____ _____ like RSS are used to notify people when new podcast content is available.

Practice Exercises

1. **Creating a Podcast Script and Recording the Podcast**

   Prior to recording a podcast, it is a good idea to create a script. Creating a script helps you to organize your thoughts and cover all your key points. For this exercise, you will write a script explaining how to open a file using Microsoft Word. You will then record the podcast based on the script.

   a. Open Microsoft Word.
   b. Create a short script, in your own words, explaining how to open a file in Word.
   c. Save your script as **Podcast Script 1_Your_Name**.
   d. Print your script.
   e. Check your recording and playback devices to be sure they are working correctly.
   f. Start Audacity and record your podcast using the script you created. Be sure to perform a sound level check. You should also make one deliberate mistake and correct it while you are still recording, using the technique explained in the chapter.
   g. Review your recording once you've completed it. Do not edit the file at this time.
   h. Save the file using the **Save Project As** option. Name the file **Podcast Practice 1_Your_Name**.
   i. Submit the **Podcast Script 1_Your_Name** and **Podcast Practice 1_Your_Name** files to your instructor. Remember that the Audacity files consist of the .aup project file and the _data project folder.

2. **Downloading Compressed Files and Editing and Exporting a Podcast**

   A new podcast has been created for Professor Schmeckendorf's class; however, it has several errors that need to be fixed. The sound check should be deleted. It runs from the beginning of the podcast up to the 4-second mark. The narrator has an error that begins at approximately the 21-second mark and lasts for 10 seconds. This is the section that begins with "The Open dialog box will appear on screen." You will need to delete this sentence and the following sentence that contains the error. Remember that the time line will adjust as portions of the recording are edited. You will also need to export the edited podcast as an MP3 file.

   a. If necessary, open **Audacity**.
   b. Navigate to the location where you saved your student data files for Chapter 2. Open the **ch2_ex2.aup** file within the ch_ex2 folder and review the podcast. Make note of the required edits.
   c. Edit the podcast as needed. Use the **Save Project As** option and save the file as **ch2_ex2_Your_Name**.
   d. Export the edited podcast as an MP3 file. Name the file **ch2_ex2_MP3_Your_Name**.

e. Use the following information to create the ID3 tags:
   Title: ch2_ex2_MP3_Your_Name
   Artist: Your Name
   Album: Podcast Practice Exercise 2
   Track Number: 1   Year: 2009
   Genre: Speech

f. Submit the edited Audacity files (project file and data folder sent as a zipped file) and the MP3 file to your instructor.

3. Creating a Video Podcast

Professor Schmeckendorf is working on a tutorial to show students how to use HTML to create web pages. You have been asked to create a video podcast using two video clips and two image files that Professor Schmeckendorf has created.

a. Start Windows Movie Maker and import the following two video clips and two image files from your Chapter 2 student data file downloads:
   - ch2_ex3_image1.jpg
   - ch2_ex3_image2.jpg
   - ch2_ex3_video1.wmv
   - ch2_ex3_video2.wmv

b. Add the imported media clips to the storyboard in the following order:
   1. ch2_ex3_video1.wmv
   2. ch2_ex3_image1.jpg
   3. ch2_ex3_video2.wmv
   4. ch2_ex3_image2.jpg

c. Play back the storyboard to ensure that everything is in place, then save the file as **ch2_ex3_Your_Name**. Submit the file to your instructor.

4. Adding Transitions and Titles and Publishing a Video Podcast

In this exercise, you'll continue working with the video podcast created in Exercise 3. Professor Schmeckendorf would like you to add transitions between the clips. He also wants you to add a title slide and credits at the end of the video. After these changes have been made, the video file must be converted to a Windows Media Video (WMV) file and published.

a. Open Windows Movie Maker and locate the file you created in Exercise 3: **ch2_ex3_Your_Name**.

b. From the **File** menu, select **Save File As** and rename the file **ch2_ex4_Your_Name**.

c. Insert the transition of your choice between each of the clips.

d. Create a title slide at the beginning of the video. Type **An Overview of HTML** in the first text box and **Presented by Professor Schmeckendorf** in the second text box.

e. Change the background color of the title slide to another color of your choice. If necessary, change the font color to ensure that there is good contrast between the background and the text.

f. Add the credits to the end of the video and be sure to add your name as the assistant and the name of your institution. Use the following text:
   - **An Overview of HTML**
   - **Presented by Professor Schmeckendorf**
   - **Assisted by Your Name**
   - **Your Institution Name**

g. Play back the storyboard to review your changes.

h. Save the file as **ch2_ex4_Your_Name**. If you receive a message indicating that the file already exists, click **Yes** to replace the file with this version.

i. Next, you'll need to **Publish** the movie, using the **Best Quality for Playback on My Computer** option, which produces a **WMV** filetype. Save it to your computer as **ch2_ex4_WMV_Your_Name**. This step may take a while due to the size of the file.

j. Due to the size of this video file, check with your instructor for instructions on how to submit the file.

Critical Thinking

1. Some podcasters like to add music to their podcasts—often as background music or as an introduction to an episode. It is important to be aware of the copyright issues that are involved when you add music to a podcast. Write a brief paper outlining the steps a podcaster should take to ensure that any music included in a podcast is in compliance with the current rules regarding copyrights. Indicate your sources, and provide at least two or three Internet resources a podcaster can turn to for guidance.

2. A podcatcher, or aggregator, can be web-based or installed on your computer. Research two examples of a web-based podcatcher and two examples of an aggregator that is installed on your computer. Write a short paper describing the advantages and disadvantages of each podcatcher.

Team Projects

1. This chapter explored the various items needed to produce audio and video podcasts. As a group, develop a list of the items you would need to equip your own podcast studio. Research the prices for these items. Create a chart listing the lowest and highest prices for each item and where it can be obtained. Indicate which items you would choose and explain why you would choose them.

2. As a group, locate one video or audio podcast on each of the following topics:
   - Music Industry
   - Computers and Technology
   - Hobby Tutorial or How-To
   - Business Ethics

Create a table that lists the title and URL for each podcast and the topic it represents. Review the podcasts and rate them using the following criteria:
   - How long was the podcast?
   - How recent was the podcast?
   - Was the podcast informative or entertaining? Did it stay on topic?
   - How was the sound and video quality? How could it have been improved?
   - Which of the four podcasts do you think is the best? Which is the worst?

Include your findings on the table and submit it to your instructor.

CHAPTER 3

Enhancing Blogs

Objectives

After you read this chapter, you will be able to:

1. Explain how to publicize a blog
2. List a blog with search engines
3. Explain how to set up RSS feeds on Blogger
4. Subscribe to blog content using an aggregator
5. Explain copyright and the possible consequences of copyright violation
6. Add images and video to a blog
7. Change a blog template
8. Describe ways of earning money by blogging
9. Add Google AdSense advertisements to a blog
10. Add Amazon Associates links to a blog
11. Describe Internet resources about enhancing blogs

The following Hands-On Exercises will help you accomplish the chapter Objectives.

Hands-On Exercises

EXERCISES	SKILLS COVERED
1. List a blog with several search engines (page 108)	**Step 1:** Start Your Browser and Navigate to the Google Blog Search Add Page and Submit Your Blog **Step 2:** Navigate to the Add Your URL to Google Page and Submit Your Blog **Step 3:** Navigate to Technorati.com, Become a Member, and Claim Your Blog **Step 4:** Navigate to IceRocket and Submit Your Blog
2. Put an RSS feed on a blog (page 116)	**Step 1:** Log In to Blogger and Access Your Blog Layout **Step 2:** Insert a Subscription Links Gadget onto Your Blog
3. Subscribe to blog content using Google Reader (page 121)	**Step 1:** Log In to Your Google Account and Access Google Reader **Step 2:** Subscribe to Professor Schmeckendorf's Blog in Google Reader
4. Create a blog post that includes a photograph (page 128)	**Step 1:** Download a Photograph **Step 2:** Access Your Blog **Step 3:** Integrate a Photograph into a Blog Post
5. Create a blog post that includes embedded video (page 136)	**Step 1:** Access Your Blog **Step 2:** Create the Basic Blog Post **Step 3:** Add the Video Embedding Code for the Video
6. Change to a new blog template (page 143)	**Step 1:** Back Up Your Existing Template **Step 2:** Choose a New Template from Blogger-Provided Templates **Step 3:** Preview a New Template from pYzam.com
7. Display AdSense ads on a blog (page 153)	**Step 1:** Register for an AdSense Account **Step 2:** Insert an AdSense Ad onto Your Blog
8. Displaying Amazon Associates links on a blog (page 163)	**Step 1:** Register for an Amazon Associates Account **Step 2:** Insert an Amazon Associates Link onto Your Blog

Objective 1

Explain how to publicize a blog

After learning about blogs in Chapter 1, you may already be writing the most insightful, funny, or informative blog ever written. However, if no one reads your blog, you really aren't accomplishing your objective. Therefore, you need to publicize your blog to attract people to it and begin to develop an audience.

How do I publicize a blog?

Publicizing blogs is just like marketing any other product or service. Think about the way soft drinks are advertised. An advertisement can be designed to create product awareness of a new type of drink, such as when Coca Cola first introduced their Full Throttle line of energy drinks. If a product is new, you need to explain what the product is and where it is available. Other advertisements are persuasive in nature and are designed to get you to purchase a product. An ad for an energy drink might show tired young people consuming an energy drink, then dancing all night at a night club. Finally, some advertisements are designed to remind people that the product exists. Displaying banners that advertise an energy drink at the X Games serves to remind the audience that the product is available rather than to generate an immediate purchase.

These same marketing principles can be applied to promoting a blog. The three basic objectives of marketing, as applied to blogs, are as follows:

- Inform – Build initial awareness of your blog with potential readers.

- Persuade – Convince readers to subscribe to your blog and keep them returning to read new content.

- Remind – *Gently* refresh people's memory about your blog so that they don't forget about it.

Reminding really isn't an appropriate option for promoting a blog unless you want to create an email list and periodically send people email about your blog. This can be rather time consuming, and you may have difficulty getting readers to provide you with their email addresses. But you can certainly inform people and persuade them to visit your blog.

How do I create initial awareness of my blog?

There are many approaches you can take to build awareness. Fortunately, most of them are relatively simple and cost nothing to implement. Here are a few suggestions to consider:

Leave Comments on Other Blogs Search for other blogs that complement or are related to your blog's topic. If you have a blog about restoring classic cars, chances are that you will find that readers who might be interested in your blog are also reading other blogs about cars. Find a blog posting to which you can add relevant information, such as confirming the user's opinion through personal experience. Then post an informative or helpful comment on that blog entry and include a link back to your blog. Readers of blogs often read comments as well as blog entries, and this can help direct readers to your blog.

For example, Professor Schmeckendorf located the Technology in Action (Figure 3.1a) blog that is written by another college professor. Similar to Professor Schmeckendorf's blog, this blog also provides information and tips about computer technology. Professor Schmeckendorf located a blog entry about a free software package called YouTube Downloader. Since he also uses this software, he posted a comment on the Technology in Action blog (Figure 3.1b), endorsing this software and directing students to his blog for more information.

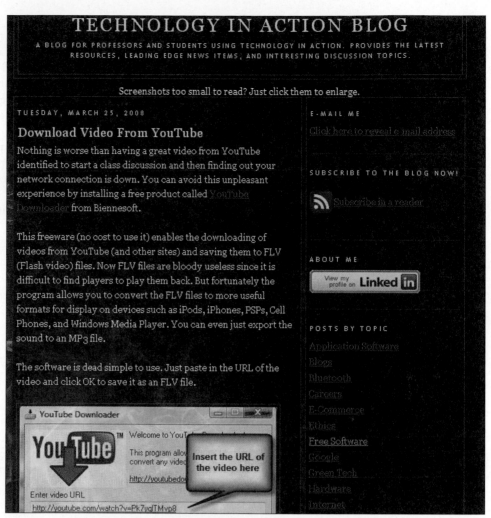

Figure 3.1a Entry on a blog with a theme similar to Professor Schmeckendorf's blog.

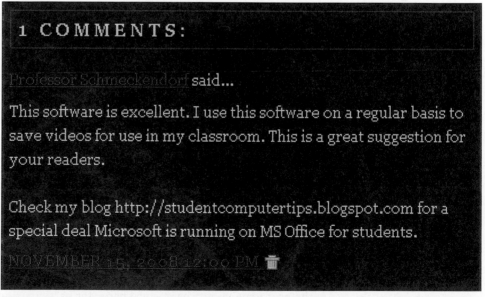

Figure 3.1b Comment posted by Professor Schmeckendorf on the Technology in Action blog.

Get Your Blog Listed in Search Engines *Search engines* are websites that are designed to search the web for information and create an index of that information. Users of a search engine can enter key words and the engine will then return a list of websites that are relevant to the search terms, called a *hit list*. You've probably used popular search engines such as Google, Yahoo!, and MSN. If your blog is indexed by major search engines, it can improve the chances that your blog will appear in the search results when people try to find information relating to your blog's topic.

With the vast increase in blogs over the past few years, blog search engines have become popular. A *blog search engine* is a specialized type of search engine that focuses on indexing and returning search results for information posted on blogs (Figure 3.2). Popular blog search engines include Technorati (www.technorati.com), Google Blog Search (http://blogsearch.google.com), and IceRocket (www.icerocket.com). It is important to have your blog indexed in these specialized search engines also.

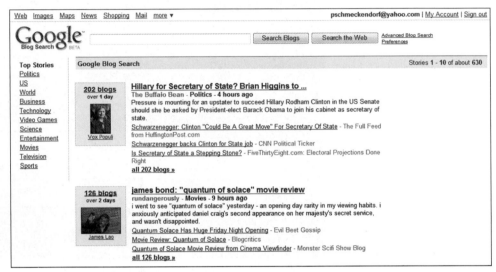

Figure 3.2 Google Blog Search (http://blogsearch.google.com) is a specialized version of the Google search engine that concentrates specifically on information found in blogs.

Enter Your Blog in Blog Carnivals A *blog carnival* is a type of online magazine (or newsletter) that is usually published on a blog on a regular basis (weekly, monthly, etc.). Blog carnivals typically have a specific topic and usually contain short descriptions of blog articles with links to those articles. Carnivals are like printed magazines because readers of carnivals browse through blog posts (articles) on related topics. It is a fast way for people to locate blog postings on a specific topic. Each blog carnival is organized by an author who solicits suggestions for content from blog owners and blog readers. Often, various blogs take turns hosting a carnival, so the carnivals are said to "travel" from place to place, similar to a real carnival.

Blog Carnival (www.blogcarnival.com) is a site that helps carnival authors solicit articles for inclusion in carnivals. The site provides a searchable listing of carnivals (http://blogcarnival.com/bc/clist.html) so that you can find carnivals that cover topics related to your blog. Each carnival—such as the Carnival of Financial Planning shown in Figure 3.3—has its own description and listing of topics that are acceptable for submission to the carnival. You can submit articles to a carnival, and the author of the carnival will decide whether or not to include your article in the next issue. Since there is no charge for participating in carnivals, and since many blog readers consult carnivals for fresh content, this is an excellent way to build readership.

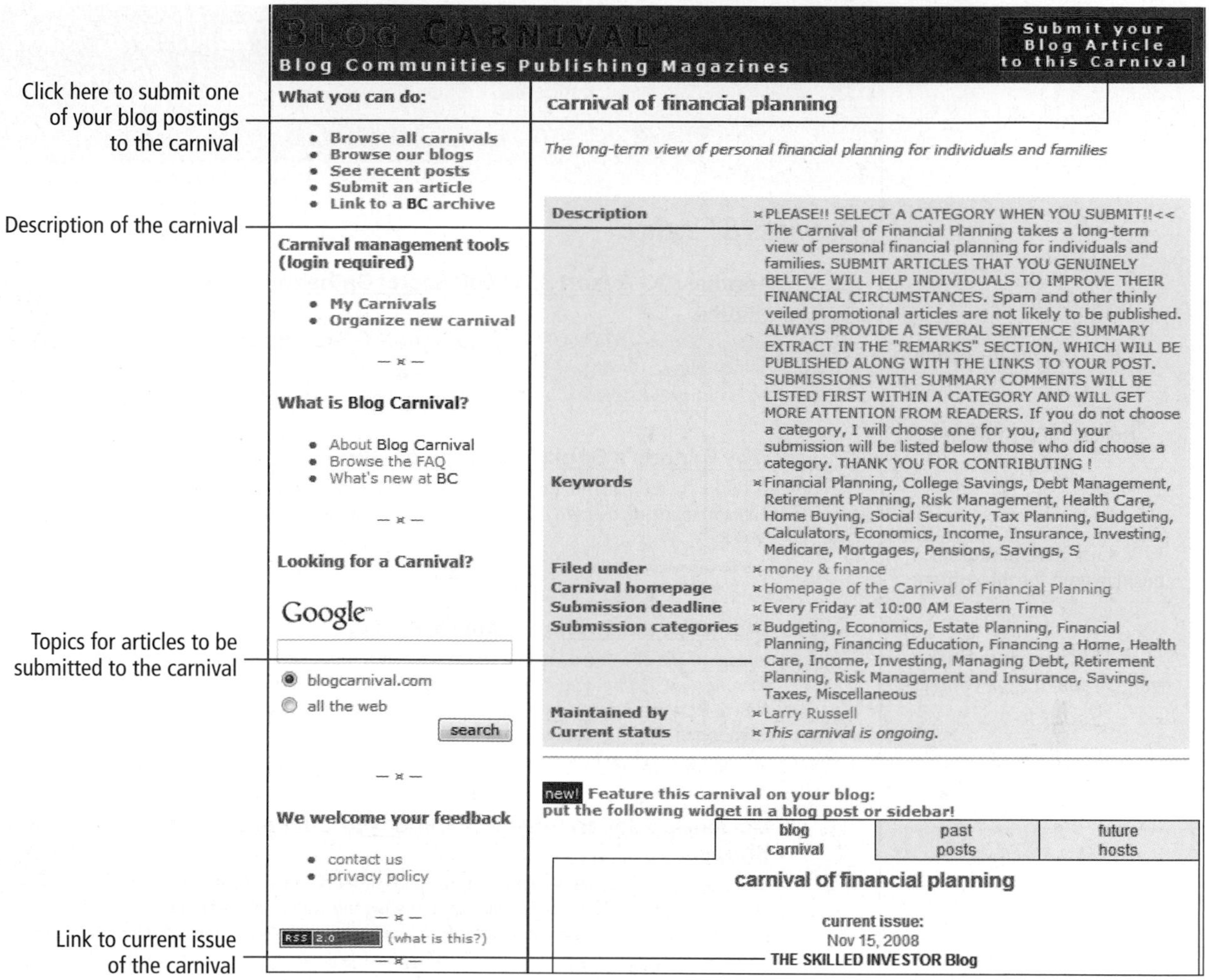

The figure shows a Blog Carnival web page with callout labels. Labels on the left point to parts of the page:

- Click here to submit one of your blog postings to the carnival
- Description of the carnival
- Topics for articles to be submitted to the carnival
- Link to current issue of the carnival

BLOG CARNIVAL
Blog Communities Publishing Magazines

Submit your Blog Article to this Carnival

What you can do:

- Browse all carnivals
- Browse our blogs
- See recent posts
- Submit an article
- Link to a BC archive

Carnival management tools (login required)

- My Carnivals
- Organize new carnival

— ✖ —

What is Blog Carnival?

- About Blog Carnival
- Browse the FAQ
- What's new at BC

— ✖ —

Looking for a Carnival?

Google

○ blogcarnival.com
○ all the web

search

— ✖ —

We welcome your feedback

- contact us
- privacy policy

— ✖ —

RSS 2.0 (what is this?)

— ✖ —

carnival of financial planning

The long-term view of personal financial planning for individuals and families

Description	✖ PLEASE!! SELECT A CATEGORY WHEN YOU SUBMIT!!<< The Carnival of Financial Planning takes a long-term view of personal financial planning for individuals and families. SUBMIT ARTICLES THAT YOU GENUINELY BELIEVE WILL HELP INDIVIDUALS TO IMPROVE THEIR FINANCIAL CIRCUMSTANCES. Spam and other thinly veiled promotional articles are not likely to be published. ALWAYS PROVIDE A SEVERAL SENTENCE SUMMARY EXTRACT IN THE "REMARKS" SECTION, WHICH WILL BE PUBLISHED ALONG WITH THE LINKS TO YOUR POST. SUBMISSIONS WITH SUMMARY COMMENTS WILL BE LISTED FIRST WITHIN A CATEGORY AND WILL GET MORE ATTENTION FROM READERS. If you do not choose a category, I will choose one for you, and your submission will be listed below those who did choose a category. THANK YOU FOR CONTRIBUTING !
Keywords	✖ Financial Planning, College Savings, Debt Management, Retirement Planning, Risk Management, Health Care, Home Buying, Social Security, Tax Planning, Budgeting, Calculators, Economics, Income, Insurance, Investing, Medicare, Mortgages, Pensions, Savings, S
Filed under	✖ money & finance
Carnival homepage	✖ Homepage of the Carnival of Financial Planning
Submission deadline	✖ Every Friday at 10:00 AM Eastern Time
Submission categories	✖ Budgeting, Economics, Estate Planning, Financial Planning, Financing Education, Financing a Home, Health Care, Income, Investing, Managing Debt, Retirement Planning, Risk Management and Insurance, Savings, Taxes, Miscellaneous
Maintained by	✖ Larry Russell
Current status	✖ *This carnival is ongoing.*

new! **Feature this carnival on your blog: put the following widget in a blog post or sidebar!**

blog carnival	past posts	future hosts

carnival of financial planning

current issue:
Nov 15, 2008
THE SKILLED INVESTOR Blog

Figure 3.3 Details of a blog carnival on financial planning.

Let Your Readers Promote Your Blog Some social networking sites, like Digg.com (Figure 3.4), encourage their members to find content on the Internet, share it with other community members, and vote on the popularity of the submission. Votes are either positive (digg) or negative (bury). The submissions with the most positive votes are displayed on the front page of various sections on Digg.com.

Many people review Digg and other social networking sites with submission and voting systems on a regular basis, so if your article becomes popular, it could be viewed by quite a few people. You can place icons on your blog that make it easy for your readers to recommend your content and share it with others through sites like Digg (Figure 3.5).

How do I persuade readers to return to my blog?

Once readers have found your blog, you need to develop strategies to keep them coming back for more. There are many approaches you can take to build a loyal following for your blog, and we recommend a few of the key ones here.

Create New, Quality Content Regularly Although this should be obvious, many new blogs fail to follow this strategy. People are looking for information, engaging content, creative discourse, or entertainment when reading blogs. If you don't produce well-written articles that pertain to the topic of your blog, readers will have no incentive to come back.

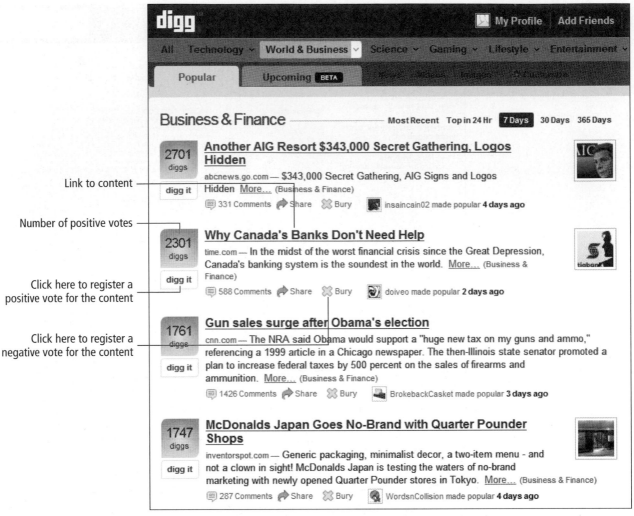

Link to content

Number of positive votes

Click here to register a positive vote for the content

Click here to register a negative vote for the content

Figure 3.4 Popular content on the business and finance page of Digg.com.

Use Images and Multimedia When Appropriate Although most blog postings contain a great deal of text, the use of visual media can stimulate interest for readers who are visual learners. Appropriate still images and videos also give your blog a more professional, polished feel.

Make It Easy For Readers to Subscribe to New Content Your readers may be reading numerous blogs on the Internet besides yours. Having to browse to your website and review it for new content might not seem like it would take much time. But what if your readers are following 50 different blogs? Will there be enough time for them to review all the blogs they are interested in every week? To make it easy to track numerous websites, blogs, and podcasts for new content, many readers use an aggregator. An *aggregator* is a type of software that is specially designed to go out and check the Internet for new content from websites, blogs, or podcasts to which you subscribe. Aggregator software can either be installed on your computer or it can be web based. An example of an installed aggregator is iTunes, while Google Reader is an example of a web-based aggregator.

When you subscribe to a blog in your aggregator, the software checks the web feed for that blog to see if any new content is available whenever you launch (or log in to) your aggregator software. A *web feed* is a specialized type of web page written in XML code that enables it to be updated whenever a blog's content is updated. Unlike regular HTML code, which is found on most web pages, a web feed page needs to be read by an aggregator. Once you have an aggregator set up to check web

Aggregator A type of software that is specially designed to go out and check the Internet for new content from websites, blogs, or podcasts to which you subscribe

Web feed A specialized type of web page written in XML code that enables it to be updated whenever a blog's content is updated

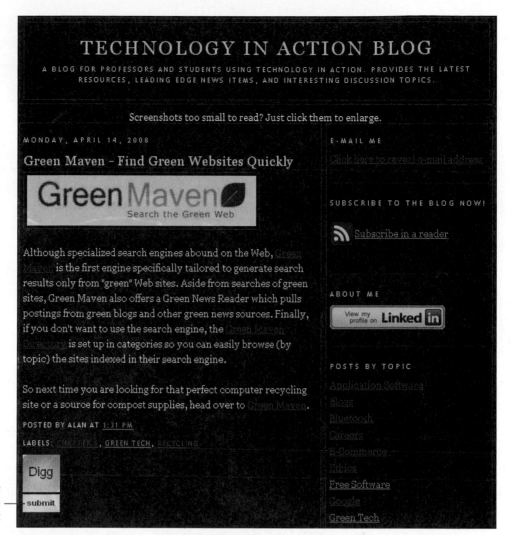

Clicking here takes a reader to the Digg website to recommend this blog post —

Figure 3.5 A blog featuring Digg submission icons.

Really Simple Syndication (RSS) A popular type of web feed that is used to syndicate content on the Internet

feeds, you are relieved of the tedium of checking numerous favorites or bookmarks in your browser to determine if a blog has been updated with new content.

RSS, which stands for *Really Simple Syndication*, is a popular type of web feed that is used to syndicate content on the Internet. Feed pages look like abbreviated versions of blogs and usually contain a portion of the most recent entries posted to a blog (Figure 3.6). A web feed is automatically generated for all sites set up on Blogger.com and most other popular blog hosting sites. You should put a link on your blog in a very obvious place (typically near the top of the blog) to enable readers to easily subscribe to your blog.

Make New Content Obvious In addition to adding subscription links, you should also consider including a list of the newest posts to your site, formatted as clickable links. This will help visitors to your blog find your latest material.

Objective 2

List a blog with search engines

For the following hands-on exercises, we'll be using Professor Schmeckendorf's blog (http://studentcomputertips.blogspot.com) in our examples. You should use the blog that you created in the Chapter 1 exercises, a blog that you currently maintain, or a

Clicking here allows you to subscribe to the blog in an aggregator

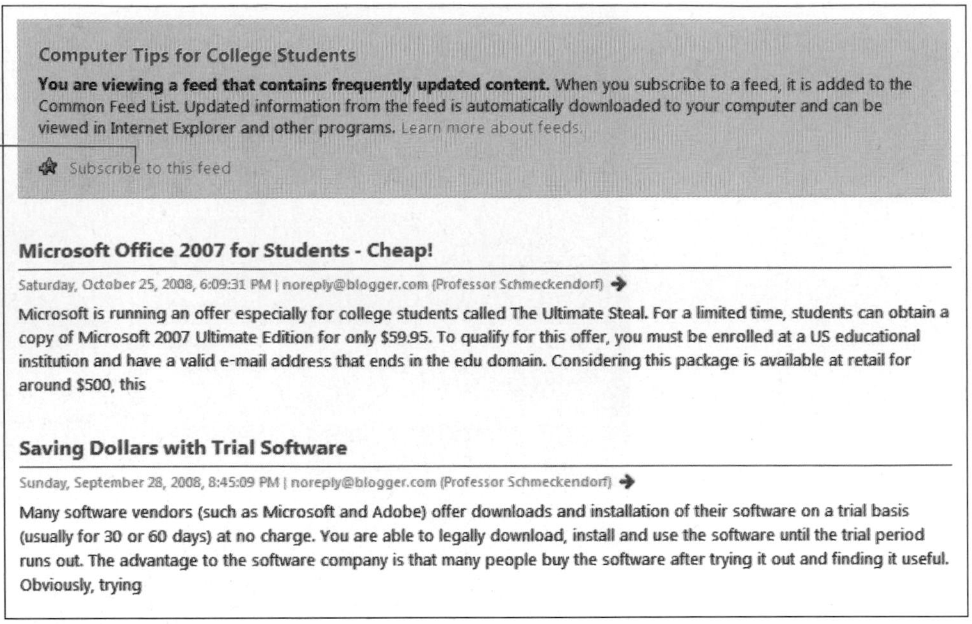

Computer Tips for College Students

You are viewing a feed that contains frequently updated content. When you subscribe to a feed, it is added to the Common Feed List. Updated information from the feed is automatically downloaded to your computer and can be viewed in Internet Explorer and other programs. Learn more about feeds.

⭐ Subscribe to this feed

Microsoft Office 2007 for Students - Cheap!

Saturday, October 25, 2008, 6:09:31 PM | noreply@blogger.com (Professor Schmeckendorf) ➜

Microsoft is running an offer especially for college students called The Ultimate Steal. For a limited time, students can obtain a copy of Microsoft 2007 Ultimate Edition for only $59.95. To qualify for this offer, you must be enrolled at a US educational institution and have a valid e-mail address that ends in the edu domain. Considering this package is available at retail for around $500, this

Saving Dollars with Trial Software

Sunday, September 28, 2008, 8:45:09 PM | noreply@blogger.com (Professor Schmeckendorf) ➜

Many software vendors (such as Microsoft and Adobe) offer downloads and installation of their software on a trial basis (usually for 30 or 60 days) at no charge. You are able to legally download, install and use the software until the trial period runs out. The advantage to the software company is that many people buy the software after trying it out and finding it useful. Obviously, trying

Figure 3.6 An excerpt of the web feed from Professor Schmeckendorf's *Computer Tips for College Students* blog.

new blog that you create for this chapter. However, if you choose to start a new blog, you should create several blog entries so that it will already have some content to work with.

Hands-On Exercises

1 | List a Blog with Several Search Engines

Steps: 1. Start Your Browser and Navigate to the Google Blog Search Add Page and Submit Your Blog **2.** Navigate to the Add Your URL to Google Page and Submit Your Blog **3.** Navigate to Technorati.com, Become a Member, and Claim Your Blog **4.** Navigate to IceRocket and Submit Your Blog

Use Figure 3.7 through 3.18 as a guide in the exercise.

 Step 1

Start Your Browser and Navigate to the Google Blog Search Add Page to Submit Your Blog

Refer to Figure 3.7 as you complete Step 1.

a. Turn on the computer.

b. Start your preferred browser (Internet Explorer, Firefox, Safari, etc.). Type **http://blogsearch.google.com/ping** in the address box of your browser and press **Enter**.

c. Type the URL for your blog in the **Your blog's address** box.

d. Click the **Submit Blog** button.

C – Enter the URL of your blog here

D – Click to submit your blog

Figure 3.7 Hands-On Exercise 1, Steps 1c and 1d.

Step 2 Navigate to the Add Your URL to Google Page and Submit Your Blog

Refer to Figure 3.8 as you complete Step 2.

a. Type **www.google.com/addurl** in the address box of your browser and press **Enter**.

b. Type the URL for your blog in the **URL** text box.

c. Type the CAPTCHA (displayed in the large box) in the smaller blank box below it.

d. Click the **Add URL** button.

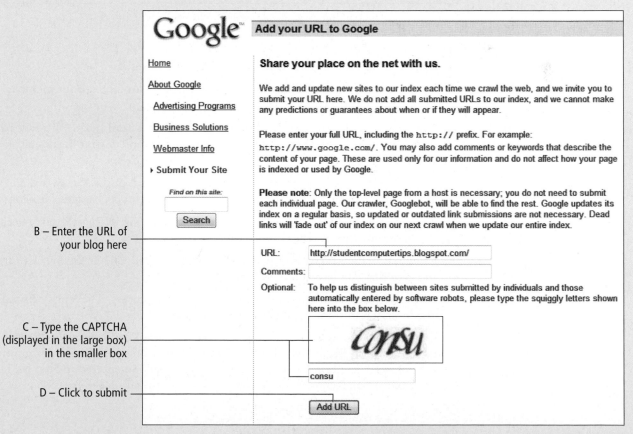

B – Enter the URL of your blog here

C – Type the CAPTCHA (displayed in the large box) in the smaller box

D – Click to submit

Figure 3.8 Hands-On Exercise 1, Steps 2b through 2d.

Navigate to Technorati.com, Become a Member, and Claim Your Blog

Refer to Figure 3.9 through 3.16 as you complete Step 3.

Technorati.com is a very popular blog search engine. Technorati also offers additional services to bloggers that match blog content with potential advertisers. So if you are serious about eventually making money with your blog, you should try to get your blog indexed in Technorati. There is no fee to join Technorati. Once you have joined, you will need to establish yourself as the owner of your blog (also known as claiming). This helps you get indexed in Technorati's search engine more quickly. In order to be eligible, your blog must meet the guidelines established by Technorati (http://support.technorati.com/guidelines).

a. Type **www.technorati.com** in the address box of your browser and press **Enter**.

b. At the top of the page, click **Join** to take you to the sign-up page.

B – Click Join to sign up ⎯

Figure 3.9 Hands-On Exercise 1, Steps 3a and 3b.

c. Type your real name in the **First** and **Last** name boxes.

d. Type a member name for yourself in the **Member Name** box. Your member name must be at least four characters in length.

e. Type your email address in the **Email** and **Confirm Email** boxes. You will need to retrieve a message from your email account to complete your Technorati registration, so make sure that this email account already exists.

f. Create a password for your account. Type the password in the **Password** and **Confirm Password** boxes. Passwords must be at least six characters in length.

g. Type the two words displayed in the ReCAPTCHA box in the text box beneath it. Be sure to separate the words with a blank space.

h. Click both **checkboxes** to agree to the terms of use for the Technorati site and to indicate that you have a blog to claim.

i. Click the **Join** button to continue the registration process. The **Verify Email Address** screen from Technorati should appear.

j. Open another browser window so that you leave the **Verify Email Address** screen from the Technorati site open in the current browser window. From the new browser window, access the email account that you entered in Step 3e. Locate the email from Technorati with your account confirmation information.

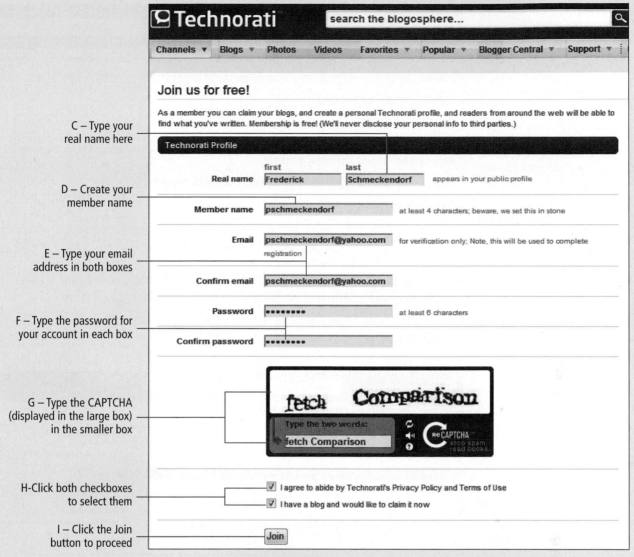

C – Type your real name here

D – Create your member name

E – Type your email address in both boxes

F – Type the password for your account in each box

G – Type the CAPTCHA (displayed in the large box) in the smaller box

H-Click both checkboxes to select them

I – Click the Join button to proceed

Figure 3.10 Hands-On Exercise 1, Steps 3c through 3i.

 Alert

The email from Technorati should arrive in your email account within a few minutes. If you cannot locate it in your inbox, check your spam or junk mail folder to see if it was identified as spam by your email system.

k. Click on the link provided in the email or copy the alphanumeric access key from the Technorati email.

l. On the **Verify Email Address** screen, type (or paste) the alphanumeric access code in the **Enter Confirmation Code** box.

m. Click the **Verify** button to confirm your Technorati account and proceed to the **My Account** screen.

L – Enter the confirmation code from the Technorati email here

M – Click to proceed

Figure 3.11 Hands-On Exercise 1, Steps 3l and 3m.

n. On the **My Account** screen, click the **Claim Your Blog Here!** link to go to the **My Account/Claim a New Blog** screen.

o. Type the URL of your blog in the URL text box. Click the **Begin Claim** button to proceed.

N – Enter the URL of your blog here

O – Click to proceed

Figure 3.12 Hands-On Exercise 1, Steps 2n and 2o.

p. Click the **Complete Claim with OpenID** button to continue the claim process by logging in to your blog account.

Review the URL carefully to ensure that you have entered it correctly. If you made a mistake, you can cancel the claim process by clicking the Cancel Claim button.

If the name you used on Technorati does not exactly match the name you used when you signed up for your blog account, you may receive an error message indicating that you are not a member or owner of the blog. Just select the option to log in with a different user account to proceed to the Blogger sign-in screen.

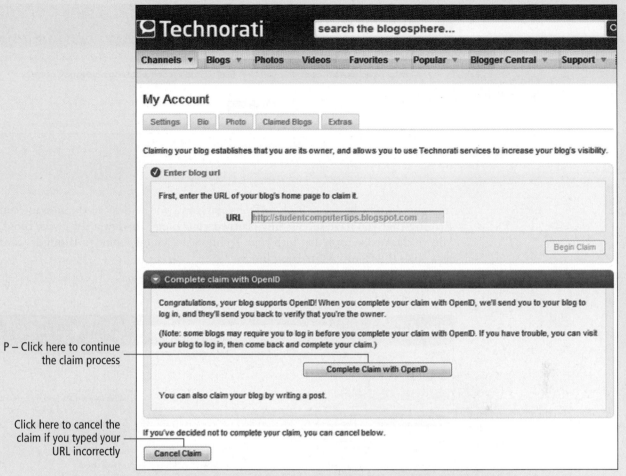

P – Click here to continue the claim process

Click here to cancel the claim if you typed your URL incorrectly

Figure 3.13 Hands-On Exercise 1, Step 3p.

q. Type your **Username** and **Password** into the appropriate boxes.

r. Click the **Sign In** button to log in to Blogger.

s. Click the **Yes, Always** button to confirm your ownership of the blog.

Q – Enter your username and password for Blogger

R – Click to sign in to Blogger

Figure 3.14 Hands-On Exercise 1, Steps 3q and 3r.

S – Click to confirm your blog ownership

Figure 3.15 Hands-On Exercise 1, Step 3s.

You should now be taken back to Technorati, and you will receive a message confirming that you have successfully claimed your blog. To view a list of the blogs you've claimed, simply log into your Technorati account, point to **Blogger Central**, and click the **Claim Your Blog** link.

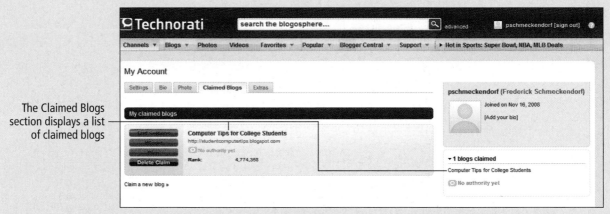

The Claimed Blogs section displays a list of claimed blogs

Figure 3.16 Technorati account for Professor Schmeckendorf showing his claimed blog.

 Navigate to IceRocket and Submit Your Blog

Refer to **Figures 3.17** through **3.18** as you complete Step 4.

IceRocket is another example of a search engine that specializes in helping visitors find information located in the blogosphere. IceRocket also provides options to search for information on the web or on MySpace or to locate news items or images. As with Technorati, there is no charge to have your blog indexed on IceRocket.

a. Type **www.icerocket.com** in the address box of your browser and press **Enter**.

b. Type the URL for your blog in the **Submit Blog** text box.

c. Click the **Go** button to submit your blog to IceRocket.

C – Click the Go button to submit your blog

B – Type the URL of your blog in this box

Figure 3.17 Hands-On Exercise 1, Steps 4b and 4c.

You should now be taken to the IceRocket Ping Us! page. There should be a message on this page thanking you for the ping. This means that they have received the URL for your blog and should schedule it to be indexed by their search engine. You do not need to click the Submit button on this page. You can now close your browser window.

Figure 3.18 IceRocket's Ping Us! screen showing the successful receipt of a blog URL.

Objective 3

Explain how to set up RSS feeds on Blogger

Now that you have begun publicizing your blog by having it indexed in search engines, you want to make sure that when readers find your blog, they can easily subscribe to your content through an RSS feed.

Blogger automatically sets up an RSS feed for each blog. All you need to do is add a gadget to your blog that provides a subscription link. Visitors to your blog can simply click this link to subscribe to your blog in their aggregator software. You should place the subscription link in a prominent place on your blog so that people can find it easily. If you are using a template with a column on the right, the top of this column is a good place to locate the link.

Hands-On Exercises

2 | Put an RSS Feed on a Blog

Steps: 1. Log In to Blogger and Access Your Blog Layout **2.** Insert a Subscription Links Gadget onto Your Blog

Use Figures 3.19 through 3.25 as a guide in the exercise.

For this hands-on exercise, we'll be modifying Professor Schmeckendorf's blog as an example. You should modify the blog you have set up in previous exercises.

Step 1 Log In to Blogger and Access Your Blog Layout

Refer to Figures 3.19 and 3.20 as you complete Step 1.

a. Start your preferred browser (Internet Explorer, Firefox, Safari, etc.). Type **www.blogger.com** in the address box of your browser and press **Enter**.

b. Type the **email address** and **password** for your Blogger account in the appropriate boxes.

c. Click the **Sign In** button to log in to Blogger.

d. On the Blogger Dashboard screen, click the **Layout** link to access the layout screen for your blog.

Figure 3.19 Hands-On Exercise 2, Steps 1b and 1c.

D – Click the Layout link

Figure 3.20 Hands-On Exercise 2, Step 1d.

 Step 2 **Insert a Subscription Links Gadget onto Your Blog**

Refer to Figures 3.21 through 3.25 as you complete Step 2.

a. Click the **Add a Gadget** link to display the Add a Gadget dialog box.

 Alert

Your layout screen may differ from the layout screen in Figure 3.21, depending upon your blog's template. You should choose an **Add a Gadget link** that is located in an appropriate place for the Subscription Links gadget to appear.

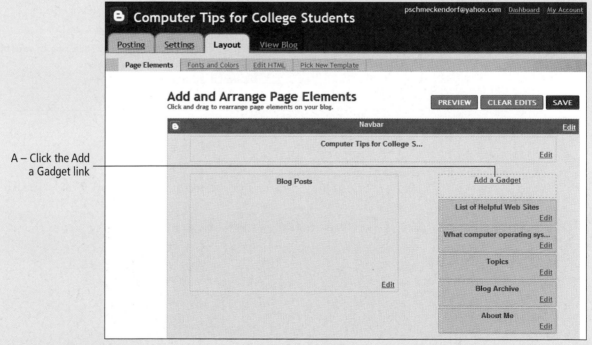

A – Click the Add a Gadget link

Figure 3.21 Hands-On Exercise 2, Step 2a.

b. In the **Add a Gadget** dialog box, click the **Basics** link to ensure that the Basics list of gadgets is displayed.

c. In the **Add a Gadget** dialog box, click the **Add** button (looks like a plus sign) next to the **Subscription Links** gadget to display the **Configure Subscription Links** dialog box.

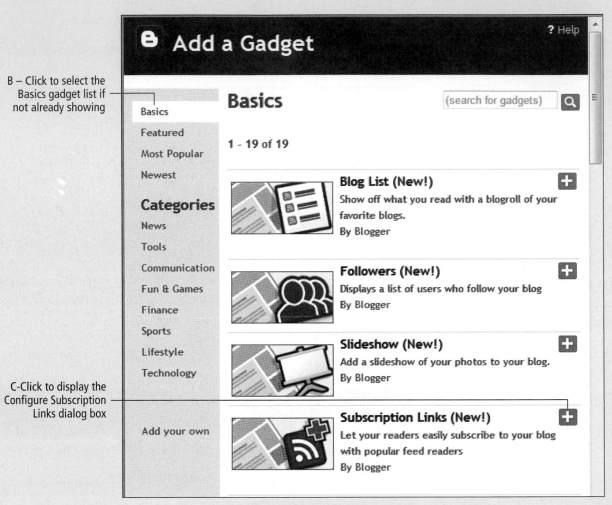

B – Click to select the Basics gadget list if not already showing

C-Click to display the Configure Subscription Links dialog box

Figure 3.22 Hands-On Exercise 2, Steps 2b and 2c.

d. In the **Configure Subscription Links** dialog box, type **Subscribe To This Blog** in the **Title** box.

e. Click the **Save** button to add the Subscription Links gadget to your blog.

D – Type **Subscribe To This** Blog here

E – Click the Save button

Figure 3.23 Hands-On Exercise 2, Steps 2d and 2e.

Notice that the gadget has now been added to the layout of the blog.

f. Click the **View Blog** link to display the blog with the new gadget installed (Figure 3.25).

g. Click the **Save** button to save the changes to the blog.

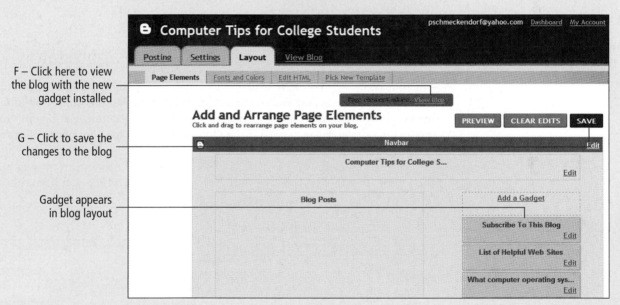

F – Click here to view the blog with the new gadget installed

G – Click to save the changes to the blog

Gadget appears in blog layout

Figure 3.24 Hands-On Exercise 2, Steps 2f and 2g.

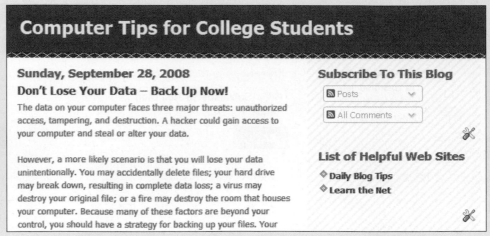

Figure 3.25 Professor Schmeckendorf's blog with the Subscription Links gadget configured.

Blog readers now have a handy link they can click to subscribe to either the posts on the blog or the comments to the posts on the blog.

Objective 4

Subscribe to blog content using an aggregator

Now that you know how easy it is to subscribe to blogs with RSS feeds, you may want to use an aggregator and start tracking blogs that you are interested in viewing. Since you already have a Google account (your Blogger account is also your Google account), it is easy to get started using Google Reader. This aggregator is provided free by Google.

Google Reader, shown in Figure 3.26, provides you with an easy way to manage numerous blogs. By clicking on the titles of the blogs to which you have subscribed,

New blog posts appear in this large window

You can filter items to show only new blog posts in the window

Clicking here allows you to email a note about the blog post to friends

Blogs to which you subscribe appear in this area

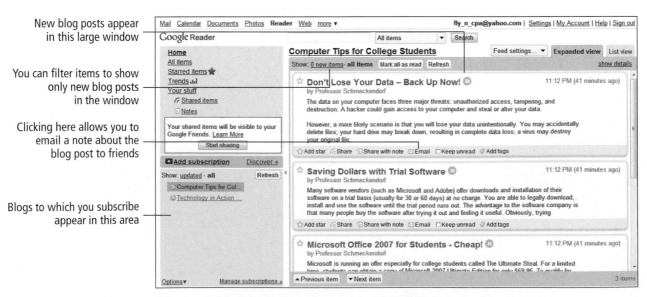

Figure 3.26 Google Reader showing subscriptions to two blogs.

new blog posts are displayed in the large window on the right. After reading these posts, you can mark them as read and they will no longer be displayed in Google Reader. You can also easily email a note about a particular blog entry to friends.

In the following hands-on exercise, you'll learn how to access Google Reader and subscribe to blogs with Google Reader.

Hands-On Exercises

3 | Subscribe to Blog Content Using Google Reader

Steps: 1. Log In to Your Google Account and Access Google Reader **2.** Subscribe to Professor Schmeckendorf's Blog in Google Reader

Use Figures 3.27 through 3.33 as a guide in the exercise.

Step 1 Log In to Your Google Account and Access Google Reader

Refer to Figures 3.27 through 3.30 as you complete Step 1.

a. Start your preferred browser (Internet Explorer, Firefox, Safari, etc.). Type **www.google.com** in the address box of your browser and press **Enter**.

b. Click the **Sign In** link to access your Google account.

B – Click to sign in to your Google account

Figure 3.27 Hands-On Exercise 3, Step 1b.

c. Type your **email** and **password** for your Google account (same as your Blogger account) in the appropriate boxes.

To remain always logged in to your Google account on the particular computer you are using, click the checkbox next to **Remember Me on This Computer** to select it. If you are using a shared computer such as a computer in a lab at school, *do not* choose this option.

d. Click the **Sign In** button to access your Google account.

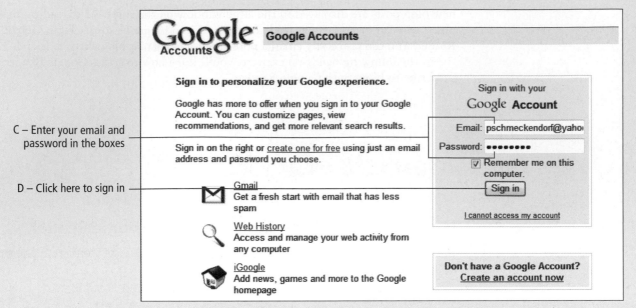

C – Enter your email and password in the boxes

D – Click here to sign in

Figure 3.28 Hands-On Exercise 3, Steps 1c and 1d.

e. Click the **More** link to display the drop-down menu. This provides you with access to many of the features offered in your Google account.

f. From the drop-down menu, click the **Reader** link to access Google Reader.

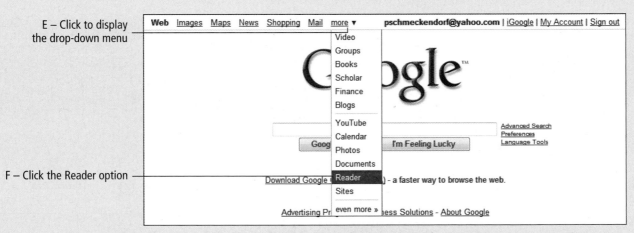

E – Click to display the drop-down menu

F – Click the Reader option

Figure 3.29 Hands-On Exercise 3, Steps 1e and 1f.

If you have never used Google Reader in this Google account before, your reader should look like the one shown in Figure 3.30. You can click on the appropriate links to view a video that explains how Google Reader works or take a tour of the features of Google Reader.

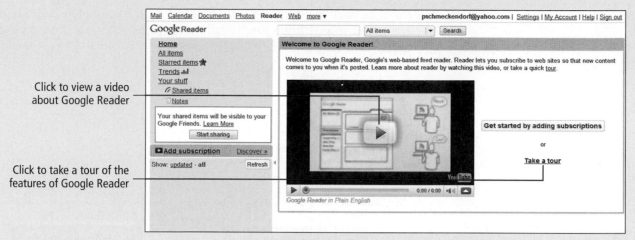

Click to view a video
about Google Reader

Click to take a tour of the
features of Google Reader

Figure 3.30 Google Reader when you first access your Google account.

You are now ready to subscribe to your first blog with Google Reader.

 Step 2 **Subscribe to Professor Schmeckendorf's Blog in Google Reader**

Refer to Figures 3.31 through 3.33 as you complete Step 2.

a. Leave Google Reader open in your browser. Open a new browser window, type http://studentcomputertips.blogspot.com in the address box of your browser, and press **Enter**.

b. Locate the **Subscribe To This Blog** section, and click the arrow in the **Posts** box to display a list of subscription choices.

c. From the list of subscription choices, click the **Add to Google** icon.

B – Click the arrow to
display the list of
subscription choices

C – Click the Add
to Google icon

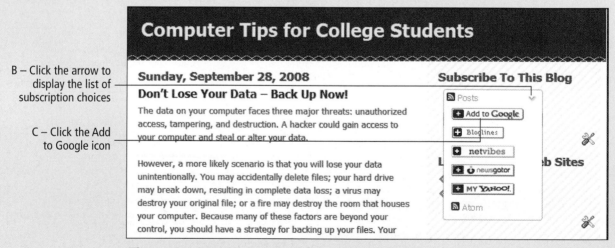

Figure 3.31 Hands-On Exercise 3, Steps 2b and 2c.

d. In the new browser window that opens, click the **Add to Google Reader** button. Alternatively, if you are using your Google home page, you could click the **Add to Google Homepage** button to display posts from this blog on your Google home page.

D – Click the Add to Google Reader button

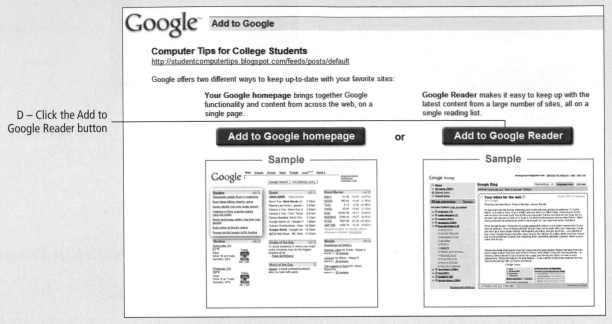

Figure 3.32 Hands-On Exercise 3, Step 2d.

The next screen may display a tip for managing your reading list. If this tip appears, simply click the **Dismiss This Message** link to remove it. Your Google Reader should now look like Figure 3.33. Professor Schmeckendorf's blog, *Computer Tips for College Students,* is now shown in the area where blog subscriptions are listed. Clicking on the title of any of the blogs in the subscription area will show partial content of posts from those blogs in the large window. Clicking on the title of a post will

Clicking this link will show only posts you haven't marked as read

After reviewing all posts, just click here to mark them as read

Click the title of any post to navigate to the blog and read it

Posts from blogs you subscribe to are shown in this large window

Blogs you subscribe to are shown here

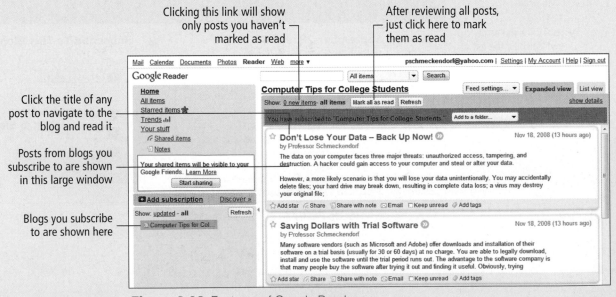

Figure 3.33 Features of Google Reader.

take you to the blog so that you can read the entire post. After reviewing all the posts you are interested in, click the **Mark All As Read** button. This indicates to Google Reader that you no longer consider these posts to be new.

You can filter the blog posts to display only the posts you haven't marked as read by clicking the **New Items** link. This makes it easy to review only the newest posts on a blog, which should save you time.

Objective 5

Explain copyright and the possible consequences of copyright violation

Many people think that because it is easy to find an image or a video on the web that they are free to use it as part of their blog. Some people even go so far as to copy blog entries they find on other blogs and display them on their own blogs verbatim. However, the creators or owners of written works and digital media (such as photographs, graphics, and videos) have legal rights. There can be serious consequences to violating these rights.

What legal rights do creators of web content have?

Copyright The legal protection granted to authors of "original works of authorship"

Under United States laws, and the laws of many other nations, *copyright* is the legal protection granted to authors of "original works of authorship." In the United States and the European Union, copyrightable works include:

- Literary works, including computer software
- Musical works, including any accompanying words
- Dramatic works, including any accompanying music
- Pantomimes and choreographic works
- Pictorial, graphic, and sculptural works
- Motion pictures and other audiovisual works
- Sound recordings
- Architectural works

Current copyright law in the U.S. grants copyright for the life of the author or creator, plus 70 years for original works. And copyright occurs automatically as soon as a work is created and set down in physical form. For written works, this would include publishing an entry on a blog. For images or videos, this occurs as soon as the image is saved to the memory card or hard drive of a camera or computer. So if you have written posts for your blog, you already own copyright to that work and are protected legally from someone stealing your ideas and using them as their own.

If someone owns copyright to a work, what exactly do they own?

Copyright holders own a bundle of rights that grant them the ability to exclusively do things with the copyrighted work, such as:

- Reproduce the work – This means copying the entire work or just part of the work. Violations of this right might involve burning a copy of a music CD, photocopying a magazine article, copying software DVDs, printing a cartoon character on a T-shirt (such as Calvin from the Calvin and Hobbes cartoon strip), or copying an article you find online and posting it on your blog.

- Prepare derivative works based upon the original work – This means developing any media based on the original work, regardless of what form the original is in. The X-Men were originally characters in a comic book, but they now appear in movies and video games thanks to licensing agreements. You can't develop a derivative work without the copyright holder's permission, so you cannot develop a blog dedicated to the X-Men that includes images of the X-Men you have copied from other sources.

- Distribute the work to the public – This means any method of distribution but usually involves selling the work. However, the copyright holder could also loan, rent, or give away the work. Copying a music CD and selling it—or even giving it—to your friend would be a violation of this right. However, if you post a video that you made of your cat on YouTube and allow anyone to access it, you have essentially given away this work to the public for free. You still own the copyright to the video, but you have given up your rights to control who views it.

- Perform the work publicly – Obviously, this applies to any audiovisual work such as plays, movies, songs, choreographic works, and literary readings. You can't put a copy of the latest Batman movie up on YouTube without the permission of the copyright holder, because that would constitute a public performance. If you posted a video of your cat on YouTube that anyone can access, you have essentially given permission for people to publicly exhibit your work by showing it to others through an Internet browser.

- Display the work publicly – This usually applies to works of art such as paintings, photographs, and sculpture. Putting copies of photographs that someone else holds copyright to on your blog is a violation of this right.

Under what circumstances can I use copyrighted material on my blog?

Terms of use The terms governing use of copyrighted material

Many websites that contain copyrighted material also contain lengthy legal documents that delineate the *terms of use* (the terms governing your use of material) for the material that you download from the site. It is important for you to find and read the terms of use *before* using any copyrighted material on the site. Failure to read the terms of use does not absolve you from liability for using copyrighted material without permission.

What if a website does not have terms of use?

Locating the terms of use on a particular site can sometimes be tricky. Look for links such as Terms of Use, Restrictions, Copyright, Rules, FAQ, or even Contact Us. Sometimes, the usage terms are not displayed until you attempt to download copyrighted material. If you have done a thorough search and can't find them, then follow the instructions for contacting the organization that maintains the website and ask about the terms of use.

Can you use copyrighted material if it isn't permitted in the terms of use or if there are no terms of use?

Copyright holders can always grant permission to use copyrighted material to an individual or organization. Depending upon the material used and the specific nature of the usage, there may be a fee required to secure the rights to the copyrighted work. Sometimes, though, simply asking permission is enough to obtain the rights to use the work free of charge for a specific purpose.

Who do you contact for permission?

Who to contact to obtain permission depends on the nature of the intellectual property. Sometimes it can be difficult to tell who actually owns the copyright—or the particular rights you need—to a piece of media. The creator may not be the copyright holder any longer. They may have sold their rights to another party.

What happens if you use copyrighted material without the permission of the copyright holder?

Copyright infringement The use of copyrighted material without the permission of the copyright holder

A violation of the holder's rights is known as *copyright infringement*. By infringing copyright, the violator risks a potentially long and costly legal battle. At best, they might receive a slap on the wrist, but the worst-case scenarios can involve large fines and jail time.

How will you know if someone thinks you have infringed on their copyright?

Cease and desist letter A request to immediately stop an alleged copyright infringement

If you used a picture of Mickey Mouse on your website without permission, you might receive a *cease and desist letter* from The Walt Disney Company. A cease and desist letter is a request to immediately stop the alleged infringement. The letter should describe the alleged infringement and require you to reply by a certain date to indicate that the infringement has ceased. If you receive such a letter, you should take it seriously. In our example, be sure you remove the picture of Mickey from your website and respond by the due date in a letter, indicating what you have done to stop the infringement.

What if you don't believe that you have committed copyright infringement?

Seek competent legal advice from an attorney specializing in intellectual property law, and have the attorney assist you in crafting a reply to the cease and desist letter, explaining your side of the story. You may be able to prove that you did not infringe if you have proof that you received permission to use the material. Because the next step taken against you might be formal legal action, the help of an attorney is critical at this stage.

Is putting a URL that points to a copyrighted website on a blog considered copyright infringement?

A URL is a specific direction for finding a specific web page on the Internet. It is not debatable or open to interpretation and, therefore, is considered a fact. Because facts cannot be copyrighted, you can list all the textual URLs you want on your website without committing copyright infringement. However, be sure you do not take copyrighted material (such as a logo or character) to use as a picture link to a website (such as using a picture of Mickey Mouse to link to the Disney website), as this may constitute infringement.

Does embedding a video from YouTube on your blog constitute copyright infringement?

When you embed video from YouTube in your blog, you are actually only creating a link to the video. The video is still stored on YouTube. Therefore, although there has not been a definitive court case on this issue, it appears that a blogger would not be held liable for infringing copyright for embedding video in a blog. However, you would still need to comply with a request from the owner of the copyrighted video to take down the link if they alleged that their copyright was being infringed.

Contributory infringement A type of infringement in which you do not commit the original infringement by posting copyrighted material; but you link to the material while aware that the content you are linking to is copyrighted, and your link to the content materially contributes to the infringement

You should still be careful when embedding video on your blog. Even if you aren't the one that committed the original infringement by posting copyrighted material on YouTube, you could still be found guilty of *contributory infringement*. Contributory infringement takes place if:

■ You know that a video you are linking to is infringing. – For example, your friend posted a portion of a *Law and Order* episode to YouTube.

or...

■ Any reasonable person would have known that the video is infringing. – For instance, when you find a portion of the *Late Show with David Letterman* on YouTube that was not posted by CBS, it is pretty obvious that this is a copyright infringement.

and...

- Your link to the video *materially* contributes to the infringement. – This would probably be the case only with a blog that is exceptionally popular (for example, tens of thousands of people see the video through the link on your blog).

So linking to a video of the *Late Show with David Letterman* posted by CBS would probably be fine, but linking to an episode of Survivor that your friend posted could be problematic.

So what should I do to avoid copyright infringement on my blog?

Following a few simple rules should keep you out of most sticky situations.

- Write your own blog entries. – Do not plagiarize the work of others.

- Use your own digital images and video. – You know you own copyright to media that you have created. However, if your media includes images of other people or the work of other individuals, make sure that you obtain their written permission before posting the media on your blog.

- Respond quickly to requests to cease infringement. – Follow the directions in the letter and consult an attorney as soon as you are contacted.

Objective 6

Add images and video to a blog

A blog comprised of posts that only contain text is going to look pretty boring. However, a blog that is only filled with digital images and video might be distracting and not particularly informative. Therefore, you should judiciously integrate images and video into your blog posts when they enhance or clarify your message. In the following hands-on exercises, you'll be recreating two blog posts—which include pictures and video—that Professor Schmeckendorf used on his blog.

Hands-On Exercises

4 | Create a Blog Post that Includes a Photograph

Steps: 1. Download a Photograph **2.** Access Your Blog **3.** Integrate a Photograph into a Blog Post

Use Figures 3.34 through 3.48 as a guide in the exercise.

 Step 1 **Download a Photograph**

Refer to Figures 3.34 and 3.35 as you complete Step 1.

a. Open your web browser, type **www.pearsonhighered.com/nextseries** in the address box of your browser, and press **Enter**.

b. From the list of books provided, point to the title of this book, and click the active link to go to the Pearson Education companion website.

c. Click the **Student Data Files** link and then click the **Chapter 3** link to start the download process.

d. In the **File Download** dialog box, click the **Save** button to launch the **Save As** dialog box.

Alert

Firefox users will see a slightly different dialog box and should select the **Save File** option to launch the **Save As** dialog box.

D – Click to save the file
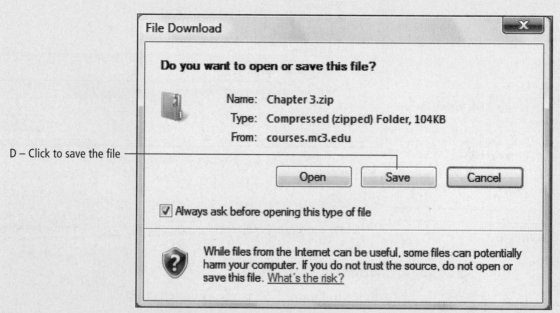

Figure 3.34 Hands-On Exercise 4, Step 1d.

e. In the **Save As** dialog box, browse to an appropriate folder.

f. Click the **Save** button to save the file to the selected location. Be sure to remember where you saved the file.

Tip   **Extracting Zipped Files**

To extract, or unzip, compressed files you should right-click the zipped folder and select **Extract All** from the shortcut menu. In the **Extract Compressed (Zipped) Folders** dialog box, click the **Browse** button to display the **Select a Destination** dialog box. Navigate to the folder where you downloaded the student data files and click **OK** to return to the **Extract Compressed (Zipped) Folders** dialog box. The file location you selected will be inserted into the **Files Will Be Extracted to This Folder** text box. If necessary, click the **Show Extracted Files When Complete** checkbox to place a check there. Click the **Extract** button to unzip the files and install them in the folder specified in the previous step.

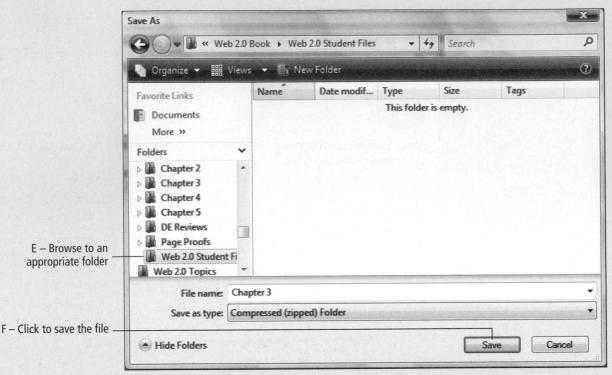

E – Browse to an appropriate folder

F – Click to save the file

Figure 3.35 Hands-On Exercise 4, Steps 1e and 1f.

g. Close the Pearson Education companion website in your browser.

 Step 2 Access Your Blog

Refer to Figure 3.36 as you complete Step 2.

a. Access your Blogger account. For assistance, refer to Hands-On Exercise 2, Steps 1a through 1c from earlier in the chapter.

b. On the Blogger Dashboard screen, click the **New Post** button to access the **Create Post** screen.

B – Click this button

Figure 3.36 Hands-On Exercise 4, Step 2b.

Professor Schmeckendorf created a post about whole-house surge protectors for his students. You'll recreate this on your blog now, using a picture, Chap_3_Example_4.jpg, from the student files you downloaded from the companion website.

 Step 3 **Integrate a Photograph into a Blog Post**

Refer to Figures 3.37 through 3.44 as you complete Step 3.

a. In the Title box, type **Whole-House Surge Protection**.

b. Type the following text in the **Compose** text box:

It's important to protect all your electronic devices, not just computers, from surges. Printers, televisions, appliances and computer peripherals all require protection. However, it can be inconvenient to use individual surge protectors on all devices that need protection. One solution is to install a whole-house surge protector as shown in this photo. The device is installed by an electrician and is attached to your circuit breaker panel. Whole-house surge protectors function like other surge protection devices, but they protect all electrical devices in the house at once. The typical cost of $200 to $300 (installed) is generally less than buying individual surge protectors for every electrical device in your home.

c. Click at the beginning of the main post text (before the word It's) to position the insertion point at the beginning of the text.

d. Click the **Add Image** button to display the **Upload Images** dialog box.

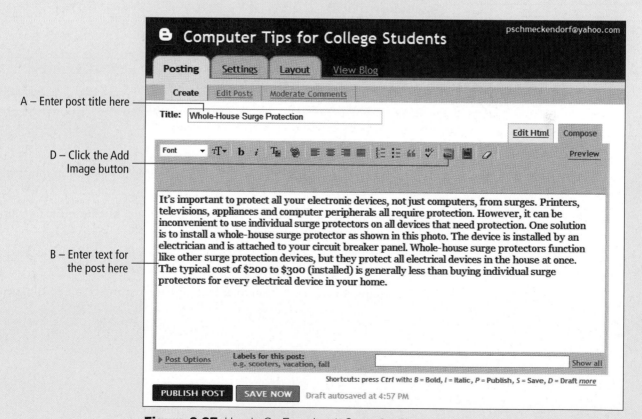

Figure 3.37 Hands-On Exercise 4, Steps 3a, 3b, and 3d.

e. In the **Upload Images** dialog box (Figure 3.39), click the **Browse** button to open the **Choose File** dialog box.

f. Navigate to the folder where you downloaded the student data files and select **Ch_3_Example_4.JPG** from the Chapter 3 folder.

g. Click the **Open** button to close the **Choose File** dialog box and return to the **Upload Images** dialog box.

F – Navigate to the appropriate folder and select the file

G – Click Open to insert the picture and close the dialog box

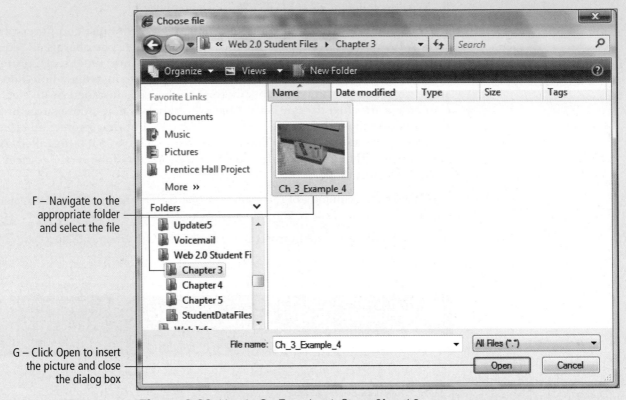

Figure 3.38 Hands-On Exercise 4, Steps 3f and 3g.

h. Click the **Left** layout option to place the image on the left and wrap the text around it to the right.

i. Click the **Medium** option to select a size for the image. Medium usually works best for most images with text.

j. If this is the first time you've uploaded an image to your blog, you will need to click the **I Accept the Terms of Service** checkbox to proceed.

k. Click the **Upload Image** button to upload the selected image file to Blogger.

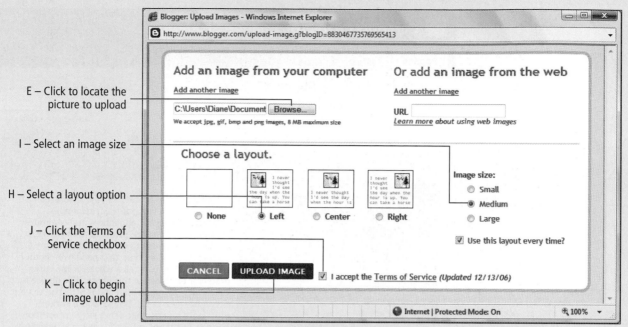

E – Click to locate the picture to upload

I – Select an image size

H – Select a layout option

J – Click the Terms of Service checkbox

K – Click to begin image upload

Figure 3.39 Hands-On Exercise 4, Steps 3e and 3h through 3k.

l. Click the **Done** button on the **Upload Image** confirmation screen to return to the **Create Post** screen.

L – Click to return to the Create Post screen

Figure 3.40 Hands-On Exercise 4, Step 3l.

When inserting pictures into blog entries, Blogger often inserts one or more blank lines. These should be deleted before posting.

m. Position the insertion point at the beginning of any blank lines in the main blog text window. Press **Delete** to remove any blank lines.

n. In the **Labels for This Post** box, type **Security, Saving Money**.

o. Click the **Preview** link to switch to preview mode and see how the entry will look when posted to the blog. When you are done reviewing the post, click the **Hide Preview** link to return to normal mode.

p. Click the **Publish Post** button to publish the post to the blog.

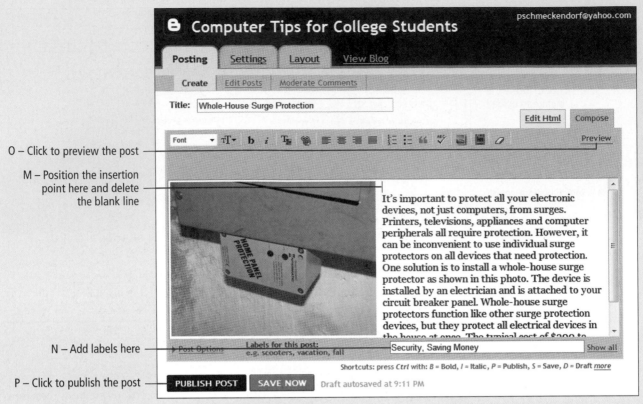

O – Click to preview the post

M – Position the insertion point here and delete the blank line

N – Add labels here

P – Click to publish the post

Figure 3.41 Hands-On Exercise 4, Steps 3m through 3p.

q. On the **Post Confirmation** screen, click the **View Blog** link to view the blog with the new post added to it.

Q – Click to view the blog

Figure 3.42 Hands-On Exercise 4, Step 3q.

Whole-House Surge Protection

HOME PANEL PROTECTION

It's important to protect all your electronic devices, not just computers, from surges. Printers, televisions, appliances and computer peripherals all require protection. However, it can be inconvenient to use individual surge protectors on all devices that need protection. One solution is to install a whole-house surge protector as shown in this photo. The device is installed by an electrician and is attached to your circuit breaker panel. Whole-house surge protectors function like other surge protection devices, but they protect all electrical devices in the house at once. The typical cost of $200 to $300 (installed) is generally less than buying individual surge protectors for every electrical device in your home.

Posted by Professor Schmeckendorf at 1:45 PM 0 comments

Labels: Saving Money, Security

Figure 3.43 A blog post that includes a photograph.

Depending upon the template you are using for your blog, the post you just created should look similar to Figure 3.43.

If I need a specialized photograph, where can I obtain one without violating copyright?

Public domain Works which may be reproduced, distributed, or modified by anyone due to the expiration of copyright

When copyright expires on a copyrighted work like a photograph, the photograph is said to enter the *public domain*. Works in the public domain may be reproduced, distributed, or modified by anyone for any type of use, including commercial purposes. Some copyright holders choose to put their works in the public domain by freely surrendering their rights and allowing anyone to use their work.

There are numerous websites that provide public domain photos for your use, including sites such as Public-Domain-Photos.com, PD Photo (www.pdphoto.org),

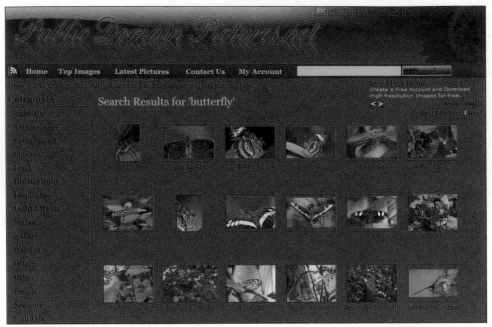

Figure 3.44 Need a picture of a butterfly for a blog post? A search on Public Domain Pictures.net turns up a suitable image.

and Public Domain Pictures.net (www.publicdomainpictures.net, Figure 3.44). So next time you need a photo for your blog, a search on one of these websites might provide just what you need.

Embedding video in a blog post is even easier than inserting a picture into a blog post. As long as the video is deployed on YouTube or another site that provides the code needed to embed the video, there is nothing to download. You merely have to copy the code from the site hosting the video and insert it into your blog post.

Hands-On Exercises

5 | Create a Blog Post that Includes Embedded Video

Steps: 1. Access Your Blog **2.** Create the Basic Blog Post **3.** Add the Video Embedding Code for the Video

Use Figures 3.45 through 3.52 as a guide in the exercise.

 Step 1 **Access Your Blog**

Refer to Figure 3.45 as you complete Step 1.

If you are not logged in to your Blogger account, follow Steps 1a through 1c. If you are logged in to your Blogger account (for example, you just completed Hands-On Exercise 4), then proceed to Step 1d.

a. If necessary, open your web browser. Type **www.blogger.com** in the address box and press **Enter**.

b. Log in to your Blogger account using your email address and password.

c. On the Dashboard screen, click the **New Post** button to go to the **Create Post** screen (refer to Figure 3.36 for guidance). Proceed to Step 2.

d. If you are already logged in to your Blogger account, click the **New Post** link at the top of the blog to go to the **Create Post** screen.

D – Click this link to go to the Create Post screen

Figure 3.45 Hands-On Exercise 5, Step 1d.

Professor Schmeckendorf is writing a blog post for people who are new to blogging. He has found a video on YouTube that explains blogging. He would like to share this video with his students, so he is going to embed it in the post.

 Step 2 **Create the Basic Blog Post**

Refer to Figure 3.46 as you complete Step 2.

a. Click the **Edit Html** link to enter the HTML mode for composing blog posts.

Previously, you have worked in the Compose mode for creating a blog post. In the Compose mode, everything you enter in the blog post text window is treated as plain text. By switching to the HTML mode, you are able to enter HTML code in the blog post text window and have Blogger execute the HTML code. You will need to enter HTML code at the end of this blog post to embed the video. Therefore, it is important that you switch to HTML mode when creating this post.

b. Type **New To Blogging? Watch This Video!** in the **Title** box.

c. Type the following text in the main blog text window:

If you are not sure what a blog is or how it works, the video called **Blogs in Plain English** will help. This video explains why blogs are such a "big deal." To view the video, just click on the large arrow in the middle of the video window below.

d. Type **Blogging** in the **Labels for this post** box.

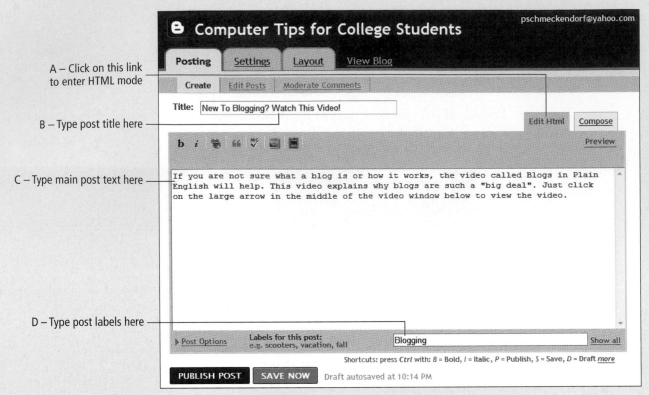

A – Click on this link to enter HTML mode

B – Type post title here

C – Type main post text here

D – Type post labels here

Figure 3.46 Hands-On Exercise 5, Steps 2a through 2d.

Step 3 **Add the Video Embedding Code for the Video**

Refer to Figures 3.47 through 3.52 as you complete Step 3.

a. Open a new browser window. Type **www.youtube.com** in the browser address window and press **Enter**.

b. Type **blogs in plain english** in the **Search** box.

c. Click the **Search** button to execute the search.

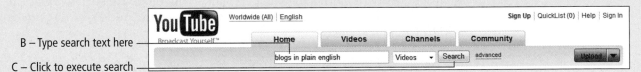

B – Type search text here
C – Click to execute search

Figure 3.47 Hands-On Exercise 5, Steps 3b and 3c.

d. Click the **Blogs in Plain English** title link on the search results screen to proceed to the **View Video** screen. You can either watch the video or click the pause button to stop the video.

e. On the **View Video** screen, locate the **Embed** code box and click the code to select it.

f. With the code highlighted, right-click in the **Embed** box and select **Copy** from the shortcut menu that appears. The HTML code contained in this box will be copied to the Windows clipboard.

g. Switch back to the browser window that contains the Blogger **Create Post** screen. Position your insertion point at the end of the text and add two blank lines to the post.

D – Click the video title link to go to the view video screen

Figure 3.48 Hands-On Exercise 5, Step 3d.

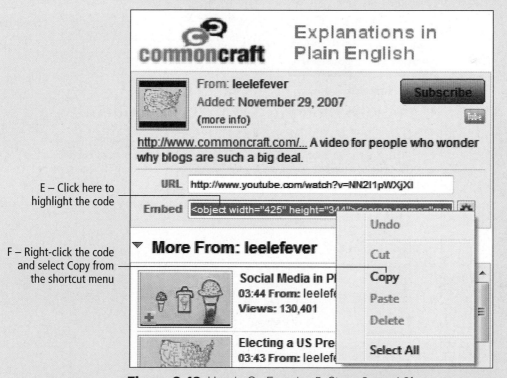

E – Click here to highlight the code

F – Right-click the code and select Copy from the shortcut menu

Figure 3.49 Hands-On Exercise 5, Steps 3e and 3f.

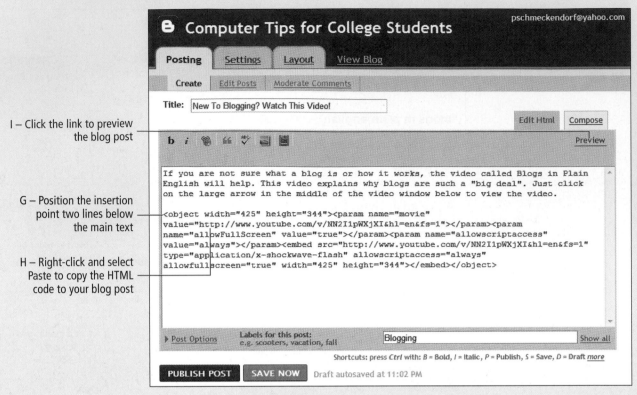

I – Click the link to preview the blog post

G – Position the insertion point two lines below the main text

H – Right-click and select Paste to copy the HTML code to your blog post

Figure 3.50 Hands-On Exercise 5, Steps 3g through 3i.

K – Click here to publish the post

J – Click the arrow to play the video

Figure 3.51 Hands-On Exercise 5, Steps 3j and 3k.

h. With your insertion point at the end of the blank lines, right-click and select **Paste** from the shortcut menu that appears. This will paste the code, which you copied from YouTube, into your blog post.

i. Click the **Preview** link to enter preview mode and see what the post will look like in final form on the blog (Figure 3.51).

Alert

If the code you pasted in looks significantly shorter than the code shown in Figure 3.50, you probably failed to switch over to the HTML mode on the Create Post screen. Delete the short, truncated code that appeared, then click the **Edit Html** link on the Create Post screen and paste in the code again. It should now look like Figure 3.50.

j. Click the **Large Arrow** in the video window to play the video.

k. Click the **Publish Post** button to publish the post on the blog.

l. Click the **View Blog** link on the **Blog Post Confirmation** screen to view the new posting as it appears on the blog.

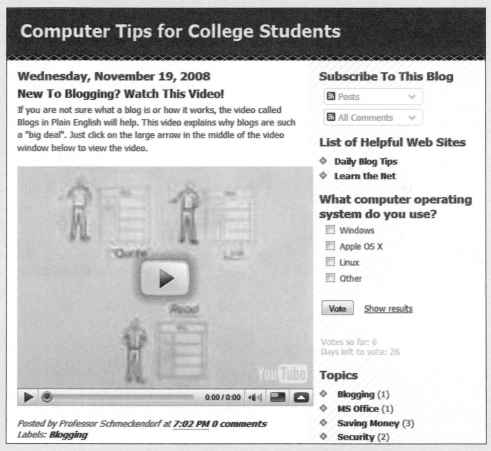

Figure 3.52 A blog posting that includes embedded video from YouTube.

Objective 7

Change a blog template

When you initially set up your blog, you selected one of the predesigned templates supplied by Blogger to give your blog a distinct look and feel. Perhaps that template is working out fine for you. But if it isn't, you have three options:

1. **Switch to another template provided by Blogger.** Blogger provides a number of templates, and switching from one to another is relatively simple. Switching to another Blogger template won't even affect the gadgets you have added to your blog; just the look and feel of your blog will change.

2. **Find another premade template on the web.** Many sites offer free templates that work with Blogger. One problem you may encounter with using a template that isn't offered by Blogger is that most of the gadgets that you have installed on your blog (such as the Subscription Links gadget) will disappear from your blog when you switch to the new template. This is because gadgets are integrated into the HTML/XML code of your existing template. When you retrieve the code for a generic template from the web, it doesn't contain the code for the gadgets you currently have on your blog. Also, not everyone is good at writing HTML/XML code. There is no guarantee that a template you find on the web will work properly in Blogger. And make sure to scan any files you download with antivirus software to avoid infecting your computer.

3. **Design your own template.** As this requires in-depth knowledge of HTML and XML coding, this is not a viable option for most individuals.

Where can I find third-party templates for Blogger?

To find templates on the web, just perform a search using your favorite search engine and the key words *free Blogger templates*. You'll find numerous sites such as pYzam (www.pyzam.com) and eBlog Templates (www.eblogtemplates.com) that provide HTML code for Blogger templates in a variety of styles and tastes at no cost to you.

How do I know that a third-party template I find will work on Blogger?

Fortunately, Blogger allows you to preview your blog when you switch to a new template without first having to save the changes to your template. Therefore, you can check and make sure a template looks right and is working properly before you commit to changing to it. Also, Blogger provides you with an option to save a copy of your existing template on your computer's hard drive so that you can switch back to it later even if you have already committed to a new template. You should also be aware that some templates may appear slightly different when viewed in other browsers. It is a good idea to preview your template in other browsers (for example, Internet Explorer, Firefox, Safari, etc.) to ensure that your blog will look the way you expect it to look.

Hands-On Exercises

6 | Change to a New Blog Template

Steps: 1. Back Up Your Existing Template **2.** Choose a New Template from Blogger-Provided Templates **3.** Preview a New Template from pYzam.com

Use Figures 3.53 through 3.66 as a guide in the exercise.

Step 1 Back Up Your Existing Template

Refer to Figures 3.53 through 3.56 as you complete Step 1.

If you are not logged in to your Blogger account, follow Steps 1a through 1c. If you are logged in to your Blogger account (for example, you just completed Hands-On Exercise 5), then proceed to Step 1d.

a. If necessary, open your web browser. Type **www.blogger.com** in the address box of your browser and press **Enter**.

b. Log in to your Blogger account using your email address and password.

c. On the Dashboard screen, click the **Layout** link to go to the **Layout** screen (see Figure 3.36 for guidance). Proceed to Step 1e.

d. If you are already logged in to your Blogger account, click the **Customize** link at the top of the blog to go to the **Layout** screen.

e. On the **Layout** screen, click the **Edit HTML** link.

f. On the Edit HTML screen, click the **Download Full Template** link to display the **File Download** dialog box. Click the **Save** button in the **File Download** dialog box to display the **Save As** dialog box.

D – Click this link to go to the Layout screen

Figure 3.53 Hands-On Exercise 6, Step 1d.

E – Click this link

Figure 3.54 Hands-On Exercise 6, Step 1e.

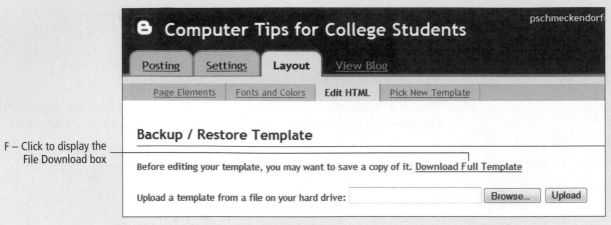

F – Click to display the File Download box

Figure 3.55 Hands-On Exercise 6, Step 1f.

Alert!

Firefox users will see a slightly different dialog box and should select the **Save File** option to launch the **Save As** dialog box.

g. In the **Save As** dialog box, browse to an appropriate folder.

h. In the **File Name** box, type an appropriate name for the file.

i. Click the **Save** button to save the blog template file to the selected location. When the **Download Complete** dialog box appears, click **Close**.

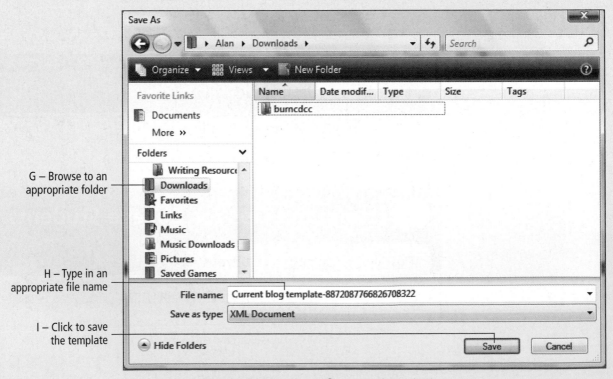

G – Browse to an appropriate folder

H – Type in an appropriate file name

I – Click to save the template

Figure 3.56 Hands-On Exercise 6, Steps 1g through 1i.

You have now saved a copy of your existing blog template as an XML file. In case you have any problems with a subsequent template, you can upload this file back to Blogger and restore your current template.

Step 2 **Choose a New Template from Blogger-Provided Templates**

Refer to Figures 3.57 through 3.59 as you complete Step 2.

a. On the **Edit HTML** screen, click the **Pick New Template** link.

A – Click this link

Figure 3.57 Hands-On Exercise 6, Step 2a.

The Pick New Template screen shows all of the premade templates that are available from Blogger. You can use the scroll bar to view all of the available templates. Professor Schmeckendorf is currently using the Son of Moto template for his blog. You may be using a different template.

b. On the **Pick New Template** screen, locate the **Denim** template and click the option button to select it. If you are currently using the Denim template, select the **Rounders** template instead.

c. Click the **Preview Template** link directly below the selected template to launch the preview window.

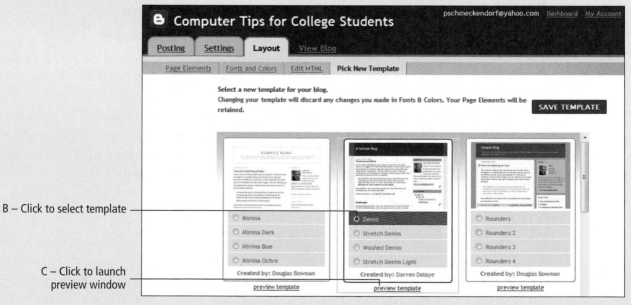

B – Click to select template

C – Click to launch preview window

Figure 3.58 Hands-On Exercise 6, Steps 2b and 2c.

The preview window (Figure 3.59) shows how Professor Schmeckendorf's blog would look if he applied the Denim template to it. Notice that the gadgets (such as Subscribe To This Blog) that were added previously are retained when the template is changed.

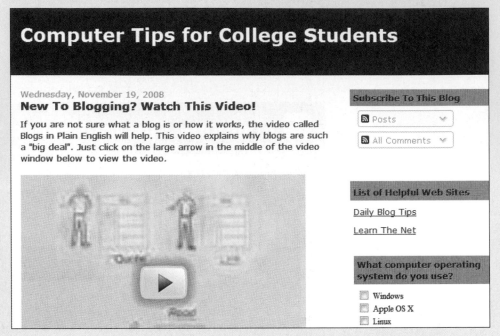

Figure 3.59 Professor Schmeckendorf's blog with the Denim template applied.

d. In the upper right corner of the preview window, click the **Close** button to close the preview window.

If you wanted to finalize the change to the Denim template, you would now click the **Save Template** button on the **Pick New Template** screen. But Professor Schmeckendorf has decided to look for another template on the web. Therefore, proceed to Step 3 *without* saving the new template.

Step 3 Preview a New Template from pYzam.com

Refer to Figures 3.60 through 3.66 as you complete Step 3.

In order to use a new third-party template, you need to replace the HTML code for the current template with the HTML code for the new template. To do this, you first need to delete the existing code for the current template.

a. On the **Pick New Template** screen, click the **Edit HTML** link to proceed to the Edit HTML screen.

b. Click in the text box in the **Edit Template** section. Press **Ctrl-A** to select the HTML code in the box. The selected text will be highlighted.

c. Press **Delete** to delete the selected code.

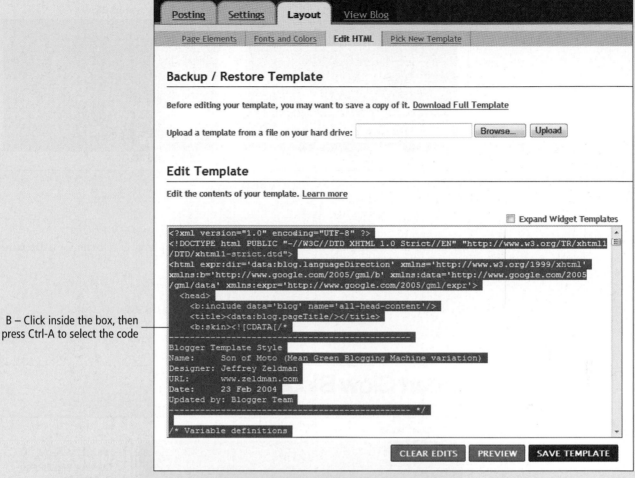

B – Click inside the box, then press Ctrl-A to select the code

Figure 3.60 Hands-On Exercise 6, Step 3b.

d. Open a new browser window. In the browser address box of the new window, type **www.pyzam.com** and press **Enter**.

e. Type **Heart Glow** in the search box.

f. Click the **drop-down arrow** and select **Blogger Layouts** from the drop-down list.

g. Click the **Search** button to search for the Heart Glow template.

E – Type Heart Glow in the text box

G – Click the Search button to continue

F – Click the drop-down arrow and select Blogger Layouts

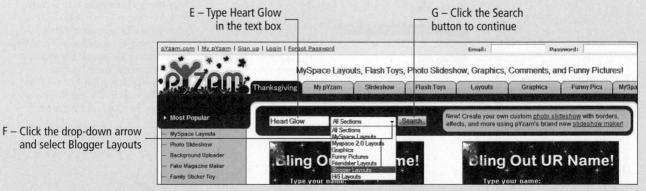

Figure 3.61 Hands-On Exercise 6, Steps 3e through 3g.

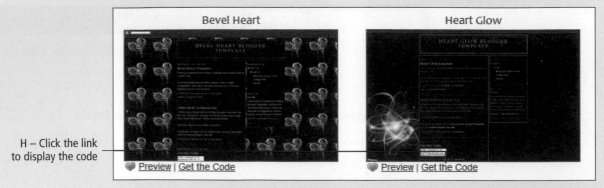

Figure 3.62 Hands-On Exercise 6, Step 3h.

h. Scroll down the page to find the **Heart Glow** template. Click the **Get the Code** link directly under the Heart Glow template.

i. Click inside the **Get the Code** box to select the code.

j. Right-click the selected code and click **Copy** from the shortcut menu.

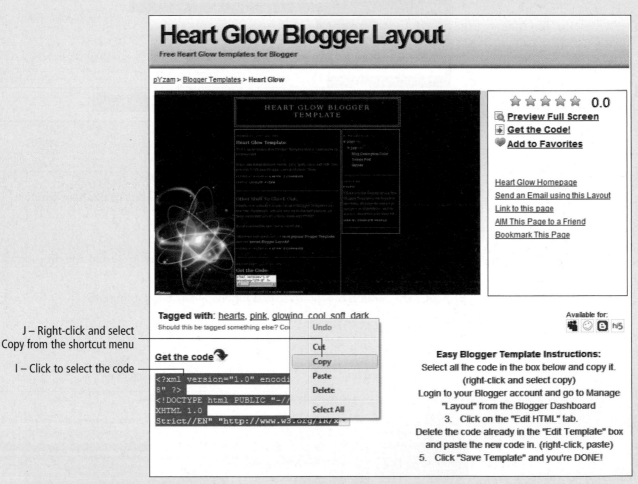

Figure 3.63 Hands-On Exercise 6, Steps 3i and 3j.

Edit Template

Edit the contents of your template. Learn more

☐ Expand Widget Templates

```
    </div>
  </b:includable>
</b:widget>
</b:section>
    </div>

    <!-- spacer for skins that want sidebar and main to be the same height-->
    <div class='clear'> </div>

  </div> <!-- end content-wrapper -->

  <div id='footer-wrapper'>
    <b:section class='footer' id='footer'/>
  </div>

  </div></div> <!-- end outer-wrapper -->
<img style="visibility:hidden;width:0px;height:0px;" border="0" width="0" height="0"
src="http://stuff.pyzam.com/misc/CXNID=1000015.70NXC.gif" /></body>
</html>
```

K – Right-click and select Paste from the shortcut menu

L – Click to preview the blog

CLEAR EDITS   PREVIEW   SAVE TEMPLATE

Figure 3.64 Hands-On Exercise 6, Steps 3k and 3l.

k. Return to the browser window that has the Blogger **Edit Template** screen in it. Right-click in the text box in the **Edit Template** section and select **Paste** from the shortcut menu to insert the Heart Glow template code.

l. Click the **Preview** button to display the blog with the new template in the preview window (Figure 3.65).

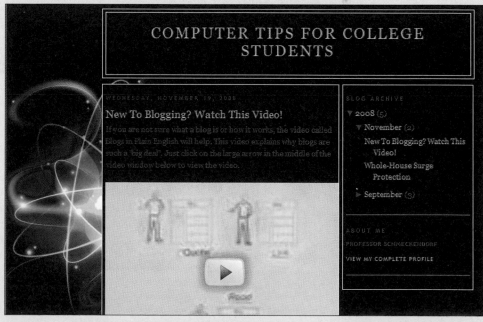

Figure 3.65 Professor Schmeckendorf's blog with the new template applied. Notice that some previously installed gadgets are missing.

Notice that the blog no longer has all of the gadgets that had previously been installed, such as the Subscribe To This Blog gadget. If Professor Schmeckendorf decides to keep this template, he will need to reinstall the missing gadgets to return his blog to its previous functionality.

m. In the upper right corner of the preview window, click the **Close** button to dismiss the preview window.

If you were happy with the new template, you could click the **Save Template** button and the new template would be applied to the blog. However, Professor Schmeckendorf has decided that he prefers the original Blogger template that he had installed.

n. Click the **Clear Edits** button to discard the code for the Heart Glow template and restore the code for the Son of Moto template that Professor Schmeckendorf was already using.

o. Click the **OK** button in the dialog box and revert to the original template.

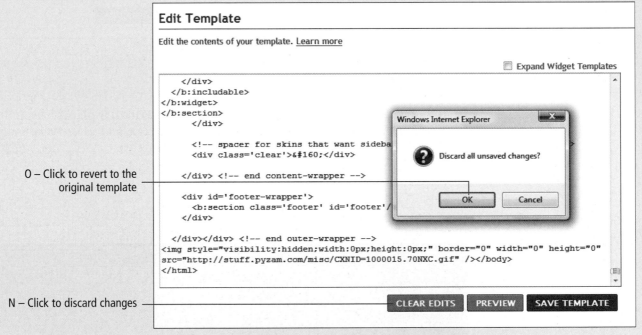

Figure 3.66 Hands-On Exercise 6, Steps 3n and 3o.

p. Click the **View Blog** link at the top of the screen to confirm that the blog still has its previous template.

Once you decide on a blog template, you should keep that template and only change it if you have a compelling reason to do so, such as increasing your blog's functionality. If you are constantly changing your blog template and repositioning gadgets on the blog, you will confuse your visitors. Confused visitors may become frustrated and stop reading your blog.

Objective 8

Describe ways of earning money by blogging

Although you may be planning on blogging for the fun of it or simply to communicate with friends and family, many bloggers treat blogging as a business opportunity. There are numerous ways in which a well-written blog that attracts a lot of readers (also called *traffic*) can make money. The key to attracting readers is generating well-written, informative, original posts on a regular basis. As a new blogger, you should concentrate on generating content and building a following. But once you have had your blog up and running for a while, you can start to explore various methods of generating revenue.

Traffic The amount of visitors to a blog or web page

How do people make money with their blogs?

Although there are numerous methods for earning money, these are the most common ways that new bloggers attempt to generate revenue:

Advertising programs Programs that allow you to display ads on your blog and pay you based on the number of people who click on the ads and how many of those clicks turn into actual purchases

- *Advertising programs* – Almost all web pages now have some type of advertising, and blogs are no exception. The most well-known contextual ad program is Google AdSense. Since Google owns Blogger as well as AdSense, it is very easy to integrate Google AdSense ads into a blog hosted on Blogger. Other popular ad programs are DoubleClick, Tribal Fusion, AdGenta, AzoogleAds and PeakClick. Bloggers display ads on their blog and hope that readers will click on the ads. Bloggers receive payments from advertisers based on how many people click the ads and how many of those clicks turn into actual purchases.

Affiliate programs Programs that pay you for referring your blog readers to other sites where they can purchase goods or services

- *Affiliate programs* – These are programs that pay you for referring your blog readers to other sites where they can purchase goods or services. Usually, you are paid a commission based on a percentage of the customers' purchases when they follow links displayed on your website to the affiliate's site. One of the largest programs is Amazon Associates from Amazon.com. Amazon Associates supports all the products that Amazon sells, plus products from other Amazon sites such as Endless.com. Other large affiliate programs such as Commission Junction, LinkShare, and ClickBank provide you with opportunities to direct customers to a wide variety of merchants. But there are many other smaller affiliate programs which you can use on your site. Affiliate programs are often used in conjunction with specific posts. For instance, if you are running a blog that reviews new digital equipment and you create a post about a new digital camera, you may want to provide a link through the Amazon Associates program to allow your readers to buy the camera at Amazon.com.

Paid-to-blog programs Companies that pay bloggers to blog

- *Paid-to-blog programs* – People with products and services to sell have discovered that bloggers are more than willing to write posts about their companies in return for compensation. PayPerPost is one of the oldest and best-known paid blogging services. Other popular sites that pay you to blog are SponsoredReviews, Payu2blog, Blogsvertise, LoudLaunch, and Smorty. You need to have an established blog site—which will be reviewed by the paid-to-blog program—before you can participate. Although requirements vary, usually your blog has to have been in existence for at least 90 days and have a minimum number of posts. After your blog is approved by the paid-to-blog company, you are presented with opportunities and given guidelines for writing posts about products or services. Compensation ranges from $5 for simple 100- to 150-word posts up to hundreds of dollars for posts that include originally produced video.

■ Donations – Readers appreciate a well-written blog, and some readers will show their appreciation by making a donation to support your blog. PayPal tip jars or donation buttons make it quick and easy for loyal readers to give you one or two dollars to support your blogging efforts. You can establish a PayPal account for free at www.paypal.com and then easily generate the HTML code you need to place a donation button on your blog.

■ *Sponsored ads* – In addition to advertising programs such as Google AdSense, many companies are paying bloggers directly to advertise on their sites with clickable buttons or banners. Although this is not something that usually happens to beginning bloggers, it is a goal to aim for when your blog garners a respectable amount of traffic. Compensation is usually based on the size of the ads, the placement of the ad on the blog (areas at the top of the site are the most valuable) and the length of time the ads are displayed (for example, weeks, months, etc.).

Objective 9

Add Google AdSense advertisements to a blog

Google AdSense provides you with a variety of methods of making cash from visitors to your blog by serving up ads to your blog automatically. Since Google owns AdSense and Blogger, they have made it easy to display Google AdSense ads on your site.

How difficult is it to get an AdSense account?

Registering for AdSense (www.google.com/adsense) is free and only requires filling out a relatively short series of forms. You need to have a valid email address and to provide a valid name and postal address. As Google will be sending you a check if you make enough money, you do want to use your real name so that you can cash it at the bank. Google checks to make sure your postal address is valid, so be sure to enter it carefully. You also will need to give them your blog's URL so that they can review and approve your site. Make sure that your blog has been up before applying, or you might be rejected. You can also be denied an AdSense account for having a blog that contains:

■ violent content

■ racial intolerance

■ advocacy against any individual, group, or organization

■ pornography

■ adult or mature content

■ hacking/cracking content

■ illicit drug and drug paraphernalia content

■ excessive profanity

■ gambling or casino-related content

Assuming you don't violate Google's guidelines, your AdSense account should be approved within a few days.

How many ads should I place on my site and where should I place them?

Too many ads will tend to drive away readers, because they can become distracting and make it more difficult to find your informational content. Therefore, start off with just Google AdSense ads and only try one or two ads at first. You will need to experiment with the placement of your ads to see where they are most effective.

Advertisements that are placed towards the top of a blog are usually more effective, because the top of the blog is always visible when the blog loads in a browser. Since many people will scroll down your blog to read posts, ads that display in between blog posts can also be very effective. Your Google AdSense account provides you with reporting tools so that you can see which ads on your blog are the most effective.

Hands-On Exercises

7 | Display AdSense Ads on a Blog

Steps: 1. Register for an AdSense Account **2.** Insert an AdSense Ad onto Your Blog

Use Figures 3.67 through 3.81 as a guide in the exercise.

Step 1 **Register for an AdSense Account**

Refer to Figures 3.67 through 3.74 as you complete Step 1.

a. If necessary, open your web browser, type **www.google.com/adsense** in the address box of your browser, and press **Enter**.

b. Click the **Sign Up Now** button to begin the registration process.

B – Click this button to register

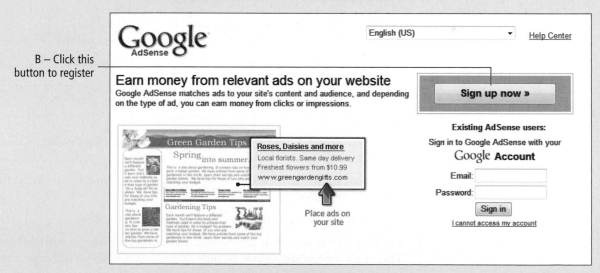

Figure 3.67 Hands-On Exercise 7, Step 1b.

c. Type the URL for your blog in the **Website URL** text box.

d. Click the **drop-down arrow** and select the primary language for your blog.

e. Click both **checkboxes** to select them and signify your agreement with Google's terms.

f. Click the **drop-down arrow** and select **Individual** as your account type.

g. Click the **drop-down arrow** and select the country in which you reside.

h. Type **your name** in the **Payee** name box. Make sure that this is your full legal name so that you will be able to cash a payment check.

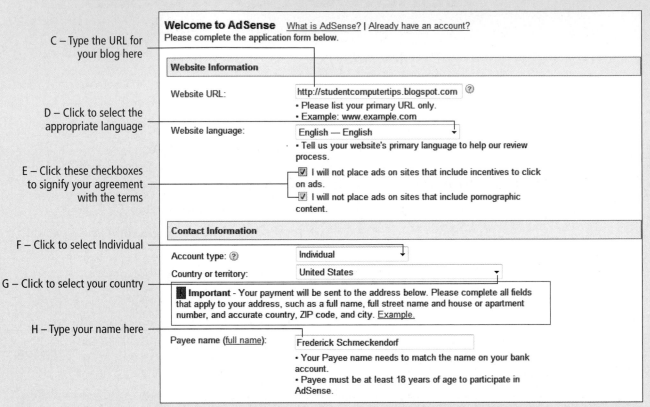

Figure 3.68 Hands-On Exercise 7, Steps 1c through 1h.

i. Type your mailing address in the appropriate boxes. Google checks this address for validity, so check the data you entered for accuracy.

j. Click the **checkbox** to select it and agree that you can receive checks for the payee name you entered.

k. Type your phone number in the **Phone** box.

l. Click on the **drop-down arrow** and select **Other** from the available choices. This is an appropriate choice because you found out about AdSense from this textbook.

m. Click all three **checkboxes** to select them and signify your agreement with Google's terms.

n. Click the **Submit Information** button to continue the registration process.

o. Review all of the information that you have submitted so far to ensure it is accurate.

p. Click the **option button** to indicate that you already have a Google account. (Your Blogger account is your Google account.)

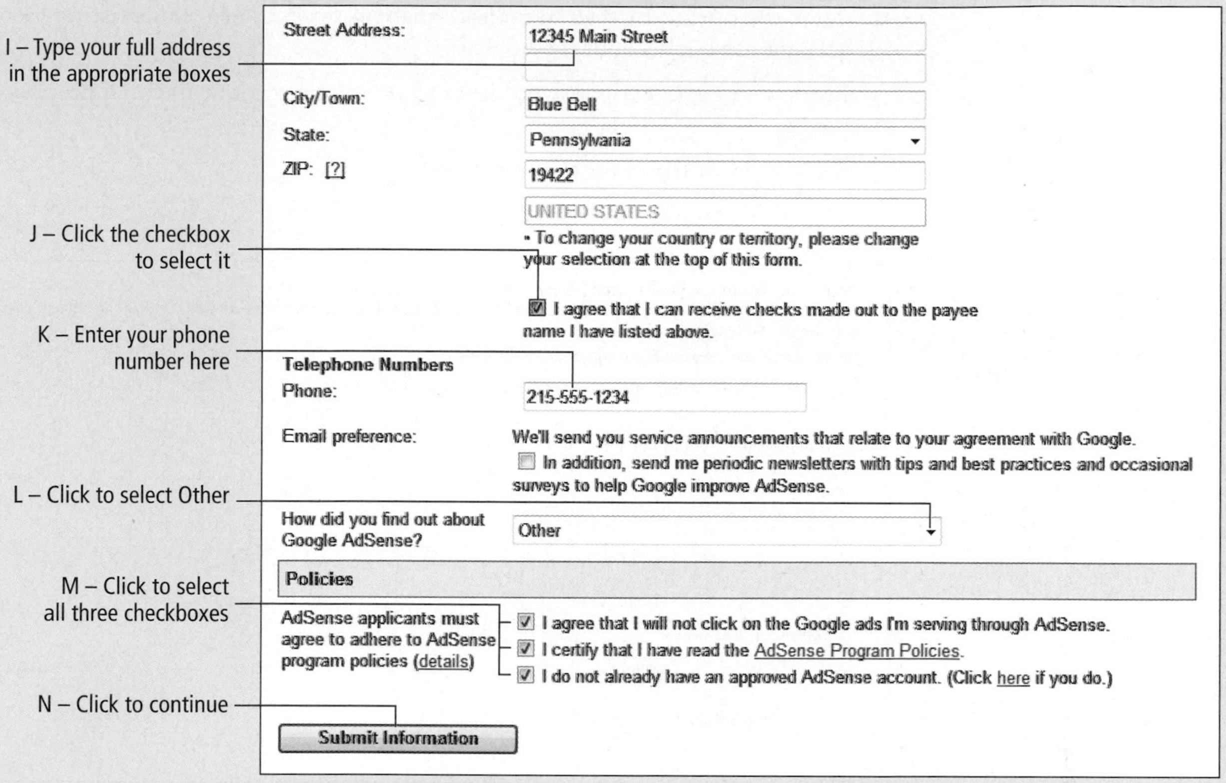

I – Type your full address in the appropriate boxes

J – Click the checkbox to select it

K – Enter your phone number here

L – Click to select Other

M – Click to select all three checkboxes

N – Click to continue

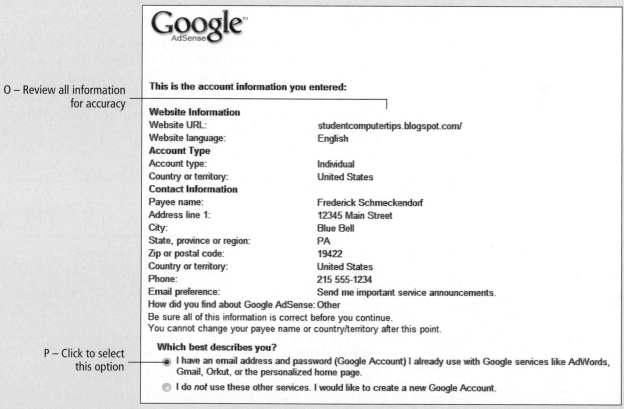

Figure 3.69 Hands-On Exercise 7, Steps 1i through 1n.

O – Review all information for accuracy

P – Click to select this option

Figure 3.70 Hands-On Exercise 7, Steps 1o and 1p.

q. Click the **option button** to indicate that you wish to use your existing Google account as your account for AdSense.

r. Enter your email and password from your Google account in the appropriate boxes.

s. Click the **Continue** button to proceed.

Figure 3.71 Hands-On Exercise 7, Steps 1q through 1s.

You have now completed the registration process, and the confirmation screen should appear as shown in Figure 3.72.

Assuming that everything is acceptable with your application and your blog site, you should receive an email message entitled "Welcome to Google AdSense" within a few days. The body of the message is shown in Figure 3.73.

t. Click on the **Sign In Link** in the email to go to the AdSense sign-in page. You can then sign in to your AdSense account with the email and password that you provided during the sign-up process.

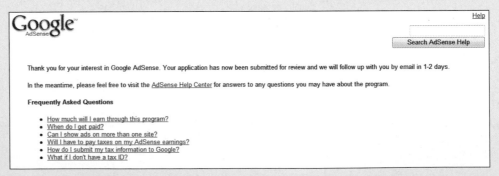

Figure 3.72 Google AdSense application submission screen indicating the successful submission of an application.

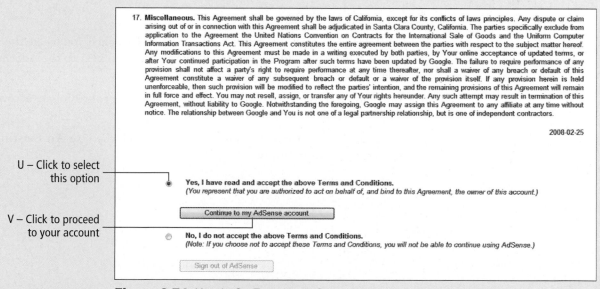

This message was sent from a notification-only email address that does not accept incoming email. Please do not reply to this message.

Congratulations!

Your Google AdSense application has been approved. You can now activate your account and get started with AdSense in minutes.

To quickly set up your account, follow the steps below. Or, for a detailed walkthrough of everything you need to know as a new AdSense publisher, visit Newbie Central: http://www.google.com/ads/newbiecentral.

STEP 1: Sign in to your account.

T – Click on the link to sign in to your account

Visit https://www.google.com/adsense?hl=en_US and sign in using the email address and password that you submitted with your application. If you've forgotten your password, visit http://www.google.com/adsensepassword for assistance.

STEP 2: Generate and implement the AdSense code.

Figure 3.73 Hands-On Exercise 7, Step 1t.

The first time you log in to your account after it has been approved, you are presented with the terms of agreement for using your AdSense account. You should review them carefully to ensure that you understand them and can abide by them.

u. Click the **Yes, I Have Read...** option to select it.

v. Click the **Continue to My AdSense Account** button to proceed.

Congratulations! Your AdSense account is now active and you are ready to place ads on your blog.

17. **Miscellaneous.** This Agreement shall be governed by the laws of California, except for its conflicts of laws principles. Any dispute or claim arising out of or in connection with this Agreement shall be adjudicated in Santa Clara County, California. The parties specifically exclude from application to the Agreement the United Nations Convention on Contracts for the International Sale of Goods and the Uniform Computer Information Transactions Act. This Agreement constitutes the entire agreement between the parties with respect to the subject matter hereof. Any modifications to this Agreement must be made in a writing executed by both parties, by Your online acceptance of updated terms, or after Your continued participation in the Program after such terms have been updated by Google. The failure to require performance of any provision shall not affect a party's right to require performance at any time thereafter, nor shall a waiver of any breach or default of this Agreement constitute a waiver of any subsequent breach or default or a waiver of the provision itself. If any provision herein is held unenforceable, then such provision will be modified to reflect the parties' intention, and the remaining provisions of this Agreement will remain in full force and effect. You may not resell, assign, or transfer any of Your rights hereunder. Any such attempt may result in termination of this Agreement, without liability to Google. Notwithstanding the foregoing, Google may assign this Agreement to any affiliate at any time without notice. The relationship between Google and You is not one of a legal partnership relationship, but is one of independent contractors.

2008-02-25

U – Click to select this option

Yes, I have read and accept the above Terms and Conditions.
(You represent that you are authorized to act on behalf of, and bind to this Agreement, the owner of this account.)

Continue to my AdSense account

V – Click to proceed to your account

No, I do not accept the above Terms and Conditions.
(Note: If you choose not to accept these Terms and Conditions, you will not be able to continue using AdSense.)

Sign out of AdSense

Figure 3.74 Hands-On Exercise 7, Steps 1u and 1v.

Step 2 Insert an AdSense Ad onto Your Blog

Refer to Figures 3.75 through 3.81 as you complete Step 2.

If you are not logged in to your Blogger account, follow Steps 2a through 2c. If you are logged in to your Blogger account, then proceed to Step 2d.

a. If necessary, open your web browser. Type **www.blogger.com** in the address box of your browser and press **Enter**.

b. Log in to your Blogger account using your email address and password.

c. On the **Dashboard** screen, click the **Layout** link to go to the **Layout** screen (see Figure 3.36 for guidance). Proceed to Step 2e.

d. If you are already logged in to Blogger, click the **Customize** link at the top of the screen to go to the **Layout** screen.

Ads are best placed at the top of the blog. So in this exercise, you'll place an advertisement at the top of the column on the right.

e. Click the **Add a Gadget** link to display the **Add a Gadget** dialog box.

E – Click to display the
Add a Gadget dialog box

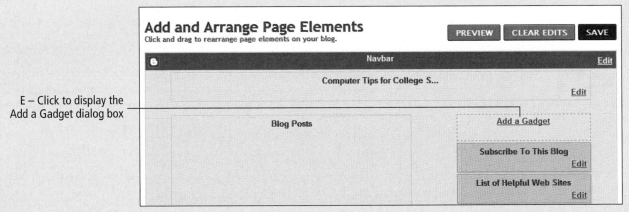

Figure 3.75 Hands-On Exercise 7, Step 2e.

f. Scroll down through the **Add a Gadget** dialog box until you locate the **AdSense** gadget. Click the **Add** button (looks like a plus sign) next to the AdSense gadget to display the **Set Up AdSense Account** dialog box.

The first time you use this gadget, you need to associate your Blogger account with your approved AdSense account.

g. In the **Set Up AdSense Account** dialog box, click the **Use An Existing AdSense Account** button.

F – Click to display the Set Up AdSense Account dialog box

Figure 3.76 Hands-On Exercise 7, Step 2f.

G – Click this button to continue

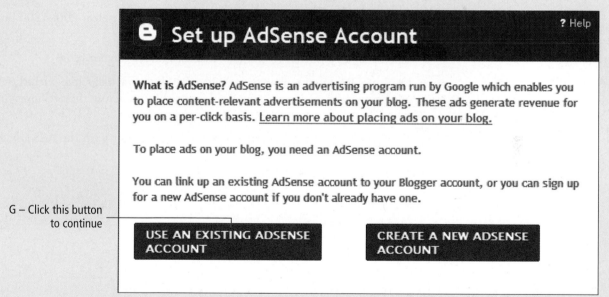

Figure 3.77 Hands-On Exercise 7, Step 2g.

h. Enter the email address associated with your AdSense account in the **AdSense Email** box.

i. Enter the zip code associated with your AdSense account in the **Postal Code** box.

j. Click the **Sign In** button to associate your AdSense account with your Blogger account and display the **Configure AdSense** dialog box.

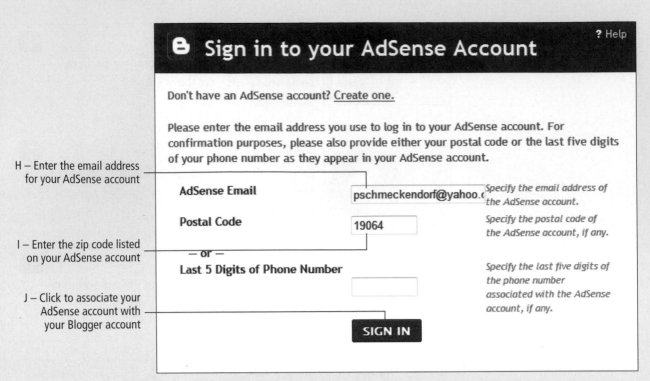

H – Enter the email address for your AdSense account

I – Enter the zip code listed on your AdSense account

J – Click to associate your AdSense account with your Blogger account

Figure 3.78 Hands-On Exercise 7, Steps 2h though 2j.

k. Click the **drop-down arrow** for the format box and select **200 x 200 Small Square** from the drop-down menu.

l. Click the **Save** button to add the AdSense gadget to your blog.

m. Click the **Preview** button to see what the blog now looks like with the AdSense ads being displayed at the top of the right column. Close the preview window when done.

n. Click the **Save** button to save the revised blog layout with the AdSense gadget now added.

Format

200 x 200 Small Square ▾

● Text And Image ○ Text Only

K – Click to select 200 x 200 Small Square

Colors

Blend Template ▾

Customize Colors

Tip: What color combinations are best for my site?

Border		#ffffff
Background		#ffffff
Text		#555544
Title		#555544
Url		#669922

Preview

Ads by Goooooogle

Apartment Search
Search here for Apartment Search
zimply.com

Apartments for rent
Quickly search online listings & submit a lead via email. aff
www.apartments.com

Advanced

Your ads are currently serving with publisher ID *ca-pub-1740103456341793*.
Switch to a different publisher ID.

L – Click to add the AdSense square to your blog

BACK   CANCEL   SAVE

Figure 3.79 Hands-On Exercise 7, Steps 2k and 2l.

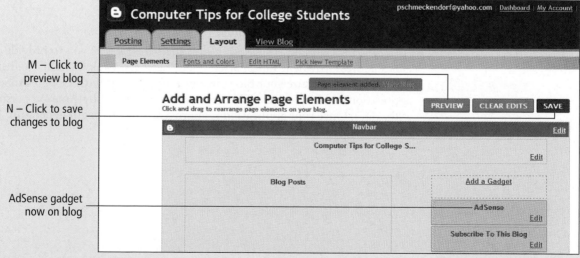

M – Click to preview blog

N – Click to save changes to blog

AdSense gadget now on blog

Figure 3.80 Hands-On Exercise 7, Steps 2m and 2n.

Contextual A type of ad in which the topic is related to the content of the website on which it is displayed

Figure 3.81 shows Professor Schmeckendorf's blog as it now looks with an AdSense ad displayed at the top of the right column. The ads shown in this space will change each time the page is loaded. AdSense ads are *contextual*, meaning that their topics are related to the content of the website on which they are displayed. The ads appearing on Professor Schmeckendorf's site should deal with some aspect of computing.

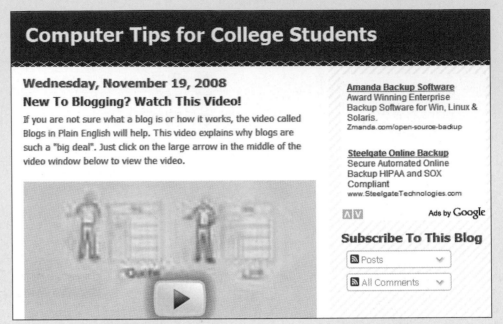

Figure 3.81 Professor Schmeckendorf's blog after adding Google AdSense ads.

Objective 10

Add Amazon Associates links to a blog

One of the best-known affiliate programs is the Amazon Associates program. This program, which is free to join, allows you to generate links and widgets to showcase Amazon products on your blog and to collect a commission when people follow the links and buy from Amazon. A *widget* is a small, interactive miniapplication that provides functionality for a blog or website.

Widget A small, interactive miniapplication that provides functionality for a blog or website

How do I join Amazon Associates?

Amazon Associates has a short sign-up page that requires you to provide a valid email address, payment information (name, address, bank account), and the URL of your blog—make sure your blog already exists. Just as with Google AdSense, your application and blog are usually reviewed and approved by Amazon personnel within a few days. Once your application is approved, you can begin generating links to display on your blog.

Hands-On Exercises

8 | Displaying Amazon Associates Links on a Blog

Steps: 1. Register for an Amazon Associates Account **2.** Insert an Amazon Associates Link onto Your Blog

Use Figures 3.82 through 3.95 as a guide in the exercise.

Step 1 Register for an Amazon Associates Account

Refer to Figures 3.82 through 3.87 as you complete Step 1.

a. If necessary, open your web browser, type **https://affiliate-program.amazon.com** in the address box of your browser, and press **Enter**.

b. Click the **Join Now for Free!** button to begin the registration process.

B – Click here to register

Figure 3.82 Hands-On Exercise 8, Step 1b.

c. On the first application screen, enter your email address in the appropriate box.

d. Click the **I Am a New Customer** option to select it.

e. Click the **Sign In Using Our Secure Server** button to continue the registration process.

f. On the registration screen, type your name in the appropriate box.

g. Type your email address in both email boxes.

h. Type a password for your account in both password boxes.

i. Click the **Continue** button to proceed to the next step of the registration process.

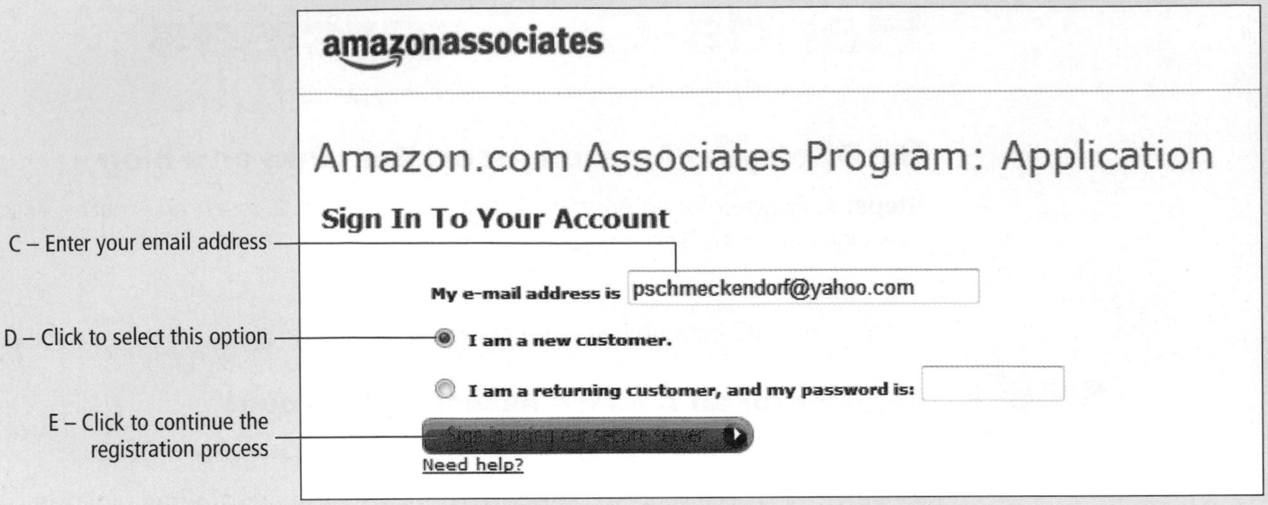

amazonassociates

Amazon.com Associates Program: Application

Sign In To Your Account

C – Enter your email address

My e-mail address is pschmeckendorf@yahoo.com

D – Click to select this option

◉ I am a new customer.

○ I am a returning customer, and my password is:

E – Click to continue the registration process

Sign in using our secure server ▶

Need help?

Figure 3.83 Hands-On Exercise 8, Steps 1c through 1e.

Registration

F – Type your name

New to Amazon.com? Register Below.

My name is: Frederick Schmeckendorf

G – Type your email address in both boxes

My e-mail address: pschmeckendorf@yahoo.com

Type it again: pschmeckendorf@yahoo.com

Birthday: Month ▼ Day ▼ (optional)

Protect your information with a password
This will be your only Amazon.com password.

H – Type a password in both boxes

Enter a new password: ••••••••

Type it again: ••••••••

I – Click the Continue button

Continue ▶

Figure 3.84 Hands-On Exercise 8, Steps 1f through 1i.

j. Enter your name, address, and phone number in the appropriate boxes.

k. Click the **Yes** option to select it.

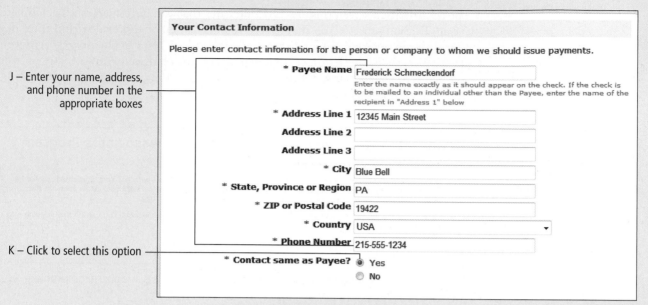

Figure 3.85 Hands-On Exercise 8, Steps 1j and 1k.

l. Type the title of your blog in the appropriate box.

m. Type your blog's URL in the **URL** text box.

n. Access the **drop-down list** and select an appropriate category for your blog.

o. Type a brief description of your blog in the box.

p. From the **drop-down list**, select **Blog** as your method of generating referrals.

q. Click the **checkbox** to select it and indicate your agreement with Amazon's terms.

r. Click the **Finish** button to complete the registration process.

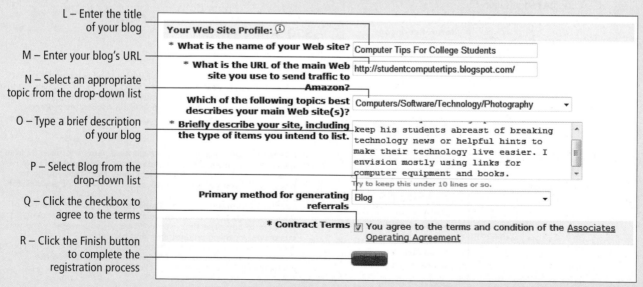

Figure 3.86 Hands-On Exercise 8, Steps 1l through 1r.

The confirmation screen (Figure 3.87) indicates that you have successfully completed the application process. You should receive notification of approval within three days after Amazon reviews your application and your blog. You can choose to specify your payment method (check, direct bank deposit, or gift certificate) now or later on when you log in to your account. Once your account is approved, you can start generating links and adding them to your blog.

Figure 3.87 Confirmation screen for the Amazon Associates registration process.

 Insert an Amazon Associates Link onto Your Blog

Refer to Figures 3.88 through 3.95 as you complete Step 2.

a. After you receive your email confirming your acceptance into the Amazon Associates program, open your web browser. Type **https://affiliate-program.amazon.com** in the address box of your browser and press **Enter**.

b. Type your email address and password in the appropriate boxes and click the **Sign In** button to access the Amazon Associates site.

c. Click the **Widgets** link to access the **Build Your Amazon Widgets** page.

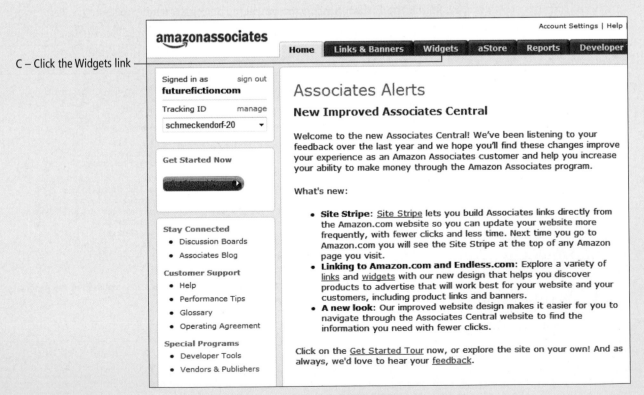

Figure 3.88 Hands-On Exercise 8, Step 2c.

D – Click to generate
code for a search box

Figure 3.89 Hands-On Exercise 8, Step 2d.

d. Scroll down the Widgets page until you locate the **Search Box** widget. Click the **Add to Your Web Page** button directly under the Search Box widget.

e. Scroll down to find the **Search Box With Dropdown** widget. Click in the **HTML Code Box** and drag to select (highlight) all of the code.

f. With the code selected, right-click in the **HTML Code Box** and select **Copy** from the shortcut menu.

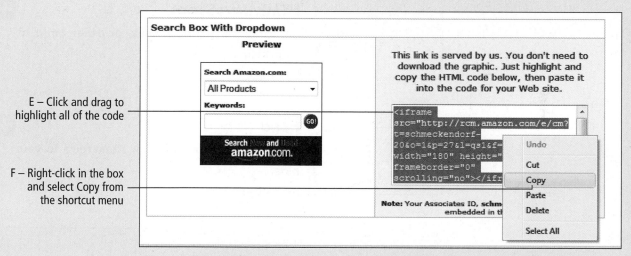

E – Click and drag to
highlight all of the code

F – Right-click in the box
and select Copy from
the shortcut menu

Figure 3.90 Hands-On Exercise 8, Steps 2e and 2f.

g. Log in to your Blogger account and click the **Layout** link on the Dashboard to take you to the **Layout** screen. If you are already logged in, click the **Customize** link at the top of your blog to access the Layout screen.

h. Click the **Add a Gadget link** to access the **Add a Gadget** dialog box.

i. In the **Add a Gadget** dialog box, scroll down until you locate the **HTML/JavaScript** gadget. Click the **Add** button to access the **Configure HTML/JavaScript** dialog box.

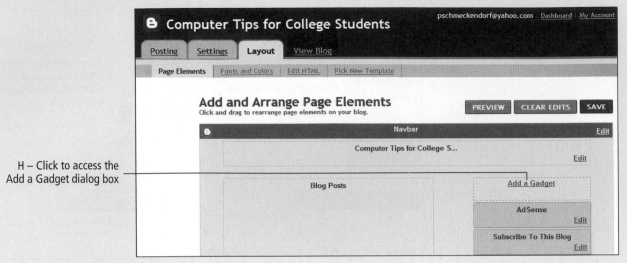

H – Click to access the Add a Gadget dialog box

Figure 3.91 Hands-On Exercise 8, Step 2h.

I – Click to access the Configure HTML/JavaScript dialog box

Figure 3.92 Hands-On Exercise 8, Step 2i.

j. In the **Configure HTML/JavaScript** dialog box, type **Find Your Favorite Things On Amazon** into the Title box.

k. Right-click in the **Content** box and select **Paste** from the shortcut menu to paste the HTML code from the Amazon Associates site into the **Content** box.

l. Click the **Save** button to add the Amazon search box to the blog.

m. Click the **Preview** button to view the blog with the new search box gadget added.

n. Click the **Save** button to save the revised blog layout.

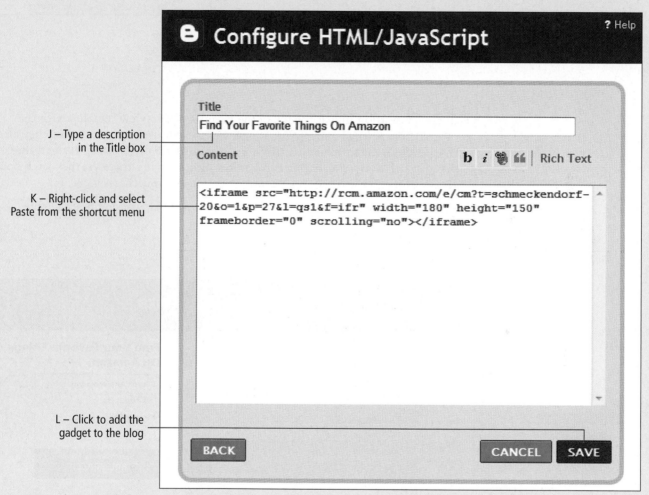

J – Type a description in the Title box

K – Right-click and select Paste from the shortcut menu

L – Click to add the gadget to the blog

Figure 3.93 Hands-On Exercise 8, Steps 2j through 2l.

M – Click to preview the blog

N – Click to save the revised layout

New gadget now added

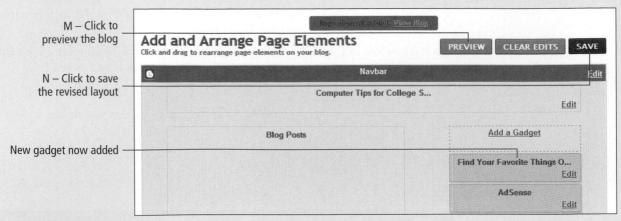

Figure 3.94 Hands-On Exercise 8, Steps 2m and 2n.

Click the **View Blog** link at the top of the Layout page to view the blog with the new search box added (Figure 3.95). Whenever a reader uses the search box, they are taken directly to the merchandise they were searching for on Amazon. If the reader makes any purchases while on the Amazon site after arriving there via the search box, Professor Schmeckendorf receives a commission on their purchases.

You can experiment with the many widgets and links that Amazon has available until you find the ones that work best on your blog.

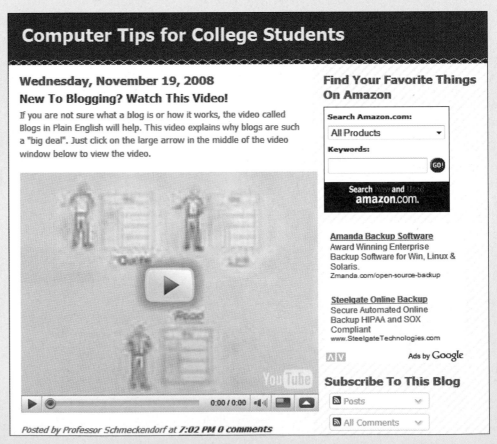

Figure 3.95 Professor Schmeckendorf's blog displaying an Amazon search box.

Objective 11

Describe Internet resources about enhancing blogs

Since blogging has become a mainstream business for many people and an avid hobby for more casual enthusiasts, a number of blogs have sprung up to assist bloggers in fine-tuning their blogs. Here are some resources you may want to explore:

- Dosh Dosh (www.doshdosh.com) – A very professional site that offers a myriad of blogging tips, Internet marketing strategies, and social media strategies. The categories on monetization strategies, link building, search engine optimization (SEO), and AdSense tips and hacks are very worthwhile.

- Pearsonified (www.pearsonified.com) – The author humbly refers to this as the "Best Damn Blog on the Planet." He provides some useful tips for improving your ranking on search engines, and his insights on website design are very refreshing.

- Problogger (www.problogger.net) – Another well-written blog that contains excellent advice on making money with your blog. Don't miss the archive "31 Days to Building a Better Blog" containing 31 daily postings that this blogger wrote to provide you with one task you can tackle per day to improve your blog.

- Blogger Tips and Tricks (http://blogger-tricks.blogspot.com) – A blog that is actually hosted on Blogger that focuses primarily on improving blogs that are hosted on Blogger. If you are sitting there scratching your head and wondering how you can do something on Blogger—like make a certain post always stay at the top of the screen, which is called a *sticky post*—try searching on this site for an answer.

- Personal Development for Smart People (www.stevepavlina.com) – In this personal development blog, the author shares his experience of getting his blog to earn $1,000 a day without spending very much money. He has some very unique opinions and ideas, and his content will usually make you think.

Summary

You have now learned how to publicize your blog and set it up to enable it to make money. But don't forget that the main thing that draws readers to a blog is new, interesting, original content. Don't be so concerned about making money from your blog that you forget to keep it updated on a regular basis. Creativity spawns readership, which in turn will provide you with the opportunity to make money if enough people are coming to your blog site. And even if you never make a dime from your blog, you can still take pride in generating quality information that keeps readers coming back for more.

Key Terms

Multiple Choice

1. If the popular political blog *Huffington Post* embedded a video clip from a new political thriller that had not yet been released in one of its posts, this would be an example of:

    (a) public domain encroachment.

    (b) a paid-to-blog program.

    (c) contributory infringement.

    (d) contextual copyright.

2. To provide additional functionality to a blog or website, you might add a:

    (a) widget.

    (b) sponsored ad.

    (c) blog carnival.

    (d) Screen tip.

3. If a blog has a high amount of traffic, which of the following statements is true?

   (a) The blog earns a lot of revenue.

   (b) The blog has a lot of readers.

   (c) The blog's author posts multiple blog entries on a daily basis.

   (d) The blog contains a number of links to other sites.

4. When the topic of an ad is related to the content of the site on which it is deployed, this ad is said to be:

   (a) sponsored.

   (b) an aggregator.

   (c) a web feed.

   (d) contextual.

5. Which of the following is *not* a method used to create awareness of a blog?

   (a) Place a widget on the blog.

   (b) Become listed in search engines.

   (c) Encourage readers to promote the blog.

   (d) Leave comments on other blogs.

6. Which type of program provides payments to a blog author based upon the referrals received from the blog?

   (a) Affiliate

   (b) Advertising

   (c) Paid-to-blog

   (d) Recommendation

7. When does a copyrighted work enter the public domain?

   (a) Ten years after its creation date.

   (b) When the copyright expires.

   (c) A copyrighted work is not eligible to be in the public domain.

   (d) Immediately upon creation.

8. What are the three basic marketing objectives that are applied to blogs?

   (a) Inform, entertain, become profitable

   (b) Notify, educate, remind

   (c) Inform, persuade, remind

   (d) Recommend, persuade, notify

9. Which of the following can be used to notify you when a blog or website has posted new content?

   (a) Blog carnival

   (b) Aggregator

   (c) Social network

   (d) Gadget

10. Which of the following statements about embedding video is *not* true?

   (a) To add the embedded code in Blogger, you need to create the post in HTML mode.

   (b) Copyright laws do not apply to embedded video.

   (c) It is not necessary to download anything to embed video on a blog.

   (d) Embedded videos can help stimulate interest for a blog's readers.

Fill in the Blank

1. To avoid copyright infringement, you should check a website's _____ _____ _____ before using any material you find there.

2. A(n) _____ _____ is similar to an online magazine and includes short descriptions of blog articles and links leading to those articles. It is often hosted by blogs that take turns publishing it.

3. An aggregator checks a blog's _____ _____ to see if there is any new content available.

4. A(n) _____ _____ is a website that locates information on the web and creates an index of the key words.

5. Under current U.S. law, _____ is assigned to a work as soon as it is created and set down in physical form.

Practice Exercises

1. **Add a Technorati Favorites Button to Your Blog**

   Many people search Technorati for blogs on topics they are interested in. Often, they are attracted to blogs that other Technorati members have tagged as their favorites. Putting a button on your blog to allow people to easily choose it as a favorite in Technorati is a good idea. For this exercise, you will place a Technorati favorites button on the blog you claimed on Technorati. You need to have completed Hands-On Exercise 1, Step 3 to complete this exercise.

   a. Open your browser.

   b. Navigate to **www.technorati.com**.

   c. Log in to the Technorati account that you created previously.

   d. After logging in, point to the **Blogger Central** link to display the drop-down menu. Click the **Claim Your Blog** link.

   e. Under the **My Claimed Blogs** list, locate the blog—if there is more than one— that you wish to work on. Click the **Edit Settings** button next to the blog you wish to work on.

   f. Scroll down to the **Favorite Buttons** section. Locate the second button, **Add This Blog to My Technorati Favorites,** and click in the box containing the HTML code. Right-click and select **Copy** from the shortcut menu to copy this HTML code onto your Windows clipboard.

   g. Open a new browser window and navigate to **www.blogger.com**.

   h. Log in to your Blogger account. On the Blogger **Dashboard**, click the **Layout** link next to your blog.

   i. Click the **Add a Gadget** link on your blog's **Add and Arrange Page Elements** screen.

   j. Find the **HTML/JavaScript** gadget in the **Add a Gadget** dialog box, and click the **Add** button next to it to display the **Configure HTML/JavaScript** dialog box.

   k. In the **Configure HTML/JavaScript** dialog box, type **Favorite My Blog** in the title box.

   l. Paste the HTML code that you copied from the Technorati site into the **Content** box. Click the **Save** button to add the gadget to your blog.

   m. On the **Add and Arrange Page Elements** screen, click the **Save** button to save your changes.

   n. On the **Add and Arrange Page Elements** screen, click one of the **View Blog** links to display your blog with the new gadget added. Go to Professor Schmeckendorf's blog at **http://studentcomputertips.blogspot.com** to see what the button should look like.

o. Print out a copy of your blog with the Technorati favorite button on it and give it to your instructor, or take a screenshot of your blog and email it to your instructor.

p. Log out of the Technorati site and your Blogger account and close your browser.

2. **Put AdSense Ads Between Posts on Your Blog**

Readers often scroll through a blog and read several posts at one sitting. Therefore, placing AdSense ads in between posts on your blog is a good strategy, because people will see them and be more likely to click on them than if the ads were located only at the top of the web page. In this exercise, you will modify your blog layout so that AdSense ads are displayed between your blog posts. To successfully complete this exercise, you must have completed Hands-On Exercise 7 and have at least two posts on your blog.

a. Open a new browser window and navigate to **www.blogger.com**.

b. Log in to your Blogger account. On the Blogger **Dashboard**, click the **Layout** link next to your blog.

c. Click the **Edit** link in the **Blog Posts** box to open the **Configure Posts** dialog box.

d. In the **Configure Posts** dialog box, click the **Show Ads Between Posts** checkbox to select it. Selecting the checkbox will cause the **Configure Inline Ads** section to appear directly below the checkbox.

e. In the **Configure Inline Ads** section, click the **drop-down arrow** and set the **Show After Every Post** option to 1.

f. Click the **drop-down arrow** in the **Format** section and select the 234 x 60 **Half Banner** option. Make sure the **Text And Image** option is selected.

g. Click the **Save** button in the **Configure Posts** dialog box to save your settings.

h. On the **Add and Arrange Page Elements** screen, click the **Save** button to save your changes.

i. Click one of the **View Blog** links on the **Add and Arrange Page Elements** screen to display your blog. Scroll down and you should see an AdSense ad displayed between the first two posts. Go to Professor Schmeckendorf's blog at **http://studentcomputertips.blogspot.com** to see what the ad should look like.

j. Print out a copy of your blog with the AdSense ad showing between posts and give it to your instructor, or take a screenshot of your blog and email it to your instructor.

k. Log out of the Google AdSense site and your Blogger account and close your browser.

3. **Putting a Google Search Box on Your Blog**

As you add more posts to your blog, it may become more difficult for readers to find what they are looking for. Adding a search feature to your blog can help visitors locate information in older posts. You can generate the code for a search box in your Google AdSense account. When your readers perform a search using this tool, the results will return links to your blog posts that match the key words. Additional Google ads will also be displayed with the search results, giving you a chance to earn more revenue.

a. Open a web browser and navigate to **www.google.com/adsense**. Log in to your AdSense account.

b. Click on the **AdSense Setup** tab to select it.

c. On the **AdSense Setup** tab, click on the **AdSense for Search** link.

d. Ensure that the **Only Sites I Select** option is active; if not, click to select it.

e. In the **Selected Sites** text box, type the URL of your blog followed by /*. For instance, Professor Schmeckendorf would type *http://studentcomputertips.blogspot.com/** in this box. Scroll down and click the **Continue** button at the bottom of the page.

f. On the **Choose Search Box Options** page, in the **Look and Feel** section, click one of the three options listed in the second column. These options put the Google Custom Search label beneath the search box. This style will work better for a search box located in a side column on a blog.

g. If necessary, type 31 in the **Text Box Length** text box. Click the **Continue** button at the bottom of the page.

h. On the **Search Results Style** page, select the **Open Results on Google in the Same Window** option. Click the **Continue** button at the bottom of the page.

i. In the **Save the Search Engine** section, click the checkbox to agree to the additional terms of Google AdSense. In the **Name Your Search Engine** text box, type the name of your blog—or as much of your blog name as will fit in the space allowed. Click the **Submit and Get Code** button.

j. Click in the **Search Code** box to select the HTML code. Right-click the selected code and choose **Copy** from the shortcut menu to copy the code onto the Windows clipboard.

k. Open a new browser window and navigate to **www.blogger.com**.

l. Log in to your Blogger account. On the Blogger **Dashboard**, click the **Layout** link next to your blog.

m. Click the **Add a Gadget** link on your blog's **Add and Arrange Page Elements** screen.

n. Find the **HTML/JavaScript** gadget in the **Add a Gadget** dialog box and click the **Add** button next to it to display the **Configure HTML/JavaScript** dialog box.

o. In the **Configure HTML/JavaScript** dialog box, type **Search This Blog** in the title box.

p. Paste the HTML code that you copied from the AdSense site into the **Content** text box. Click the **Save** button to add the gadget to your blog.

q. On the **Add and Arrange Page Elements** screen, click the **Save** button to save your changes.

r. On the **Add and Arrange Page Elements** screen, click one of the **View Blog** links to display your blog with the new gadget added. Go to Professor Schmeckendorf's blog at **http://studentcomputertips.blogspot.com** to see what the search box should look like.

s. Print out a copy of your blog with the Google Custom Search box on it and give it to your instructor, or take a screenshot of your blog and email it to your instructor.

t. Log out of the Google AdSense site and your Blogger account and close your browser.

4. **Put an Amazon Banner Beneath the Title of Your Blog**

The top of your blog is premium advertising space, as visitors will see any ads placed there as soon as your blog loads in their browser. An Amazon banner generated from your Amazon Associates account will be a great addition to the blog if it is placed directly under the title of your blog. However, the HTML code of most Blogger templates requires a bit of tweaking to enable the creation of additional gadgets at the top of the blog.

a. Open your browser and navigate to **https://affiliate-program.amazon.com**. Log in to your Amazon Associates account.

b. Click on the **Links & Banners** tab at the top of the screen. Scroll down the Links and Banners page to the **Banners** section and click the **Add Banners Now** link.

c. In the **Banner Links by Category** section, click on a link that most closely matches the content of your site. Professor Schmeckendorf chose **Computers and Accessories**.

d. On the next page, find a banner that you like with a size of **468 x 60**. Click on the **Highlight HTML** button beneath the selected banner. Right-click the selected code and select **Copy** from the shortcut menu to copy the HTML code to the Windows clipboard.

e. Open a new browser window and navigate to **www.blogger.com**.

f. Log in to your Blogger account. On the Blogger **Dashboard**, click the **Layout** link next to your blog.

g. Click on the **Edit HTML** link at the top of the screen to display the HTML code for your blog's template.

h. If desired, you can click the **Download Full Template** link and save a copy of the blog's HTML code before making any changes.

i. In the **Edit Template** text box, search for the HTML code that looks similar to the following code. Note that your HTML code may differ slightly depending upon the template you are using.

```
<div id='header-wrapper'>
<b:section class='header' id='header' maxwidgets='1' showaddelement='no'>
<b:widget id='Header1' locked='true' title='Computer Tips for College Students
(Header)' type='Header'/>
</b:section>
</div>
```

j. Change the number following *maxwidgets* to 3,change the *no* after *showaddelement* to **yes**, and then change the *true* after *locked* to **false.** The line of code should now look like this (changes shown in red):

```
<b:section class='header' id='header' maxwidgets='3' showaddelement='yes'>
<b:widget id='Header1' locked='false' title='Computer Tips for College Students
(Header)' type='Header'/>
```

k. Click the **Save Template** button to save the changes that you made to your blog's template. Then click the **Page Elements** link at the top of the page. Your blog should now have an **Add a Gadget** link at the very top.

l. Click the **Add a Gadget** link at the top of your blog's **Add and Arrange Page Elements** screen.

m. Find the **HTML/JavaScript** gadget in the **Add a Gadget** dialog box and click the **Add** button next to it to display the **Configure HTML/JavaScript** dialog box.

n. You do not need to add a title for this gadget. Paste the HTML code you copied from the Amazon Associates site into the **Content** text box. Click the **Save** button to add the gadget to your blog.

o. On the **Add and Arrange Page Elements** screen, notice that the HTML/JavaScript gadget you just added is now above the Title gadget for your blog. Click and drag the **HTML/JavaScript** gadget below the Title gadget to position it below the title of your blog.

p. On the **Add and Arrange Page Elements** screen, click the **Save** button to save your changes.

q. Click on one of the **View Blog** links to display your blog with the new gadget added. Go to Professor Schmeckendorf's blog at **http://studentcomputertips. blogspot.com** to see what the banner under the title should look like.

r. Print out a copy of your blog with the Amazon ad banner displayed beneath the title and give it to your instructor, or take a screenshot of your blog and email it to your instructor.

s. Log out of the Amazon Associates site and your Blogger account and close your browser.

Critical Thinking

1. When you signed up for Google AdSense, you had to agree to several statements. In particular, you agreed that you would not place ads on sites that offered visitors incentives to click on the ads and that you would not click on the Google ads that appear on your own blog. Why would Google ask you to agree to these terms? Explore these issues and write a brief paper explaining your thoughts and identifying where you found your information.

2. There are many sites that offer free blog templates. Some of these sites add special HTML code to their templates to indicate that the blog was created by someone other than you. Other sites may not include any special code but may request that you add a link on your blog that leads back to the site from which you obtained the template. What are the ethical and legal ramifications of removing the HTML code or neglecting to add the requested link on your blog? Would you modify the template or comply with the layout creator's wishes? Write a brief paper detailing your findings and explaining your decision.

Team Projects

1. In this chapter, you learned how to use an aggregator (Google Reader) to subscribe to blogs and other types of web content. There are a number of other aggregator programs available. Divide your team into two groups. One group should research aggregator software that is installed on your computer; the other group should research web-based aggregators. Create a chart listing the aggregators you found and the advantages and disadvantages of each type. Present your findings to the class.

2. In this chapter, you learned how to submit your blog to several search engines, including Google, Technorati, and IceRocket. As a group, identify three other search engines to which you can submit your blog. Research and answer the following questions:

   • Why did you select these particular search engines?

   • Are any of your choices blog search engines?

   • Do any of the search engines cater to a particular audience (for example, health care, science, etc.)?

   • How popular are these search engines? If possible, locate and list information about their market share.

   • What is the submission process?

   Write a brief paper detailing your findings.

CHAPTER 4

Wikis

Objectives

After you read this chapter, you will be able to:

1. Explain what a wiki is and why you would use a wiki

2. Describe Wikipedia and how it works, and explain how to create and edit content on Wikipedia

3. Explain how to evaluate information found on the Internet

4. Discuss websites you can use to start a wiki

5. Set up an account and a wiki on PBwiki

6. Edit a wiki page and add pages to a wiki

7. Add internal and external links to a wiki

8. Upload content to or embed content on a wiki

9. Describe Internet resources that educate people about wikis

The following Hands-On Exercises will help you accomplish the chapter Objectives.

Hands-On Exercises

EXERCISES	SKILLS COVERED
1. Create an account on PBwiki and configure a wiki (page 191)	**Step 1:** Sign Up for an Account on PBwiki **Step 2:** Configure a Wiki on PBwiki
2. Edit a wiki page on PBwiki and add pages to a wiki (page 201)	**Step 1:** Log In to Your PBwiki Account **Step 2:** Edit the FrontPage of Your Wiki **Step 3:** Add Pages to Your Wiki
3. Add internal and external links to wiki pages (page 210)	**Step 1:** Create a Navigation Scheme for a Wiki Using Internal Links **Step 2:** Insert External Links to Content on a Wiki Page
4. Upload images to a wiki and embed video on a wiki page (page 216)	**Step 1:** Upload an Image to PBwiki **Step 2:** Embed a YouTube Video on a Wiki Page

Objective 1

Explain what a wiki is and why you would use a wiki

What is a wiki?

Chances are that you've looked at a website and noticed information that was incorrect or incomplete. When you found such a site, didn't you wish you had the ability to change the information on that website? This is the idea behind wikis.

A *wiki* is essentially a collection of web pages in which each page has its own edit button. Unlike a website, which is usually edited and maintained by a specially designated person or department, wikis were designed to allow groups of people to collectively generate and edit textual information. The text can be viewed by anyone with access to the wiki, which is often anyone with a browser who can find the URL of the wiki. One page on a wiki is known as a *wiki page*, whereas a group of wiki pages is known collectively as a *wiki*. Wikis are a Web 2.0 application because they foster content creation and interaction among a group of people. Wikis are designed to be viewed and edited using nothing more than a web browser, and they require no knowledge of HTML coding.

Who invented wikis?

Ward Cunningham is generally credited as inventing the wiki in 1995 when he deployed the software to power the WikiWikiWeb on his company's website (www.c2.com). The WikiWikiWeb was designed to facilitate the sharing of information between programmers. *Wiki* is a Hawaiian word that means *fast*. The original wiki was named after the WikiWiki shuttle, a bus service that operates out of the Honolulu airport and provides a quick way to go from the airport to downtown Honolulu. Wikis grew quickly in popularity with computer programmers but did not become known to the mainstream public until the creation of Wikipedia in 2001.

Why would I use a wiki?

It is likely that you have already used one of the world's most popular wikis: Wikipedia. Wikipedia is basically an online encyclopedia, but its unique feature is that it is written by people just like you from all around the globe. Businesses and individuals are finding that wikis have benefits for many different purposes aside from encyclopedias.

Personal Uses of Wikis

- Note taking – Take notes in your college classes on your laptop and post them to your wiki (either during class or after class). Get your friends who are taking the same class to add their notes to the wiki. Then you will have a collaborative study guide that should be more comprehensive than your notes alone. And most wikis have search features that facilitate locating specific information.

- Group projects – Students are often required to work in groups to complete assignments. Using a wiki facilitates communication and planning among group members. Wikis also can be used to keep track of who did how much work on a particular project. This is especially useful for providing objective evidence to your instructor when one group member is not doing a sufficient share of the work.

- To-do lists – We all have tasks to accomplish every day. A wiki is a great place to manage a to-do list because you can easily edit it as tasks change, and you can access it from any device (such as your phone) that has access to the Internet.

Wiki A collection of web pages that are designed to be edited by groups of individuals.

Wiki page One page on a wiki.

- Event planning – Need to plan a 25th wedding anniversary party for your parents? How about a bridal shower for your best friend? Events are easy to organize through a wiki, as you can set up different parts of the wiki to handle various segments of the event: planning, physical location, gifts, decorations, seating charts, contact information, etc.

- Creating a knowledge base – Perhaps you are passionate about a particular subject such as the television shows *Heroes* (Figure 4.1) or *Buffy the Vampire Slayer*. It is likely that there are fans throughout the world who share your interest. A wiki gives fans a chance to build a knowledge base and to speculate about developments in specific areas of interest.

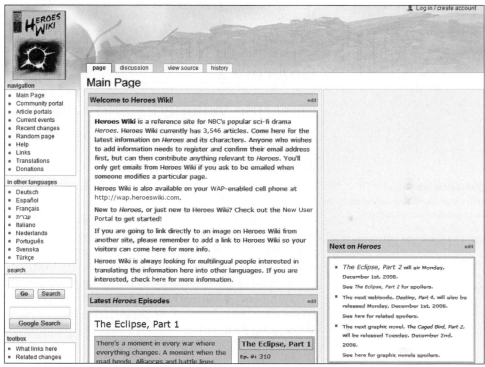

Figure 4.1 The Heroes Wiki (www.heroeswiki.com) provides fans a place to share their knowledge and opinions about the popular television show *Heroes*.

Business or Organizational Uses of Wikis

- Project management and planning – Coordinating projects, especially when people who are involved in a project are located at widespread geographic locations, is often done through wikis. A wiki can provide everyone involved in a project with access to all planning documents, schedules, timelines, and images necessary to manage the project.

- Operations and training manuals – There is a great deal of documentation that workers consult to learn how to operate machinery or manage business processes. Distributing paper manuals is a waste of natural resources and time, especially if the manuals are frequently updated. Putting this information on a wiki provides access and makes frequent updates simple. You'll always be looking at the current version of the manual if it is updated on the web whenever changes occur.

- Checklists – Operations with multiple steps are often repeated frequently. Having a checklist to refer to ensures that operations are carried out consistently and that the actions are taken in the correct order. Wiki checklists can be easily updated by multiple people.

- Development of business plans – Business plans (to launch a new business, product, or service) are developed by teams of individuals such as accountants, marketing professionals, attorneys, salesmen, manufacturing personnel, logistics specialists, etc. Coordination of complex business plans, where the input from many individuals is required, can be carried out more efficiently with the use of a wiki.

- Frequently Asked Questions (FAQ) documents – Time can be saved by generating answers to frequently asked questions and posting them on a wiki. Using a wiki allows people to easily generate new questions or post answers to questions that others have already asked.

- Community news and announcements – Small towns often start wikis to keep residents abreast of news and activities in the local community.

To understand how wikis work, we'll use Wikipedia as an example to explain the basic concepts of wikis.

Objective 2

Describe Wikipedia and how it works, and explain how to create and edit content on Wikipedia

What exactly is Wikipedia?

Wikipedia (www.wikipedia.org) is an online encyclopedia that is deployed in many languages and is accessible at no cost to its users (Figure 4.2). Wikipedia's name is a combination of the words *wiki* and *encyclopedia*. Unlike conventional encyclopedias, which are written by paid writers, Wikipedia's content can be generated by anyone who wishes to add to it, and the current content of Wikipedia has been written by unpaid volunteers. It was launched in January 2001 by Jimmy Wales and Larry Sanger, and it was originally supported by Jimmy Wales' company, Bomis.

Wikipedia is currently hosted, funded, and managed by the Wikimedia Foundation, Inc., a nonprofit organization located in San Francisco, California. The Wikimedia Foundation operates a variety of wiki projects in addition to Wikipedia.

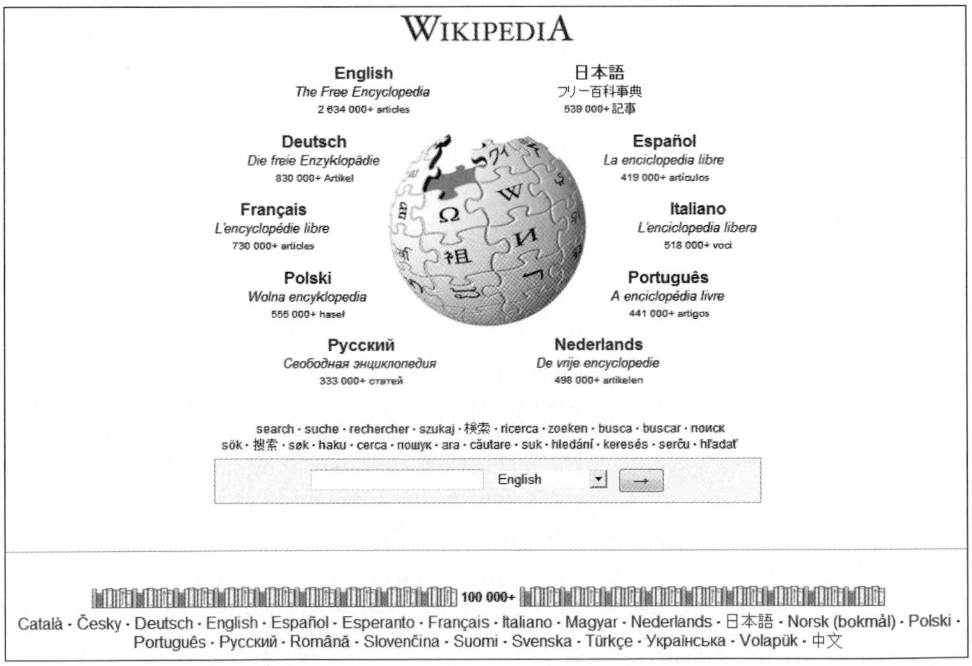

Wikipedia An online encyclopedia that is deployed in many languages and is accessible at no cost to its users.

Figure 4.2 Wikipedia now features articles in over 260 languages, although the majority of articles are written in English.

The foundation's mission is to encourage people to collaboratively develop information and provide that information to the general public free of charge. Although the foundation receives some grant money, it relies heavily on donations, which is why you will frequently see appeals for donations on Wikipedia pages.

What is the goal of Wikipedia?

Wikipedia strives to be a repository of factual knowledge. Its contribution guidelines state that topics submitted to Wikipedia must be encyclopedic in nature. To Wikipedia, this means that a topic must be *notable*, which is defined as having significant coverage in other reliable media sources (such as conventional media outlets or scholarly journals). In addition, Wikipedia is supposed to cover knowledge that is already established and recognized. . . in other words, facts. Wikipedia is not a forum for publishing new information, speculation, or original works (such as fictional stories). Wikipedia stresses that statements made in an article must be supported by appropriate references to other published sources of information that are deemed reliable.

Most importantly, since Wikipedia is designed to deal with facts, articles in Wikipedia should not express opinions or take sides. If an article is about a topic that has opposing views, each view should be given a roughly equal share of coverage.

How does Wikipedia differ from traditional encyclopedias?

Peer review or refereeing
A process by which experts in a given field review another author's scholarly work to determine that the output is valid and substantially correct.

Traditional encyclopedias, such as *Encyclopedia Britannica*, have formal peer review processes to review content **before** it is published in the encyclopedia. *Peer review* (also called *refereeing*) is a process by which experts in a given field review another author's scholarly work to determine that the output is valid and substantially correct. For example, this textbook underwent a peer review process prior to publication. Professors with Web 2.0 expertise reviewed what the authors had written to confirm its validity and to make suggestions about improvements (or corrections) to the content. Wikipedia has no such formal peer review process. Articles or edits to articles are published right after they are written and become available almost immediately on the Internet. Therefore, Wikipedia *does not guarantee* the validity or accuracy of the information it contains.

The copyright (rights to copy, publish, and distribute) to articles that are written for publication are usually owned by the authors or publishers of the work. The copyright for articles on Wikipedia is not owned by the authors of the articles. When you provide content to Wikipedia, you surrender your rights to hold the copyright to your work. Also, Wikipedia is not censored. Content that some people may find objectionable or pornographic is published in it.

Who enforces the guidelines set down for contributing articles to Wikipedia?

Wiki community The users and contributors to a wiki.

The users and contributors to Wikipedia make up its *wiki community*. A community is critical to a wiki because the community is what generates content for a wiki. Sometimes a community might only consist of three or four people, such as a group of students planning a project for their class. With large wikis like Wikipedia, the community is comprised of millions of people spread around the globe. Each person who visits Wikipedia can take on one or more of the following roles:

- Readers – Readers merely access Wikipedia, search for the information they need, and leave. Most people who visit Wikipedia are readers.

- Writers – Some readers eventually choose to become writers by generating content for Wikipedia. Anyone can write for Wikipedia. There is no test or minimum standards for becoming a writer, and you can start writing for Wikipedia right now by generating a page. All you need to do to generate a new page for Wikipedia is create a free account.

- Editors – Most pages in Wikipedia can also be edited by anyone. Editors correct mistakes they see on a page or make additions and changes to content on a page.

Watchlist A list of web pages that are being monitored.

Regular editors and contributors often maintain watchlists of pages. A *watchlist* is a list of pages that are being monitored. Anytime updates are made to those pages, the person maintaining the watchlist is informed of the changes. A watchlist makes it easier to keep track of the pages that you are interested in monitoring. You can edit pages anonymously because editing does not require a Wikipedia account; however, you must have an account to create a watchlist.

- Administrators – People who have been contributing to Wikipedia for a long time and who consistently do quality work either writing or editing are sometimes given administrator status on Wikipedia (currently about 1,600 people). This gives them the ability to delete or undelete pages, lock pages to keep them from falling prey to vandals, and block certain users from contributing to Wikipedia.

Aren't people tempted to put false information up on Wikipedia to further a cause or paint themselves in a positive light?

Human nature being what it is, this is not an infrequent occurrence on Wikipedia and other sites like it. Wiki vandals and Internet trolls sometimes post inappropriate information on Wikipedia. *Wiki vandals* deface pages in a wiki by one of these methods:

- Deleting legitimate information

- Inserting irrelevant or nonsensical information

- Violating the policies of the wiki (such as adding content that is speculative on Wikipedia)

- Inserting links to commercial sites in an attempt to sell products or services

Wiki vandals Individuals who deface pages in a wiki by deleting legitimate information, inserting irrelevant or nonsensical information, violating the policies of the wiki (such as adding content that is speculative on Wikipedia), or inserting links to commercial sites in an attempt to sell products or services.

Vandals are usually seeking amusement, furthering a political or hate-speech agenda, or just trying to see if their damage gets detected. *Internet trolls* are individuals who write inflammatory, controversial, or irrelevant content in online communities such as Wikipedia just to provoke emotional responses from readers.

The most famous case of vandalism on Wikipedia was false and defamatory content placed there about John Seigenthaler, an American journalist and political figure. The vandalism went undetected for four months but was finally reported and fixed. Mr. Seigenthaler then published an article criticizing Wikipedia for being inaccurate, which was certainly a justifiable reaction based on his experience.

Internet trolls Individuals who write inflammatory, controversial, or irrelevant content in online communities such as Wikipedia, just to provoke emotional responses from readers.

How does Wikipedia prevent vandalism?

Community members take responsibility for policing the content and eliminating false or erroneous information. Certain pages that are subject to constant vandalism have been locked by administrators so that they can't be edited by just anyone. Other pages that suffer from occasional vandalism are closely monitored by editors who are notified when changes are made so that they can review them for correctness and appropriateness. However, because the community can't be watching everything at once, vandalism or accidental additions of erroneous information aren't always detected right away on Wikipedia.

What does a Wikipedia page look like?

On Wikipedia's home page (Figure 4.2), if you type the word *carousel* in the search box and click the search button (looks like an arrow pointing to the right), you will be taken to a wiki page about carousels (Figure 4.3).

Click here to edit this page

Information about carousels created by one or more contributors

Picture of carousel horses uploaded by a contributor

Figure 4.3 A wiki page about carousels from Wikipedia.

How do you edit a Wikipedia wiki page?

At the top of most pages is a link that says Edit This Page. You may have new information about carousels that you wish to add to the page, or you may have a picture of a carousel figure that you want to upload to the page (uploading requires a Wikipedia account). If you click the Edit This Page link, you are taken to the editing page for the carousel wiki page (Figure 4.4). This page has an edit box that contains HTML code for the carousel page. There is a toolbar that provides functionality to make editing easier (such as adding HTML tags for references). You can add or change text wherever you need to on this page.

Editing toolbar

Editing box contains the HTML code for the page

Professor Schmeckendorf decides to add zebras to this list here

Figure 4.4 The carousel wiki page in the editing mode.

Professor Schmeckendorf knows quite a bit about carousels, and he has decided to expand the list of animals (other than horses) that are commonly found on carousels to include zebras. Below the editing area is a Save Page button. Clicking this button will save the change Professor Schmeckendorf makes to the carousel page. The change will immediately be posted to the web, and the page now includes zebras in the list of animals.

How do you know who has contributed to a page?

On Wikipedia, in most cases you will never know exactly who contributed to a page, because editing can be performed anonymously. However, wikis contain a feature called *revision history* that tracks which users (even anonymous ones) have made changes to a page. The **revision history page** (Figure 4.5) provides a chronological listing (most recent first) of the edits to the page. On Wikipedia, you can access this page by clicking the History link at the top of a wiki page. Edits made by contributors logged in to their Wikipedia accounts show the screen names for their accounts. Anonymous edits are identified only by the IP (Internet Protocol) address of the computer from which the edit was made. An **IP address** is a unique number assigned to devices connected to the Internet. The IP address is similar to the street address of your house. It helps data find its way from one device to another on the Internet.

Revision history page A chronological listing (most recent first) of the edits to a wiki page.

IP address A unique number assigned to devices connected to the Internet.

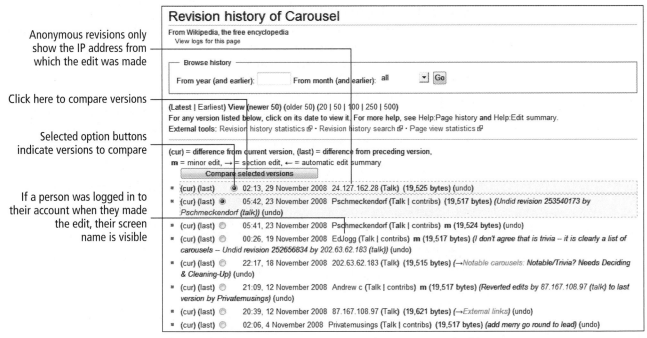

Figure 4.5 The revision history page for the carousel wiki page.

The revision history page allows a user to compare two versions of a wiki page, such as the current version and a previous one. This makes it easy to see exactly what was changed on the page in the most recent edit (Figure 4.6). It also makes it very convenient for an editor to revert to the previous version of the page if the editor determines that the revisions were unnecessary, incorrect, or a result of vandalism. Professor Schmeckendorf's edit is shown in red text on the left side of Figure 4.6.

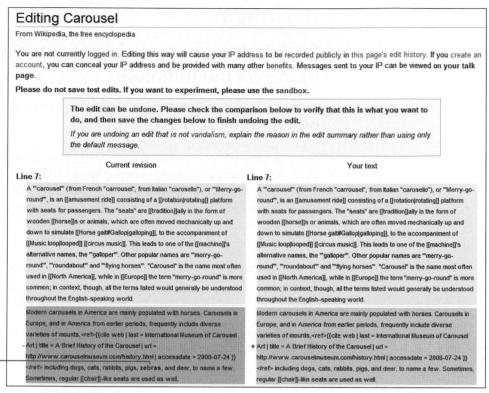

Changes in the current version from the previous version are shown as red text

Figure 4.6 A comparison of the current version of the carousel wiki page to the previous version of the page.

How can I become familiar with the editing process on Wikipedia?

The best way to become familiar with editing Wikipedia is to try it yourself. You can follow these steps as a guideline:

1. Think of a topic about which you are very knowledgeable.
2. Search for a page on Wikipedia that contains information about your topic.
3. Read the page carefully.
4. Locate a section of the page which you think might benefit from additional information, or find something on the page with which you disagree.
5. Click the **Edit This Page** link at the top of the page and make some changes to the page.
6. Click the **Save Page** button at the bottom of the editing page to submit your edits to Wikipedia.

Remember to check back in a couple of days to see what has happened to your edit. By then, the community should have responded in some way to your edit. An editor may have changed your wording slightly to make your meaning clearer. Or an editor may have deleted your change if they felt it was inappropriate or off topic. Or you might find that nothing has been changed, signaling that the community agrees with your edit.

Objective 3

Explain how to evaluate information found on the Internet

Because anyone can edit Wikipedia, how do I know that the information I find on it is accurate?

Wikipedia can be very accurate. At the end of 2005, the journal *Nature* conducted a study to compare Wikipedia's accuracy with that of *Encyclopedia Britannica*. The study found that for scientific articles, Wikipedia had about as many errors as the *Encyclopedia Britannica*. However, at any given time, an article that you are reviewing on Wikipedia could be biased, factually incorrect, or contain outdated information. You need to evaluate the accuracy of what you find on Wikipedia in exactly the same way you would evaluate any other information you find on the Internet.

What criteria should you use for evaluating the suitability of a website?

Evaluation criteria are similar to those you use for printed resources that you would find in your school library. You need to consider the following:

- **Who is the author?** Is information about the author—including contact information—readily available on the site? If you know the author's name, you can search the Internet or other resources to consider the expertise of the author. Is the author a noted leader in the field she or he is writing about and recognized as an authority by others you respect? Does the author have appropriate credentials (such as college degrees or relevant work experience) that indicates expertise in that particular field? Although you might find what you consider to be good information on an anonymous blogger's website, you don't have any information about the blogger to consider that person an authority on a subject. Obviously, this isn't applicable to Wikipedia, where you never really know the author's name.

- **Who is the publisher of the information or the owner of the website?** Is the organization that owns or sponsors the website clearly identified? Is that entity an appropriate source of information for the topic you are researching? Is the publisher respected in the field and relied upon by others? Obviously, a respected journalistic body like the *New York Times* (www.nytimes.com) has more credibility than Billy Bob's Bodacious Blog!

- **What is the relationship of the author to the publisher?** Is the author an employee of the publishing entity? Or does the author have a more casual relationship with the publisher, possibly as a freelance author or independent contractor? Employees *might* be held to a more stringent level of competence and be required to have more appropriate credentials than freelancers or independent contractors.

- **Is the viewpoint biased?** Writers tend to use information that helps them make their points to the reader. A good writer is objective and provides different points of view, even when those points are detrimental to the writer's argument. The writer should also acknowledge when he or she is presenting an opinion as opposed to facts, and controversial theories should be identified as such. Consider the organization sponsoring the website and how it might be affected by the information. If you are reviewing information about products that the company publishing the website sells, be aware that the information presented may be intended to persuade people to buy the product. Corporate websites tend to paint the corporation in the most positive light, whereas a site not sponsored by the corporation might provide a more objective opinion about the company's operations and products. Also consider whether the publisher has a particular political, religious, or philosophical agenda that may encourage the author to slant the information that is presented to support the publisher's causes.

- **Does the work cite sources?** Just as your professors expect you to use footnotes and a bibliography in your research papers, scholarly publications on the Internet should also list their sources of information. When presented with a list of sources, check them. Are the sources respected publications or from authoritative and reliable authors on other websites? This is critical for evaluating information found on Wikipedia. Footnotes are located at the bottom of each wiki page on Wikipedia, so check them out for legitimacy.

- **Is the accuracy of the work verifiable?** Can you find the sources listed in the bibliography? Do hyperlinks to other articles work so that you can review the sources? For articles involving research, were the research methods, the data collected, and the interpretation of the results provided so that the research study could be reproduced if necessary?

- **Is the information presented current?** Are dates of publication clearly indicated on the website? When the work is updated, are updates clearly identified and dated? Are the dates when research information was gathered presented (for example, "based on a study conducted by XYZ Consultants in May, 2011")? You can check the history on Wikipedia to help determine how current the information is on that wiki page.

Finally, after following these steps, take a step back and consider what you have found. Decide why the page was placed on the web. Was the main goal of the page to inform, persuade, or sell? Consider whether the page was intended to be a parody or a satire. The best indicator for this is the tone of the writing. Was the writer sarcastic? Did the author tend to use a lot of humor or exaggerate to make points? Was the page supplemented with outlandish or humorous photographs? Decide if there are better places to find your needed research sources than on the Internet. Are the websites you are evaluating as credible as respected published periodicals or texts that you would consult in your college library? If, after all of this analysis, you feel comfortable with the quality of the material you have reviewed, then you may have found a good source of reliable information on the web.

Objective 4

Discuss websites you can use to start a wiki

What do you need to start a wiki?

Server A computer that provides services to other computers upon request.

In the early days of wikis, you needed to install wiki hosting software on a *server* (a computer that provides services to other computers upon request) and connect that server to the Internet. Maintaining a wiki server is not a job for novices. Fortunately, the popularity of wikis gave rise to the creation of hosted wiki service providers, known as wiki farms, that can be used by individuals who lack technical knowledge.

Wiki farm A server (or a group of connected servers) that runs wiki software and is designed to host multiple wikis at the same time.

A *wiki farm* is a server (or a group of connected servers) that runs wiki software and is designed to host multiple wikis at the same time. Some wiki farms charge a fee for hosting a wiki. However, many wiki farms offer free wiki hosting and support their companies by displaying advertising, such as Google AdSense ads, on the wikis they host. Often, you can pay a monthly fee to eliminate the ads placed by the hosting company and even place ads of your own on your wiki so that you can generate revenue.

Where can you find a wiki hosting service?

In an online search engine, just type in the phrase *free wikis* and you should find a long list of wiki hosting providers. Two popular sites for educators and students are PBwiki (www.pbwiki.com) and Wikispaces (www.wikispaces.com), as they offer free wiki hosting, a good range of features, and easy setup (Figure 4.7). Wikidot (www.wikidot.com) is another free wiki hosting provider that offers wikis with a more robust set of features and is a great place to set up a full-featured business wiki. However, the learning curve is a bit steeper for Wikidot, so we don't recommend it for setting up your first wiki.

Figure 4.7 PBwiki provides a free wiki hosting solution that is perfect for novice wiki designers.

How can you host a wiki that looks like Wikipedia or the Heroes wiki?

If you look closely at Wikipedia and the Heroes wiki (www.heroeswiki.com), you will notice that they look very similar in many aspects. This is because both sites use a software package called *MediaWiki* (Figure 4.8) to host their wikis. MediaWiki (www.mediawiki.org) is software that was originally developed to power Wikipedia. It is now available free of charge under a ***GNU General Public License (GPL)***. GPL licenses specify that a software program can be distributed to and modified by anyone, even for commercial purposes (i.e., you are allowed to make money from it). The software is designed to run on large wiki farms and handle millions of user requests per day. MediaWiki requires technical expertise to deploy and maintain, so it is not used by beginners to host a wiki. But if you happen to develop a wiki that becomes

GNU General Public License
A license that specifies that a software program can be distributed to and modified by anyone, even for commercial purposes.

Figure 4.8 Although it requires technical expertise to deploy, MediaWiki is free, full-featured software that can be used to host a robust wiki site such as Wikipedia.

wildly popular, with some help, you could eventually use the MediaWiki software to host your wiki.

For the rest of this chapter, we'll be using PBwiki to show you how to set up and host your first wiki.

Objective 5

Set up an account and a wiki on PBwiki

What details should you consider before setting up a wiki?

Before taking the plunge and launching your first wiki, there are some decisions that you should make.

- **What is the purpose of your wiki?** Determining the goals for your wiki will help you decide if a wiki is really the best type of vehicle to accomplish your goals. Projects that involve collaborative writing (such as building a knowledge base), documentation that requires frequent revisions, providing information to employees who are geographically dispersed, or events that need planning are good candidates for a wiki. If you are merely trying to share files (such as spreadsheets) between individuals, an application such as Google Docs might be a better choice.

- **Should your wiki be visible to everyone?** Wikis do not have to be visible to anyone with a browser. A wiki can be made private so that only authorized individuals can view the wiki. This is often appropriate with proprietary information or a project that is not yet completed.

- **Who should be able to edit or add to your wiki?** Unlike Wikipedia, you can set up your wiki to allow editing access to authorized individuals only. In the case of a wiki that is used by a group of students to plan a class project, probably only the students in the group need the ability to edit the wiki.

- **Who will manage the wiki?** Although wikis can exist without formal management, setting responsibilities for certain wiki tasks can facilitate the completion of a project.

After you make the above decisions, you are ready to sign up for a wiki account on a hosting service and begin constructing your wiki.

Hands-On Exercises

Professor Schmeckendorf has decided to set up his first wiki to facilitate research and information sharing for one of his computer literacy classes. In the Hands-On Exercises in this chapter, you'll recreate Professor Schmeckendorf's wiki on your own wiki site. You can always delete this site from your wiki account or change it to eliminate the wiki pages added in the Hands-On Exercises after you have completed the class for which you are performing these exercises.

1 | Create an Account on PBwiki and Configure a Wiki

Steps: 1. Sign Up for an Account on PBwiki **2.** Configure a Wiki on PBwiki

Use Figures 4.9 through 4.21 as a guide in the exercise.

Step 1   Sign Up for an Account on PBwiki

Refer to Figures 4.9 through 4.13 as you complete Step 1.

a. Turn on the computer.

b. Start your preferred browser (Internet Explorer, Firefox, Safari, etc.). Type **www.pbwiki.com** in the address box of your browser and press **Enter**.

c. At the top of the page, click the **Sign Up** link to begin the sign up process.

C – Click to begin the sign up process

Figure 4.9 Hands-On Exercise 1, Step 1c.

d. In the **Your Name** box, type your name. You do not have to use your real name if you are concerned about protecting your identity.

e. In the **Your Email Address** box, type your email address. This needs to be an email address that already exists, as PBwiki will be sending a confirmation code to this address.

f. Type a password in both the **Enter a Password** and **Confirm Password** boxes.

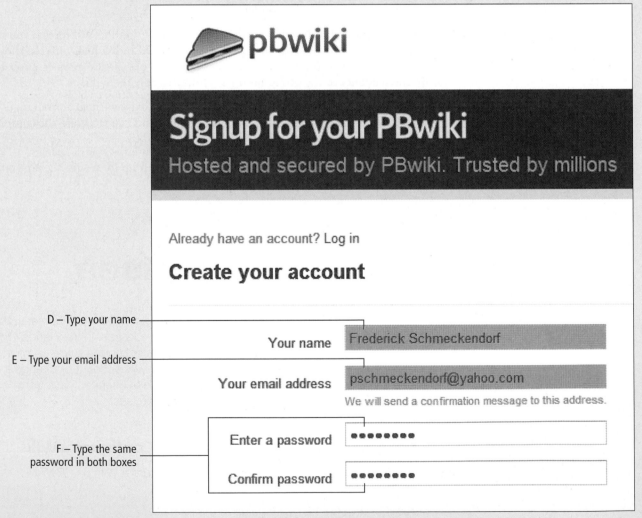

D – Type your name

E – Type your email address

F – Type the same password in both boxes

Figure 4.10 Hands-On Exercise 1, Steps 1d through 1f.

g. In the **Choose a Wiki Name** box, type a URL for your wiki. A suggestion for the URL name is to use a combination of the course number of the course you are currently taking, the first initial of your first name, and your entire last name.

You cannot use cis110fschmeckendorf as your URL. This URL is already in use by Professor Schmeckendorf's Wiki. You will receive an error message if you try to use a URL that is already being used by someone else.

h. Click the **For Individuals** option to select it. Even though you are a student, the educational use option is geared towards teachers; so identifying yourself as an individual is appropriate.

i. If necessary, click the **Yes, Please Make This a PBwiki 2.0 Wiki** checkbox to select it. This creates a wiki with all of the latest features.

j. Click the **Create My Wiki** button to continue the registration process.

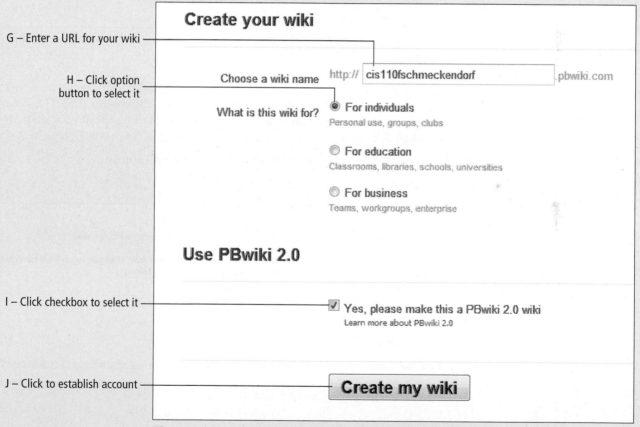

Figure 4.11 Hands-On Exercise 1, Steps 1g through 1j.

Your screen should now reflect that your account information has been processed, as shown in Figure 4.12. You now need to check the email account that you used to sign up for your PBwiki account for a confirmation email. You need the link in this email to activate your PBwiki account.

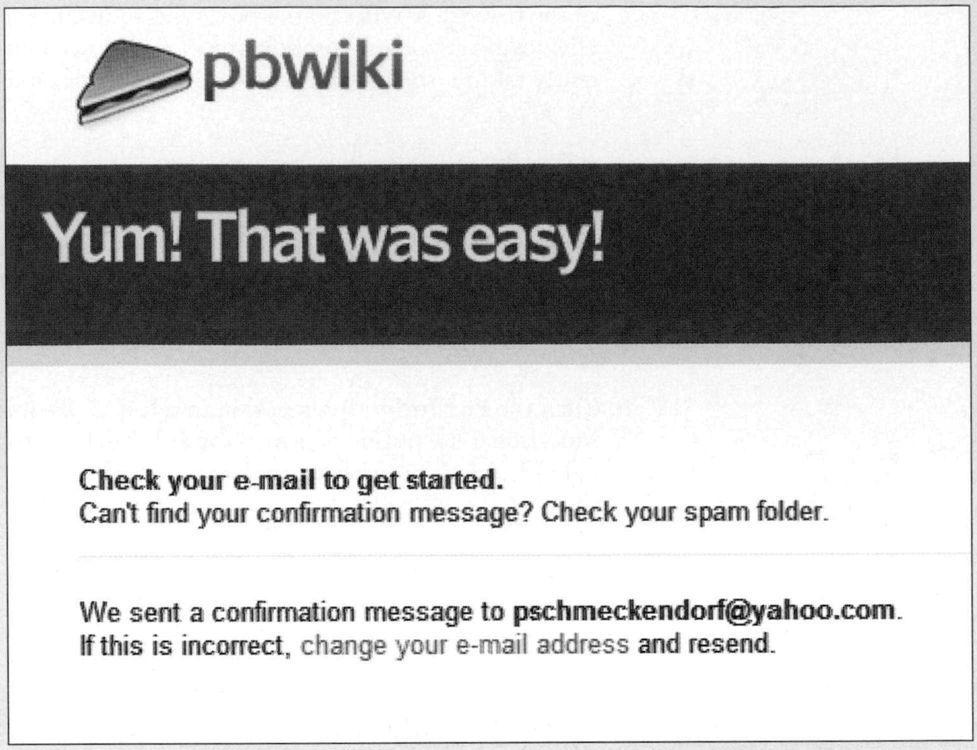

Yum! That was easy!

Check your e-mail to get started.
Can't find your confirmation message? Check your spam folder.

We sent a confirmation message to **pschmeckendorf@yahoo.com.**
If this is incorrect, change your e-mail address and resend.

Figure 4.12 Confirmation screen showing that your wiki sign up information has been processed.

k. Check your email account for an email message with the subject line "Use your new PBwiki now." If you don't see the email in your inbox, check your spam or junk mail folder.

l. Click on the link in the email to activate your PBwiki account.

Hi!

Thanks for creating a PBwiki at pbwiki.com. You're almost ready to start rolling with your wiki! :)

We won't finish actually making your wiki until you log in, so please do that now. Until you log in for the first time, someone else could still take this name. To finish creating your wiki, click below:

L – Click to activate
your PBwiki account ———— http://cis110fschmeckendorf.pbwiki.com/?pwd=mHjRGKGBGw

We hope you enjoy PBwiki and please do tell all your friends about it!

Cheers,
David, Ramit, Nathan & The PBwiki Team

PS: If you have questions or comments, contact support: http://pbwiki.com/help.php?wiki=cis110fschmeckendorf

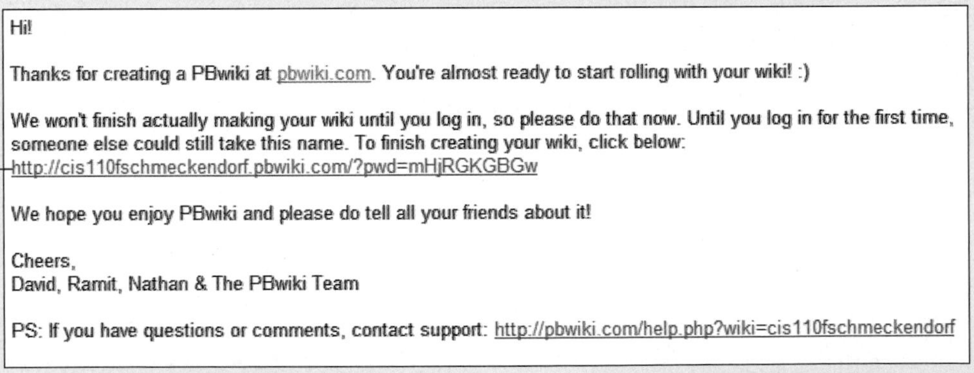

Figure 4.13 Hands-On Exercise 1, Step 1l.

A separate browser window should now open and a welcome screen on PBwiki should be displayed. Notice that the URL for your wiki is displayed at the top of this welcome screen (Figure 4.14).

Step 2   Configure a Wiki on PBwiki

Refer to Figures 4.14 through 4.21 as you complete Step 2.

a. Click the **Anyone** option to make your wiki visible to anyone who wishes to see it, such as your professor.

b. Click the **Only People I Invite or Approve** option to place restrictions on who can edit your wiki.

c. Click the **I Agree to the PBwiki Terms of Service** checkbox to select it and agree to the terms of service set by PBwiki.

d. Click the **Take Me to My Wiki** button to view your wiki and continue configuring it.

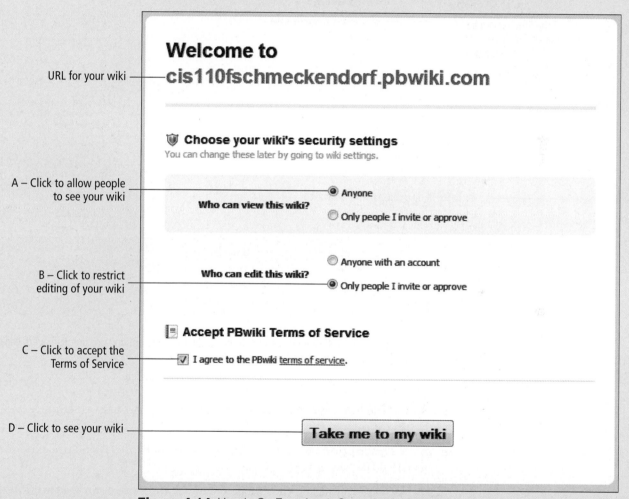

URL for your wiki

A – Click to allow people to see your wiki

B – Click to restrict editing of your wiki

C – Click to accept the Terms of Service

D – Click to see your wiki

Figure 4.14 Hands-On Exercise 1, Steps 2a through 2d.

The wiki you created should look very similar to Figure 4.15. This is the basic wiki configuration that PBwiki sets up when a wiki is first created. The only page that currently exists in the wiki is the FrontPage. It has text on it that was placed there by PBwiki, but this can easily be edited or removed. By default, the title of the wiki is the URL, which is not very descriptive of the wiki. You'll fix the title first and also edit some other settings for the wiki.

e. On the wiki, click the **Settings** link to access the wiki settings screen.

Default title for wiki

E – Click here to edit settings for the wiki

Text placed on the FrontPage by PBwiki can be edited or removed

The Sidebar can be edited just like other wiki pages

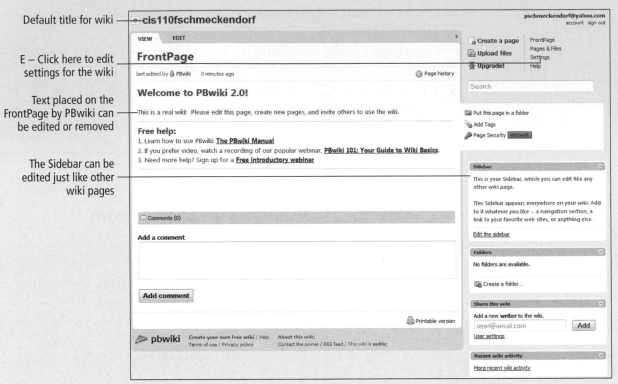

Figure 4.15 Hands-On Exercise 1, Step 2e.

When you enter the Wiki Settings screen, if the About This Wiki options are not displayed, click the About This Wiki link on the left side of the screen.

f. In the **Title** box, replace the default title by typing **Professor Schmeckendorf's CIS110 Wiki**.

g. In the **Description** box, type **A wiki created by Professor Schmeckendorf for his CIS 110 class at GSU**.

h. Check that the time and the keyboard language are correct for your wiki. If they are not, click the **drop-down arrows** next to the appropriate options and change them.

i. If necessary, click the **Show Contact Form for This Wiki** checkbox to select it. Professor Schmeckendorf wants students to be able to contact him if they are having problems with the wiki.

j. Click the **Save** button to save the changes you just made to the wiki.

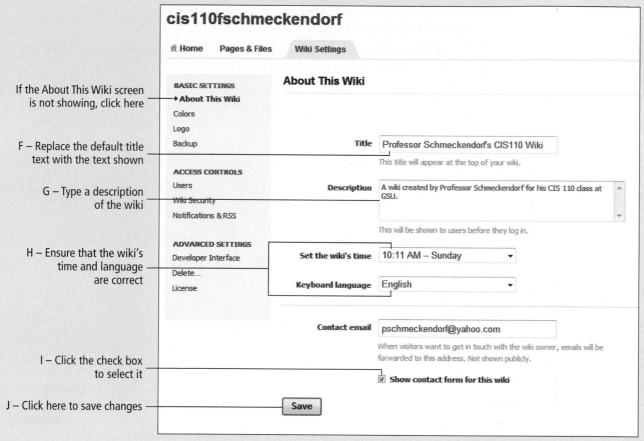

Figure 4.16 Hands-On Exercise 1, Steps 2f through 2j.

Professor Schmeckendorf wants to give access privileges to the wiki to one of his graduate students, Hans Grindeldorf, who will be assisting him in maintaining the wiki. There are five different permission levels that you can grant to other people who will be accessing your wiki:

- Administrator – An administrator can rename or delete anything on the wiki, add users, change user permission levels, or delete users. Administrators are the only users who have access to the wiki's Settings page. Use this level of permission carefully.

- Editor – An editor can rename or delete pages, files, and folders. Editors are able to make deletions that cannot be recovered, so they should be highly trusted individuals.

- Writer – A writer can edit pages, revert pages to previous versions, upload new files, and create new pages. This is the recommended level of access for community members for a wiki, because writers cannot perform any action that cannot be undone.

- Reader – A reader cannot make any modification to the wiki, but they can view the content.

- Page Level Only – Users with this permission level can only access the parts of the wiki for which you have granted them access. You can restrict their access to a particular page if necessary.

Because you created the wiki, you have administrator-level permissions for the wiki, which means that you can do everything to the wiki, including deleting the entire wiki. For most people who will be working on your wiki, you should grant them writer-level permission so that they can't make any changes to the wiki that an administrator cannot undo.

k. On the **About This Wiki** screen, in the **Access Controls** section, click the **Users** link to access the **Manage Users** screen.

l. Type the email of one of your classmates into the **Email Address** box. If you are not working with classmates, use a friend or family member's email address. **Do not** type Professor Schmeckendorf's assistant's email address into the box as shown in the figure!

m. If necessary, click the **drop-down arrow** and select **Writer** from the available permission levels.

n. Click the **Add User** button to add your classmate as a user to your wiki.

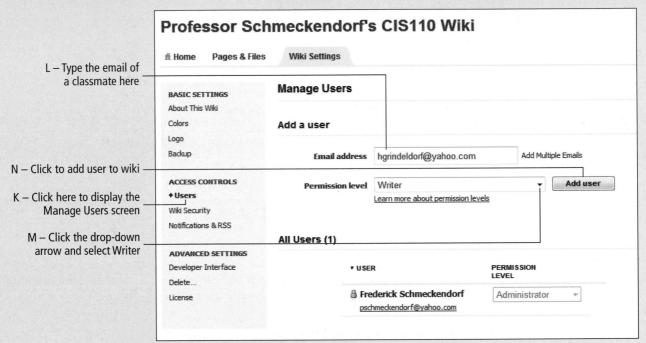

Figure 4.17 Hands-On Exercise 1, Steps 2k through 2n.

Figure 4.18 shows the results of adding a new user to your wiki. The user you just added should now be displayed under the list of users. Administrators on your wiki can change user permission levels for other users.

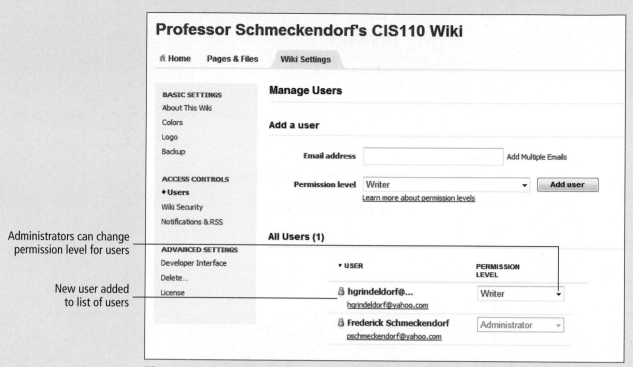

Administrators can change permission level for users

New user added to list of users

Figure 4.18 Manage Users screen listing users authorized for a wiki.

The person you added to your wiki as a user will receive an email inviting them to join the wiki (Figure 4.19). The new user will need to check their email box for this message (check the spam or junk mail folders if the message is not in the inbox). If they click the link in the email, they will be taken to PBwiki to log in.

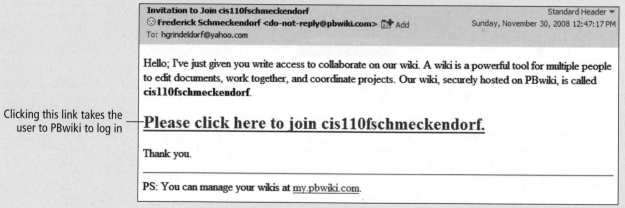

Clicking this link takes the user to PBwiki to log in

Figure 4.19 Email inviting a user to join a wiki.

After clicking on the link, the user you invited is taken to the **Set Up Your Account** screen on PBwiki (Figure 4.20). The user is asked to enter a name and password. Clicking the **Save** button takes the user to the next step in the sign up process.

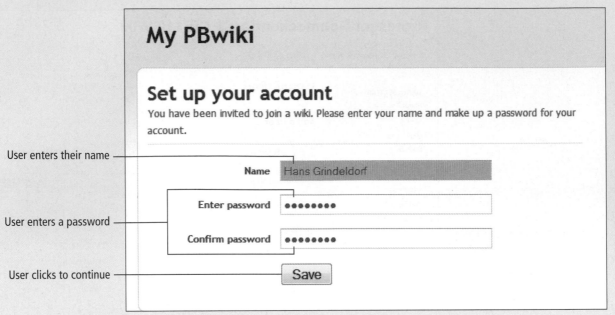

User enters their name

User enters a password

User clicks to continue

Figure 4.20 The user set-up screen on PBwiki.

The user you invited has now established an account on PBwiki. The My Wikis screen shows all of the wikis that an account holder is a member of or has created. Since Hans has not created any wikis yet, only Professor Schmeckendorf's wiki will appear on this list of wikis (Figure 4.21). Clicking on the link to Professor Schmeckendorf's wiki will take Hans to the wiki. Once the friend you have invited to your wiki follows the link in the email they received and creates their PBwiki account, their My Wikis screen should list your wiki on it.

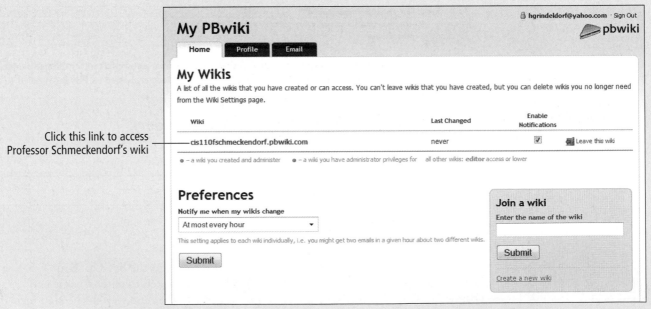

Click this link to access Professor Schmeckendorf's wiki

Figure 4.21 The My Wikis screen for Hans Grindeldorf, who was invited to join Professor Schmeckendorf's wiki.

o. On the **Manage Users** screen, click the **Sign Out** link in the upper right corner to sign out of your PBwiki account.

p. Close your browser.

Professor Schmeckendorf's wiki is now set up and configured. In the next Hands-On Exercise, you will modify Professor Schmeckendorf's wiki by editing the FrontPage and adding pages to the wiki.

Objective 6

Edit a wiki page and add pages to a wiki

In Hands-On Exercise 1, you set up Professor Schmeckendorf's wiki. Now it is time to start modifying the wiki to get the functionality that Professor Schmeckendorf requires. First, you'll edit the FrontPage to change the default text that PBwiki places on all initial web pages. Then you'll add pages to the wiki to make it more functional.

Hands-On Exercises

2 | Edit a Wiki Page on PBwiki and Add Pages to a Wiki

Steps: 1. Log In to Your PBwiki Account **2.** Edit the FrontPage of Your Wiki **3.** Add Pages to Your Wiki

Use Figures 4.22 through 4.35 as a guide in the exercise.

Step 1   Log In to Your PBwiki Account

Refer to Figures 4.22 through 4.24 as you complete Step 1.

a. Turn on the computer.

b. Start your preferred browser (Internet Explorer, Firefox, Safari, etc.). Type **www.pbwiki.com** in the address box of your browser and press **Enter**.

c. At the top of the site, click the **Log In** link to sign in to your PBwiki account.

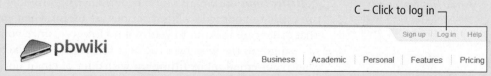

Figure 4.22 Hands-On Exercise 2, Step 1c.

d. Type your email address in the **Email Address** box (or confirm that the address already showing in the box is yours).

e. Type your password in the **Password** box.

f. Click the **Log In** button to sign in to your account.

Click this link if an email address other than yours is showing, to clear it

D – Type your email address

E – Type your password

F – Click to log in

Figure 4.23 Hands-On Exercise 2, Steps 1d through 1f.

Notifications Emails sent out by your wiki provider to alert you when changes are made to your wikis.

One of the preferences you can set for your wikis is the notification preference. *Notifications* are emails sent out by your wiki provider to alert you when changes are made to your wikis. Notifications are useful when you want to review changes that others are making to your wiki. However, since you are going to be making a lot of changes to the wiki over the next few Hands-On Exercises, you probably don't want your email inbox filling up with a lot of email notifications advising that you have changed your own wiki. Therefore, you should change the notification preference to Never to avoid this issue. You can always reset this preference later on.

g. Click the **drop-down arrow** in the preferences section and select the **Never** option.

h. Click the **Submit** button to save the change to your preferences.

i. Click the link to the wiki you set up in Hands-On Exercise 1 to access the wiki. Note that the name of your wiki will not match the one shown in Figure 4.24, as you have created a unique URL for your wiki.

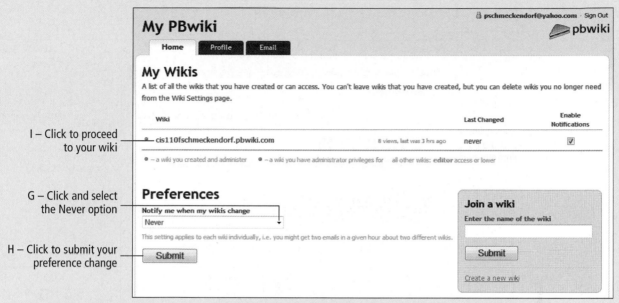

I – Click to proceed to your wiki

G – Click and select the Never option

H – Click to submit your preference change

Figure 4.24 Hands-On Exercise 2, Steps 1g through 1i.

Step 2 Edit the FrontPage of Your Wiki

Refer to Figures 4.25 through 4.29 as you complete Step 2.

Your wiki should now be displaying the FrontPage because you should not have added any other pages to your wiki yet. The FrontPage needs to be modified by deleting the default text that PBwiki creates when an account is set up and replacing it with more useful text.

a. Click the **Edit** link to edit the FrontPage of your wiki.

A – Click to edit the FrontPage

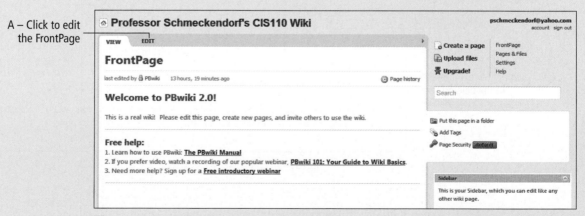

Figure 4.25 Hands-On Exercise 2, Step 2a.

The FrontPage of the wiki is now in the editing mode. Notice that a group of icons representing various editing tools has appeared at the top of the page. Many of these icons will look familiar, as they are very similar to icons used for editing in other software programs, such as Microsoft Word.

b. Click anywhere in the text. Press **Ctrl-A** to select all of the text on the FrontPage. Press **Delete** to delete the text.

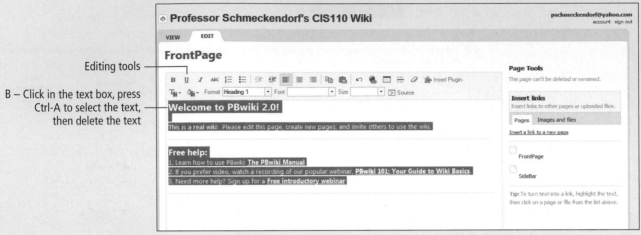

Figure 4.26 Hands-On Exercise 2, Step 2b.

c. Type the following in place of the text that you just deleted from the FrontPage.

Welcome to Professor Schmeckendorf's CIS110 Wiki!

This wiki has been set up for the CIS110 students in Professor Schmeckendorf's CIS110 class to facilitate better communication by the class members and to help organize group research projects.

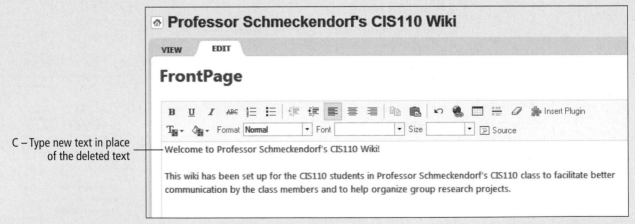

Figure 4.27 Hands-On Exercise 2, Step 2c.

The heading should be enlarged so that it is more noticeable.

d. Click and drag to select the text in the heading.

e. Click the drop-down arrow next to the **Format** box and select **Heading 1** from the available choices.

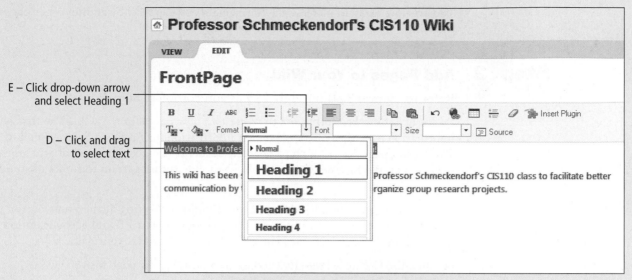

E – Click drop-down arrow and select Heading 1

D – Click and drag to select text

Figure 4.28 Hands-On Exercise 2, Steps 2d and 2e.

Notice that the heading of the page is now displayed in a much larger font (Figure 4.29). The contents of this page are sufficient for now, so you should save the changes made to the FrontPage.

f. Click on the **Save** button to save the edits that were made to the FrontPage. This also exits the editing mode for the page and returns you to the view mode.

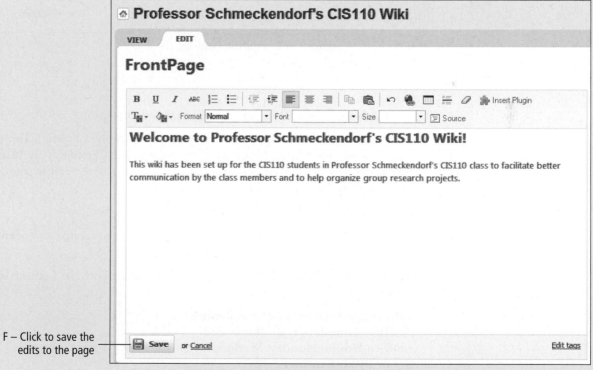

F – Click to save the edits to the page

Figure 4.29 Hands-On Exercise 2, Step 2f.

You are now ready to increase the functionality of the wiki by adding other pages to the wiki.

Step 3 Add Pages to Your Wiki

Refer to Figures 4.30 through 4.35 as you complete Step 3.

Professor Schmeckendorf wants to create two new pages for the wiki. The first is an information page that provides contact information for Professor Schmeckendorf. The second page is a research page where students can post abstracts of articles that they find on the Internet or provide links to videos that pertain to topics of study in the course.

a. If you have just completed Step 2, you should be looking at the FrontPage of your wiki in the view mode. If you have logged out of your PBwiki account, follow the directions in Step 1 of this Hands-On Exercise to access your wiki.

b. Click the **Create a Page** link to begin creating a new page for your wiki.

B – Click to create a new page

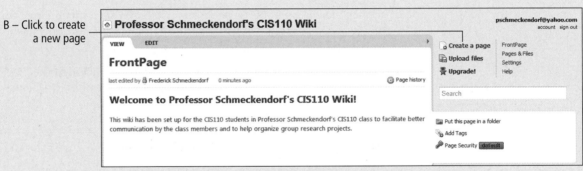

Figure 4.30 Hands-On Exercise 2, Step 3b.

c. In the **Name Your Page** box, type **Contact Information**.

d. If necessary, click the **More Options** link to display the **Choose a Template** section. Ensure the **Blank Template** option is selected. Templates can help save time when setting up some types of pages. But as this is a fairly simple page, you can use a totally blank page from which to work.

e. Click the **Create Page** button to create the page.

A new page entitled **Contact Information** has now been created and opens in edit mode. Now you will add content to the page.

f. Type Professor Schmeckendorf's contact information onto the Contact Information page:

Professor Frederick Schmeckendorf
Office: Founders Hall, Room 222
Office Hours: Monday, Wednesday and Friday – 1 pm to 3 pm
**   or by appointment**
E-mail: pschmeckendorf@yahoo.com

g. Click the **Save** button to save the page.

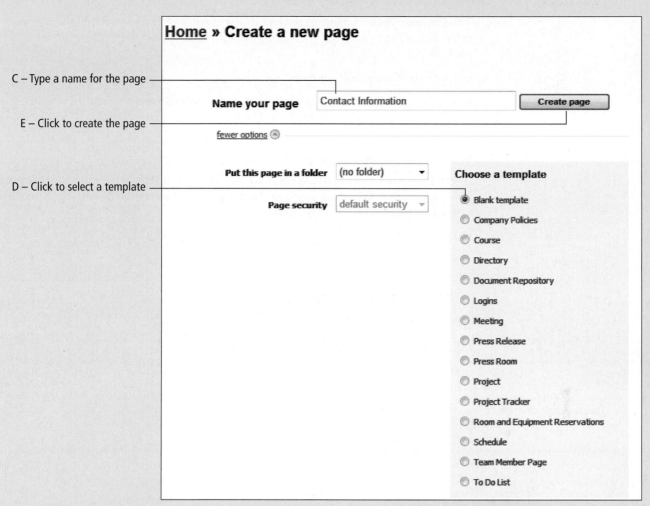

Figure 4.31 Hands-On Exercise 2, Steps 3c through 3e.

C – Type a name for the page

E – Click to create the page

D – Click to select a template

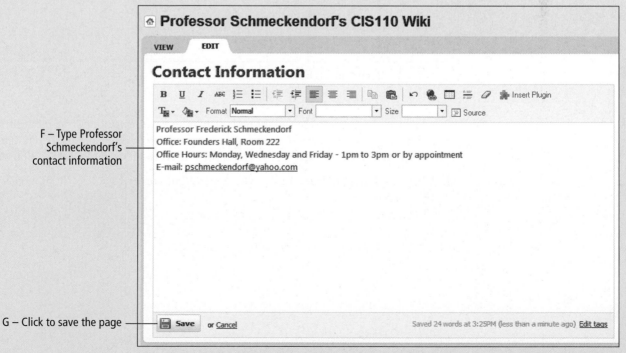

Figure 4.32 Hands-On Exercise 2, Steps 3f and 3g.

F – Type Professor Schmeckendorf's contact information

G – Click to save the page

The **Contact Information** page should now display in the view mode. Now you'll create the second page that Professor Schmeckendorf wants for student research projects.

h. Click the **Create a Page** link.

i. On the **Create a New Page** screen, type **Student Research** for the page title, and again select a blank template. Click the **Create Page** button to create the page.

j. Type the following description onto the page:

On this page, please place links to articles or embed videos that pertain to topics we are covering in class. Sharing information with your classmates is part of your grade for the semester.

k. Click the **Save** button to save the page.

J – Type the page description

K – Click to save the page

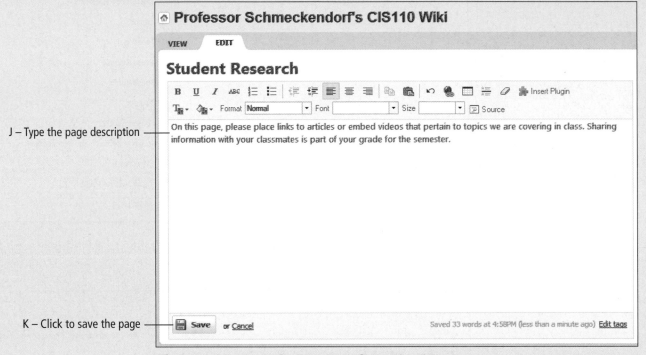

Figure 4.33 Hands-On Exercise 2, Steps 3j and 3k.

The Student Research page should now display in the view mode. It can be difficult to tell how many pages are in your wiki when looking at one page in the view mode. To review all pages currently on your site, you need to view the Pages & Files screen.

l. Click the **Pages & Files** link in the upper right corner to access the **Pages & Files** screen.

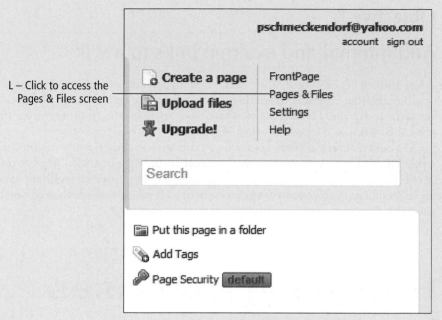

L – Click to access the Pages & Files screen

Figure 4.34 Hands-On Exercise 2, Step 3l.

The **Pages & Files** screen (Figure 4.35) shows you all pages that are currently part of your wiki. From this screen, you can edit and rename pages by following the appropriate links. You can even delete pages by clicking the checkbox next to the page name to select it and then clicking the **Delete** button.

m. Click the **Home** link to return to the FrontPage of the wiki.

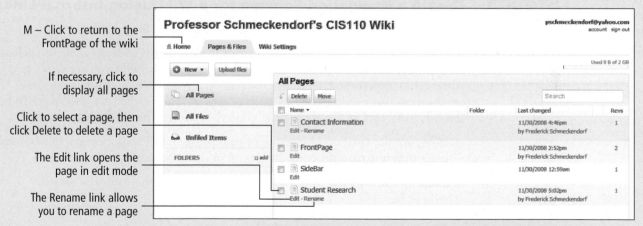

M – Click to return to the FrontPage of the wiki

If necessary, click to display all pages

Click to select a page, then click Delete to delete a page

The Edit link opens the page in edit mode

The Rename link allows you to rename a page

Figure 4.35 The Pages & Files screen allows you to manage the pages on a wiki. Hands-On Exercise 2, Step 3m.

You may now log out of the PBwiki site or continue on to the next Hands-On Exercise. In the next section, you'll learn how to add clickable links to pages to improve their functionality and usefulness.

Objective 7

Add internal and external links to a wiki

Hyperlink Text or an image that connects to another document on the web or to another location on the same web page.

Internal links Hyperlinks that connect one wiki page to another point within the wiki.

External links Hyperlinks that connect to web pages that are located outside of the wiki.

A key feature of the World Wide Web is the hyperlink (or link). A *hyperlink* is text or an image that connects to another document on the web or to another location on the same web page. Hyperlinks facilitate navigation on the Internet. Links are just as critical to wikis as they are to other web pages.

On wikis, *internal links* connect a wiki page to another point within the wiki. The link could connect to another location on the same wiki page or might connect to a different wiki page. Internal links are often used to facilitate navigation for users of a wiki. *External links* connect to web pages that are located outside of the wiki.

Hands-On Exercises

3 | Add Internal and External Links to Wiki Pages

Steps: 1. Create a Navigation Scheme for a Wiki Using Internal Links
2. Insert External Links to Content on a Wiki Page

Use Figures 4.36 through 4.43 as a guide in the exercise.

Create a Navigation Scheme for a Wiki Using Internal Links

Refer to Figures 4.36 through 4.40 as you complete Step 1.

Sidebar A feature of PBwiki, this is a small section that is always visible (by default) on the right side of your wiki no matter what page of the wiki you are viewing.

A feature of PBwiki is the *Sidebar*, a small section that is always visible (by default) on the right side of your wiki no matter what page of the wiki you are viewing. Although it appears smaller than a conventional wiki page, it still has the same attributes as other wiki pages, so it can be edited. The Sidebar is a good place to put internal links that will assist your wiki users in navigating through your wiki.

a. If you are not currently logged in to your account at PBwiki, open a browser, navigate to **www.pbwiki.com**, and log in to your account.

b. Click on the **Edit the Sidebar** link to enter the edit mode for the Sidebar wiki page.

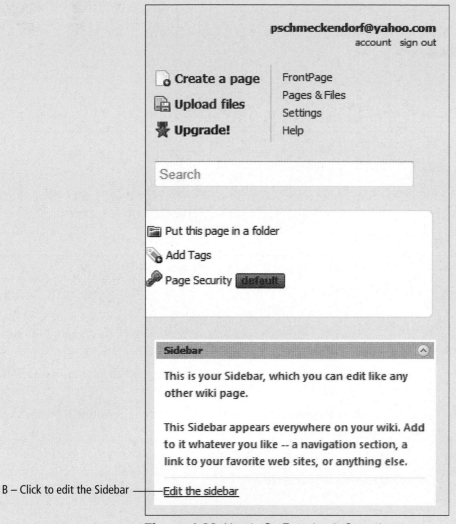

pschmeckendorf@yahoo.com

account   sign out

 Create a page   FrontPage
 Upload files   Pages & Files
 Upgrade!   Settings
                      Help

Search

 Put this page in a folder
 Add Tags
 Page Security default

Sidebar

This is your Sidebar, which you can edit like any other wiki page.

This Sidebar appears everywhere on your wiki. Add to it whatever you like -- a navigation section, a link to your favorite web sites, or anything else.

B – Click to edit the Sidebar ——— Edit the sidebar

Figure 4.36 Hands-On Exercise 3, Step 1b.

c. Click somewhere in the text that is currently on the Sidebar and press **Ctrl-A** to select it. Press **Delete** to delete this text.

Currently, there are two pages in the wiki besides the FrontPage. You need to create links in the Sidebar to both of those pages, as well as a link to return to the FrontPage.

d. Type **Wiki Navigation** on the Sidebar. Press **Enter** to place the insertion point on the line below the words *Wiki Navigation*.

e. Click the **Insert a Link to a New Page** link to display the **Insert Link** dialog box.

f. Click the **Link Type** drop-down arrow and select **PBwiki page**. This indicates that the link will be an internal link to another page on the wiki. Click the **Page** drop-down arrow and select **Contact Information** from the available choices.

g. Click the **OK** button to insert the link.

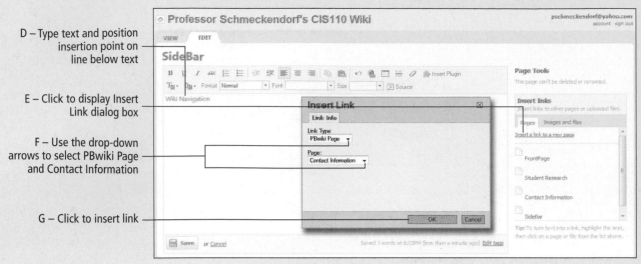

D – Type text and position insertion point on line below text

E – Click to display Insert Link dialog box

F – Use the drop-down arrows to select PBwiki Page and Contact Information

G – Click to insert link

Figure 4.37 Hands-On Exercise 3, Steps 1d through 1g.

Notice that a hyperlink called *Contact Information* has been inserted on the Sidebar page (Figure 4.38). A user clicking this link will navigate to the Contact Information page.

h. Position the insertion point on the line underneath the **Contact Information** link.

i. Click the **Student Research** link to insert a link to the **Student Research** page on the Sidebar page.

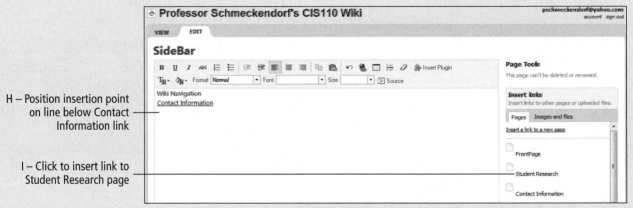

H – Position insertion point on line below Contact Information link

I – Click to insert link to Student Research page

Figure 4.38 Hands-On Exercise 3, Steps 1h and 1i.

A link to the Student Research page has been inserted below the link for the Contact Information page (Figure 4.39). You also need to insert a link back to the FrontPage. However, since *FrontPage* is a term unique to PBwiki and may not be familiar to all users of the wiki, Professor Schmeckendorf feels that the link back to the FrontPage should say *Home* instead.

j. Type **Home** below the **Student Research** link. Click and drag to select the Home text.

k. With the Home text selected, click the **FrontPage** link to turn the word *Home* into a link to the FrontPage wiki page.

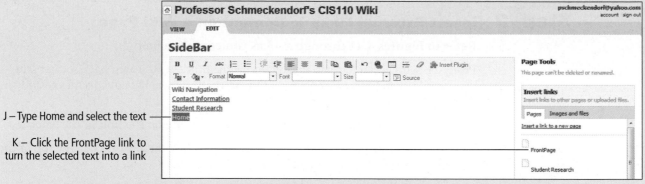

J – Type Home and select the text

K – Click the FrontPage link to turn the selected text into a link

Figure 4.39 Hands-On Exercise 3, Steps 1j and 1k.

You should now have links to all three wiki pages on the Sidebar page.

l. Click the **Save** button to save the Sidebar page.

The Sidebar page will now display in view mode. Notice that the Sidebar area now contains navigation links for the wiki (Figure 4.40). Clicking any of these links will take you to the appropriate page on the wiki. As you add pages to your wiki, you should also add links to those pages in the Sidebar so that users can locate pages easily.

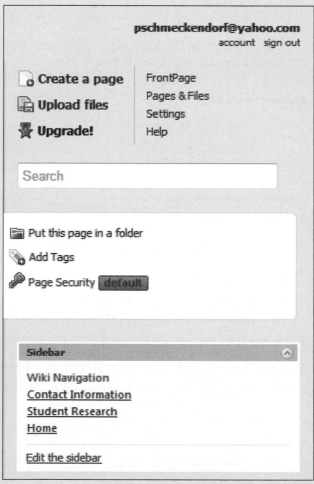

Figure 4.40 The Sidebar with a wiki navigation scheme in place.

Step 2 Insert External Links to Content on a Wiki Page

Refer to Figures 4.41 through 4.43 as you complete Step 2.

Professor Schmeckendorf has already set up the Student Research page so that students could share information they locate on the Internet. He now decides to add an example on that page for them to follow.

a. Navigate to the **Student Research** page by clicking on the link in the Sidebar.

b. When the Student Research page is displayed, click the **Edit** link at the top of the page to display the page in edit mode.

c. Type the following text beneath the existing text on the Student Research page. Use Figure 4.41 as a guide for text placement. Use the formatting buttons to bold the text "Surfing Safely on Wireless Hotspots".

> **Here is an example of what I'm expecting on this page:**
>
> **Surfing Safely on Wireless Hotspots - Many people surf on wireless hotspots but are unaware of precautions they need to take in order to protect themselves from hackers. This article from Microsoft contains seven good tips for protecting yourself while surfing.**

d. In the last sentence, select the text **"article from Microsoft"**. This text will be turned into a hyperlink to the article.

e. With the text selected, click the **Insert a Link to a New Page** link to display the **Insert Link** dialog box.

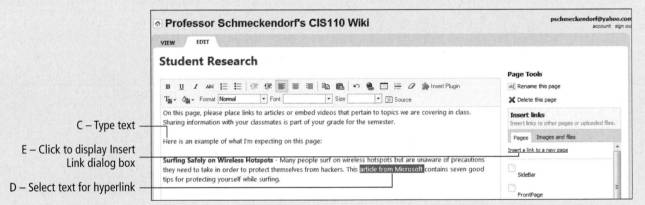

Figure 4.41 Hands-On Exercise 3, Steps 2c through 2e.

f. Click the **Link Type** drop-down arrow and select **URL** from the available choices. This indicates that the link will be an external link to another website.

g. Type the URL for the article into the URL box. The URL is:

www.microsoft.com/atwork/stayconnected/hotspots.mspx

h. Click the **OK** button to insert the link on the wiki page.

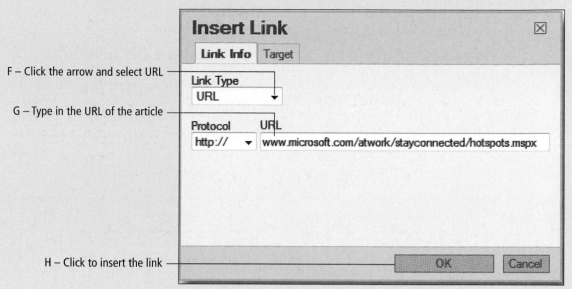

F – Click the arrow and select URL

G – Type in the URL of the article

H – Click to insert the link

Figure 4.42 Hands-On Exercise 3, Steps 2f through 2h.

Notice that the text has now been turned into a hyperlink to the article on Microsoft's website (Figure 4.43).

i. Click the **Save** button to save your edits to the Student Research page.

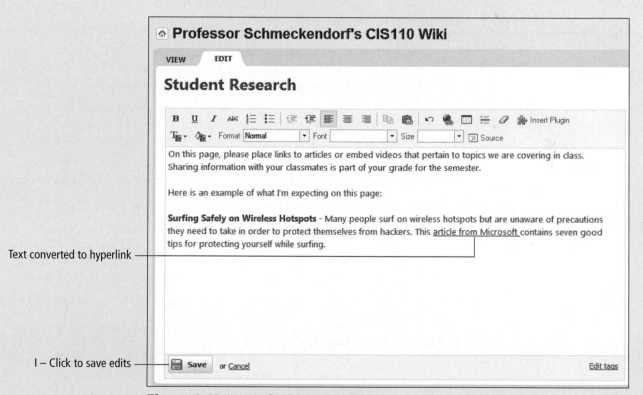

Text converted to hyperlink

I – Click to save edits

Figure 4.43 Hands-On Exercise 3, Step 2i.

You may now log out of PBwiki or continue on to the next Hands-On Exercise. In the next section, you'll learn how to upload images to a wiki and display them on a wiki page and how to embed video on a wiki page.

Objective 8

Upload content to or embed content on a wiki

Like other web pages, wikis are more interesting and exciting when they contain relevant images or videos. Professor Schmeckendorf has decided that he should upload the logo for his university, Ginormous State University, to the FrontPage of his wiki. He also has found a video that he wants his students to view, so he needs to embed it on the Student Research wiki page.

Hands-On Exercises

4 | Upload Images to a Wiki and Embed Video on a Wiki Page

Steps: 1. Upload an Image to PBwiki **2.** Embed a YouTube Video on a Wiki Page

Use Figures 4.44 through 4.53 as a guide in the exercise.

Step 1 Upload an Image to PBwiki

Refer to Figures 4.44 through 4.46 as you complete Step 1.

a. Open your web browser, navigate to **www.pbwiki.com** and log in to your account. Make sure you are viewing the FrontPage of your wiki.

b. Download the Chapter 4 student data files from the companion website at **www.pearsonhighered.com/nextseries**. Instructions for downloading the files can be found on the companion website. Save the files to your hard drive or another appropriate location and then extract them.

c. Click the **Edit** link at the top of the FrontPage to enter edit mode for the page.

d. Click the **Images and Files** link to display the **Browse** button.

e. Click the **Browse** button to display the **Choose File** dialog box. Navigate to the folder where you saved the Chapter 4 student data files and select the GSU_Logo.jpg file. Click the **Open** button on the **Choose File** dialog box to upload the file to the wiki. A link for the file will appear in the area below the Browse button.

f. Insert two blank lines above the text that is already on the FrontPage. Position the insertion point at the top left corner of the page.

g. Click the **GSU_Logo.jpg** link to insert the file on the FrontPage.

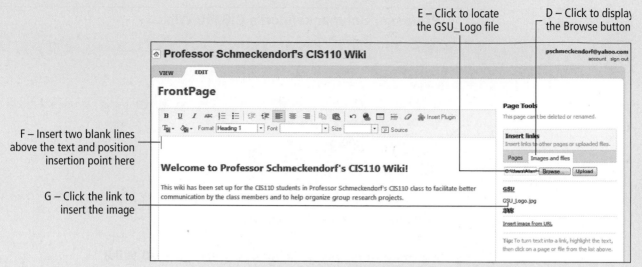

E – Click to locate the GSU_Logo file

D – Click to display the Browse button

F – Insert two blank lines above the text and position insertion point here

G – Click the link to insert the image

Figure 4.44 Hands-On Exercise 4, Steps 1d through 1g.

The logo image may be too large for the space available and look disproportionate (Figure 4.45). If this occurs, complete the following steps. If the logo appears to be the correct size and proportion, skip to Step 1j.

h. Click the logo image to select it and display the sizing handles.

i. Click the lower right sizing handle and drag it up and to the left to adjust the image to a smaller size.

j. When you have adjusted the image to the appropriate size, click the **Save** button to save your edits to the FrontPage.

H – Click the image to select it

I – Click the sizing handle and drag to make the image smaller

Figure 4.45 Hands-On Exercise 4, Steps 1h and 1i.

Image is now an appropriate size

J – Click to save edits

Figure 4.46 Hands-On Exercise 4, Step 1j.

Step 2 **Embed a YouTube Video on a Wiki Page**

Refer to Figures 4.47 through 4.53 as you complete Step 2.

Professor Schmeckendorf located an interesting video on YouTube about increasing a Wi-Fi signal when using your laptop. He has decided to embed the video on the Student Research page so that students can view it.

a. Open a new browser window and type **www.youtube.com/watch?v= LY8Wi7XRXCA** in the address window. This will take you to the video on the YouTube site. You can watch the video or click the Pause button to stop it.

b. Click anywhere in the **Embed** box to select the code. Right-click in the **Embed** box and select **Copy** from the shortcut menu to copy the code.

B – Click to select the code; right-click and select Copy

Figure 4.47 Hands-On Exercise 4, Step 2b.

c. On the wiki, navigate to the Student Research page. Click the **Edit** link at the top of the page to enter the edit mode.

d. Type the following text at the bottom of the page:

Here is a helpful video on extending your Wi-Fi signal.

e. Position the insertion point two lines below the text you just typed.

f. Click the **Insert Plugin** link to display the **Insert Plugin** dialog box.

F – Click to display Insert Plugin dialog box

D – Type this text

E – Position insertion point two lines below text

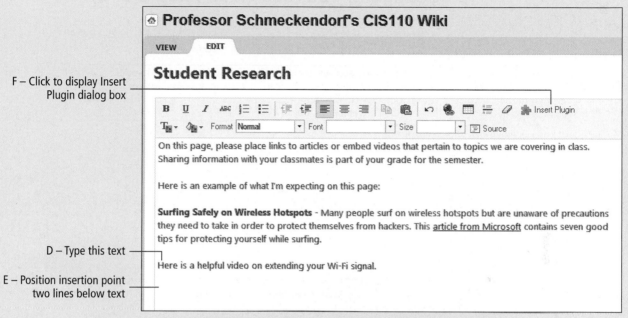

Figure 4.48 Hands-On Exercise 4, Steps 2d through 2f.

g. Point to the **Video** box with the cursor to display the video options. Click the **YouTube Video** link to proceed with embedding the video.

G – Point to the Video box to display choices and click the YouTube Video option

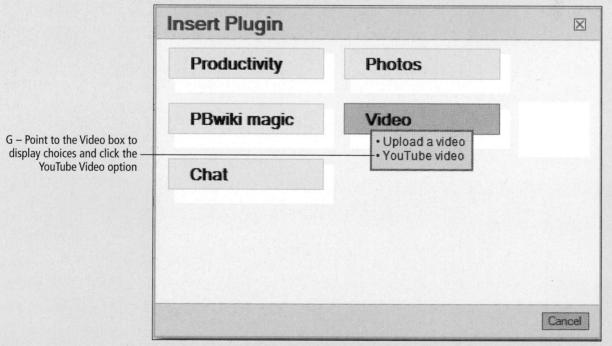

Figure 4.49 Hands-On Exercise 4, Step 2g.

h. In the empty box, paste the embed code that you copied from the YouTube site.

i. Click the **Preview** button to preview the YouTube video. This ensures that the embed code is working properly.

H – Paste the embed code copied from YouTube here

I – Click to preview the video

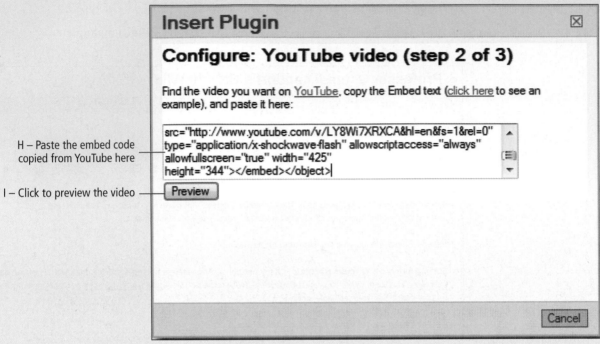

Figure 4.50 Hands-On Exercise 4, Steps 2h and 2i.

The video should display in the **Insert Plugin** dialog box in a way similar to how it appears on YouTube.

j. Click the **Play** button (large arrow) to test the video and ensure that it is working properly. If it does not work, click the **Back** button and try copying and pasting the embed code from YouTube again.

k. If the video appears to play properly, click the **OK** button to embed the video on the wiki page.

There should now be a large shaded box on the wiki page with a YouTube logo in the center of it (Figure 4.52). This indicates that the video has been embedded on the page.

l. Click the **Save** button to save your edits of the page.

J – Click the Play button to test the video

K – Click to embed the video on the wiki page

Figure 4.51 Hands-On Exercise 4, Steps 2j and 2k.

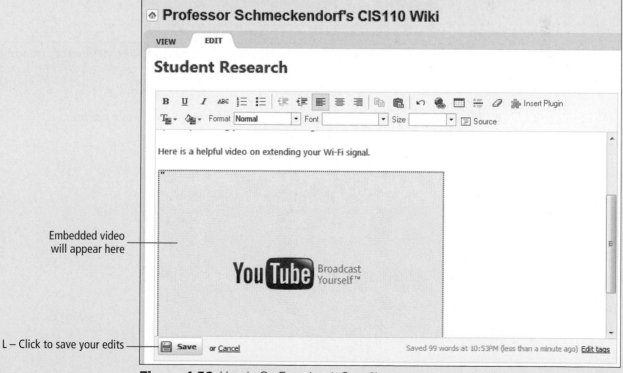

Embedded video will appear here

L – Click to save your edits

Figure 4.52 Hands-On Exercise 4, Step 2l.

The Student Research page should display in view mode (Figure 4.53). The video is embedded and ready to be viewed by anyone accessing the Student Research page.

Figure 4.53 Student Research page with a YouTube video embedded and ready for viewing.

You may now log out of your PBwiki account and close your browser.

Objective 9

Describe Internet resources that educate people about wikis

Many people are using wikis for a variety of reasons. Consequently, there is a wealth of information on the Internet that can help you learn more about creating wikis or help you locate wikis with information that may be of interest to you. Here are some resources you may want to explore:

- pbwikimanual (http://pbwikimanual.pbwiki.com) – There are other features available on PBwiki that you can explore as you develop wikis for your own use. The *pbwikimanual* is a Help file that contains more information on using the PBwiki site.

- Wikipatterns (www.wikipatterns.com) – A site geared towards making wikis viable business tools. The authors identify useful methodologies for increasing wiki readership and contributor participation. They also identify negative patterns that can drive people away from your wiki.

- Future Changes: Grow Your Wiki (www.ikiw.org) – This blog, written by Stewart Mader (a well-known wiki expert and author of books about wikis), focuses on wikis and other forms of social media and how you can improve your wiki content, encourage readership, and garner more contributions. The series of video posts entitled "21 Days of Wiki Adoption" is especially instructive.

- Wikis in Education (http://wikisineducation.wetpaint.com) – A wiki that helps educators and students figure out effective ways to use wikis in the educational process. The wiki is hosted on Wetpaint, which is another free wiki hosting service that is easy to learn to use.

- How To Use Wikis For Business (www.informationweek.com/news/management/showArticle.jhtml?articleID=167600331) – Although a few years old, this is an excellent article from *Information Week* magazine about how to use wikis in a business setting. In addition to covering why a wiki might be right for your organization, it also explains why a wiki won't always work in every situation.

Summary

You have now learned many of the basic skills needed for creating and managing wikis. The main thing that makes a wiki effective is the community that is behind the wiki. If you attract committed, knowledgeable individuals who are willing to contribute to and edit information on your wiki, it can be very successful. Remember that the basis of most wikis is collaborating on the development of textual information. Yes, you can add images and videos to wikis, but use them sparingly and only when they are most effective for communicating information. Gratuitous use of multimedia can detract from an otherwise effective wiki.

Key Terms

Multiple Choice

1. A group of computers set up to host multiple wikis at the same time is known as a wiki:
   (a) forest.
   (b) farm.
   (c) community.
   (d) silo.

2. Readers, writers, and editors are the basic people who make up a wiki:
   (a) editorial team.
   (b) dream team.
   (c) commune.
   (d) community.

3. Links from one page on a wiki to another page on the same wiki are known as:

   (a) internal links.

   (b) wiki links.

   (c) external links.

   (d) page links.

4. Erroneous information intentionally posted on a wiki is a type of wiki:

   (a) error.

   (b) uncertainty.

   (c) vandalism.

   (d) validation problem.

5. A process by which experts in a given field review another author's scholarly work to determine that the output is valid and substantially correct is known as:

   (a) wiki comparison.

   (b) peer review.

   (c) editing.

   (d) author review.

6. Which is the recommended permission level to grant users of a PBwiki account?

   (a) Administrator

   (b) Reader

   (c) Editor

   (d) Writer

7. A common use for wikis by individuals is:

   (a) note taking in a college class.

   (b) coordinating group projects for a college class.

   (c) planning a wedding.

   (d) all of the above.

8. Wikipedia:

   (a) is never accurate.

   (b) is an online encyclopedia written by unpaid volunteers.

   (c) can only be edited by people who have a Wikipedia account.

   (d) refuses to accept donations for funding.

9. Which of the following would *not* be acceptable to add to Wikipedia?

   (a) Speculation about the plot line of the next *Spiderman* movie

   (b) Information about potential victims of the Holocaust who were rescued by German citizens during World War II

   (c) The results of a research project that measured tidal flows at the New Jersey shoreline

   (d) Blueprints of experimental weapons that were developed by the United States during the Vietnam War

10. Individuals who write inflammatory messages on wikis just to provoke emotional responses from readers are known as:

    (a) Internet vandals.

    (b) wiki wise guys.

    (c) wiki haters.

    (d) Internet trolls.

Fill in the Blank

1. The word *wiki* in the Hawaiian language means _____.

2. The page for a Wikipedia entry that shows which individuals have worked on writing and editing the page is known as the _____ _____ _____.

3. MediaWiki, the software that powers Wikipedia, is available to anyone who wants to use it because it is published under the _____ _____ _____ _____.

4. Links on a wiki that lead to web pages that are not part of the wiki itself are known as _____ _____.

5. The _____ is the first page that is set up on a wiki hosted by PBwiki.

Practice Exercises

Note: Successful completion of these exercises assumes that the student has completed all of the Hands-On Exercises in this chapter.

1. **Extending the Student Research Page of Professor Schmeckendorf's Wiki**

   Professor Schmeckendorf's vision for the Student Research page on his wiki is to make it a resource for students who want to learn more about information technology. In this exercise, you will add information to the Student Research page on the wiki you created in the Hands-On Exercises.

   a. On the Internet, find an article on an information technology ethics issue (such as green computing, content filtering, plagiarism, copyright infringement, etc.).

   b. Search YouTube and locate one video that teaches about some aspect of information technology (such as how to build your own computer).

   c. Open your preferred browser and navigate to PBwiki.com.

   d. Log in to your PBwiki account and access your wiki.

   e. Navigate to the Student Research page. Click the **Edit** link at the top of the page to enter the editing mode.

   f. Write a short synopsis of the ethics article you found on the Internet and enter it on the Student Research page.

   g. Create an external link to the article as a textual link in the synopsis.

   h. Write a short sentence or two introducing the video you found and enter it on the Student Research page.

   i. Using the techniques you learned in this chapter, embed the YouTube video on the Student Research page.

   j. Click the **Save** button to save the edits you have made to the page.

   k. Print out the completed page and submit it to your instructor, or take a screenshot of the completed page and email it to your instructor. Log out of PBwiki and close your browser.

2. **Create a New Page for Professor Schmeckendorf's Wiki**

   Professor Schmeckendorf has decided that each student in the class should introduce himself or herself to the other class members through the wiki. In this assignment, you will set up a new page on the wiki to facilitate this interaction.

   a. Open your preferred browser and navigate to PBwiki.com.

   b. Log in to your PBwiki account and access your wiki.

   c. Click on the **Create a Page** link.

   d. Type **Student Introductions** in the **Name Your Page** box.

   e. Click the **Blank Template** option to select it.

f. Click the **Create Page** button to create the new page.

g. Type the following at the top of the new page:

On this page you should write your name, explain your goals in taking this class and write a brief summary of your computer skills.

h. On the second line (under the sentence you just typed), type your name and provide the information requested by Professor Schmeckendorf. Your goals should relate to the class for which you are completing this assignment.

i. Click the **Save** button to save your edits to the Student Introductions page.

j. Print out the completed page and submit it to your instructor, or take a screenshot of the completed page and email it to your instructor. Log out of PBwiki and close your browser.

3. **Add a Picture to Professor Schmeckendorf's Contact Information**

Professor Schmeckendorf has located an old picture of himself during his early days at GSU. He would like you to place it on his Contact Information page on the wiki.

a. Open your preferred browser and navigate to PBwiki.com.

b. Log in to your PBwiki account and access your wiki.

c. Navigate to the **Contact Information** page in your wiki. Click the **Edit** link at the top of the page to enter the edit mode.

d. Click the **Images and Files** link to display the Browse button.

e. Click the **Browse** button to display the **Choose File** dialog box. Navigate to the folder where you saved your Chapter 4 student data files and select the Professor_Schmeckendorf.jpg file. Click the **Open** button in the **Choose File** dialog box to upload the file to the wiki. A link for the file will appear in the area below the Browse button.

f. Insert two blank lines above the text that is already on the Contact Information page. Position the insertion point at the top left corner of the page.

g. Click the **Professor_Schmeckendorf.jpg** link to insert the file on the **Contact Information** page.

h. Resize the photo as needed by clicking it and using the sizing handles.

i. When you have adjusted the image to an appropriate size, click the **Save** button to save your edits to the Contact Information page.

j. Print out the completed page and submit it to your instructor, or take a screenshot of the completed page and email it to your instructor. Log out of PBwiki and close your browser.

Critical Thinking

1. Including images on a wiki can help readers understand ideas and concepts. However, just taking images that you find on the Internet and using them is usually not appropriate, because most images are subject to copyright protections. Write a brief paper outlining the steps a wiki user should take to ensure that any images found on the Internet can be used on the wiki and do not violate someone's copyright.

2. There are numerous wiki hosting services that provide free wiki hosting to individuals and businesses. Other than PBwiki, investigate at least two other free wiki hosting services. Write a short paper describing the advantages and disadvantages of each hosting service, and compare and contrast their features to those of PBwiki.

Team Projects

1. As a small group, consider how you could benefit from setting up a wiki as a study aid for a class that you are all taking. Write a short paper explaining how your wiki would be set up, what pages you would have in your wiki, and the duties and responsibilities of each member of the wiki community (frequency of contributions, expectations for editing other member's contributions, etc.).

2. As a group, locate at least four wikis (not including Wikipedia) that pertain to computers and technology. Create a table that lists the title and URL for each wiki and the main topics that it covers. Review the contents of the wiki, focusing on wiki pages that are up to date. Your instructor may determine a time frame for articles, but anything edited within the last six months may be acceptable. Remember that this can be determined by checking a wiki's history pages. Rate each of the wikis using the following criteria:

   - How current is the information on the wiki?

   - Does the wiki contain sufficient depth for all topics that it is supposed to cover?

   - Is the wiki well written? Are there a lot of spelling and grammatical errors? Is it easy to understand?

   - How would you suggest improving the wiki?

   - Which of the four wikis do you think is the best? Which is the worst?

   Include your findings on the table and submit it to your instructor.

CHAPTER 5

Social Networking

Objectives

After you read this chapter, you will be able to:

1. Explain what a social network is, what social networks are used for, and the typical features of social networks

2. Describe the advantages and disadvantages of social networks

3. Take appropriate measures to maintain your safety and privacy

4. Set up an Orkut account and create your profile

5. Invite a friend to join your Orkut network

6. Modify your Orkut account settings

7. Create your own social network using Ning, add features, and change its appearance

8. Moderate and promote your Ning social network

9. Describe Internet resources that educate people about social networking

The following Hands-On Exercises will help you accomplish the chapter Objectives.

Hands-On Exercises

EXERCISES	SKILLS COVERED
1. Set up an Orkut account and create a profile (page 238)	**Step 1:** Start Your Browser and Navigate to Orkut **Step 2:** Create an Orkut Account **Step 3:** Fill Out Your Orkut Profile
2. Invite a friend to join Orkut (page 242)	**Step 1:** Review the Find Friends Page and Navigate to the Home Page **Step 2:** Identify the Components of the Home Page and Invite a Friend
3. Modify Orkut account settings (page 247)	**Step 1:** Set Your Status **Step 2:** Navigate to the Profile Page **Step 3:** Edit Your Profile and Save Your Changes
4. Create a social network using Ning (page 252)	**Step 1:** Create a Ning Account **Step 2:** Name Your Social Network and Create a URL **Step 3:** Describe Your Social Network, Add Features, and Change Its Appearance
5. Moderate and promote your social network (page 259)	**Step 1:** Log In to Your Social Network **Step 2:** Adjust the Settings **Step 3:** Invite a New Member and Create an Administrator **Step 4:** Create a Badge

Objective 1

Explain what a social network is, what social networks are used for, and the typical features of social networks

What is a social network?

Social network A community made up of people, groups, or organizations that are connected by one or more common interests.

A *social network* is a community made up of people, groups, or organizations that are connected by one or more common interests. Social networks are not new; communities are the building blocks of society. In fact, you are already a member of at least one social network. Take a look at the people you interact with regularly. Chances are that you have at least one best friend and several other good friends, as well as your immediate family members. From there, your network begins to branch out to include casual friends and acquaintances, classmates, teachers, coworkers, and others. Some of these people may know each other, while others may be strangers, but they all have one thing in common: they know you! With the advent of Web 2.0, social networking has moved online. In this chapter, you will be exploring the various types of online social networks that exist.

What are social networks used for?

The primary purpose of online social networks is to help people make connections within a community and put those connections to good use. For example, Steve had two tickets to see The Machine, a Pink Floyd tribute band, but his friend had to cancel at the last minute. Steve called several of his friends, but everyone already had plans. Luckily, Steve is a member of an online social networking site and his friend Jessie is also friends with Doug. Steve remembered that Doug's profile indicated that he was a big fan of Pink Floyd. Steve had met Doug before and thought he seemed like a good guy, so he got in touch with him. Doug was happy to buy Steve's extra ticket, and they both had a great time at the concert. By using the social networking site to make connections, Steve was able to find someone with similar interests to go to the concert with.

What types of social networks are there?

There are many different types of social networks. Some—such as Facebook (www.facebook.com), MySpace (www.myspace.com), Bebo (www.bebo.com), and Orkut (www.orkut.com)—are used to create communities of friends and people with similar interests. These social networks help members to communicate with one another in many different ways. Many organizations and groups have also created social networking sites as a way to interact with current members and attract new members. One of the earliest social networks was Classmates (www.classmates.com), which enabled users to identify their high schools and years of graduation so that they could reconnect with former classmates (Figure 5.1). Classmates still exists, but its scope has broadened considerably. Members can now connect with classmates from elementary schools, high schools, and colleges, as well as with former colleagues from the military and various employers.

Figure 5.1 Classmates was one of the first social networking sites and helps members reconnect with former classmates.

Are there other types of social networks?

Some sites—such as LinkedIn (www.linkedin.com) or Plaxo (www.plaxo.com)—are referred to as *professional networks*. A **professional network** connects business people and other professionals in an online community and allows them to showcase their talents and skills. Rather than being used for entertainment purposes, such sites are used to manage and develop professional relationships with colleagues and potential employers. Other sites—such as YouTube (www.youtube.com), Twitter (www.twitter.com), Flickr (www.flickr.com), and Match.com (www.match.com)—are also considered to be social networks. Although not always as full-featured as sites like Facebook or MySpace, these sites also give you the opportunity to become part of an online community and share videos, photos, opinions, information, and other personal details about yourself with other members. On a less frivolous note, Change.org (www.change.org) is an example of an *issues-focused network*: a social action network that provides members with information and opportunities to help with causes that range from global warming and animal rights to fair trade and peace in the Middle East. Additionally, some sites, such as Ning (www.ning.com), allow members to create their own online communities.

Can anyone join a social network?

Social networks can be open or closed communities. In an *open community*, anyone is free to join, regardless of their interests or who they might know. Most social networking sites fall into this category. However, to connect with other members on these sites, you may still need to obtain a member's permission before adding them to your network. In a *closed community*, members typically must be invited by the site organizer or pre-existing members. Closed communities often represent special interest groups or may be used in corporate or educational settings.

Professional network A social network that connects business people and other professionals in an online community and allows them to showcase their talents and skills.

Issues-focused network A social action network that provides members with information and opportunities to help with causes that range from global warming and animal rights to fair trade and peace in the Middle East.

Open community A social network in which anyone is free to join, regardless of their interests or who they might know.

Closed community A social network to which members typically must be invited by the site organizer or pre-existing members.

What are the features of a social network?

Although each social network tries to differentiate itself from its competition, most sites have some similar features (Figure 5.2); they may, however, refer to those features using different names. To a first-time user, the vast array of features available on a social network can be overwhelming, but here are some of the typical features you might find:

- Home Page – Once you've logged in, the home page is typically the page that provides an overview of your activities within the network.

- Profile – A *profile* is used to provide information about a member. Although some details may be mandatory, such as your name or email address, many can be added or skipped at your discretion.

- Friends – A social network may have millions of members. The individuals that you have connected with are often identified as friends or contacts. These are the people who make up your portion of the online community. Typically, this area will display your friend's name and an image selected by that person. Clicking the name or image will take you to your friend's home page.

- Communication Areas – Depending upon the site, there may be several different types of communication areas. Many sites include one or more sections— such as a message wall, discussion forum, or comments area—to allow members to leave messages and comments for one another. News feeds, status updates, activity streams, and other areas often allow you to see when others have made changes to their pages (such as posting a photo or video) or posted comments on the sites of mutual friends. These areas also allow you to update your own status to let others know what you are doing. Some networks include an icon to indicate when you are online and enable live chatting through the use of an instant messaging application. Message and notification areas provide ways to communicate privately—similar to email messages—and are not visible to others in the network.

- Video and Pictures – Part of the fun of social networks is the ability to post pictures and videos to share with your friends. Members of your network can view and comment on the media you post and may also be able to view items your friends have posted.

- Groups – In addition to your friends and contacts, many organizations have become involved with social networking. You can join one of these groups or create your own special interest group. Some groups are open to everyone, while others are by invitation only.

- Applications – There are a number of other features, known as applications or *widgets*, which can be added to your social network. *Internal applications* are developed by the creators of the network, while *external applications* are created by third-party developers, sometimes for commercial purposes. Some applications are for entertainment purposes and allow you to play games, throw snowballs, take quizzes, poke your friends, or listen to music. Others have been developed to promote special causes. For instance, prior to the 2008 presidential election, over one million Facebook members added an application to their pages encouraging others to vote on Election Day. Still other widgets have more everyday uses and allow members to track events, organize website bookmarks, or coordinate schedules.

Profile A feature of a social network that is used to provide information about a member.

Widgets Applications or features which can be added to your social network.

Internal applications Features that can be added to a social network that are developed by the creators of the network.

External applications Features that can be added to a social network that are created by third-party developers, sometimes for commercial purposes.

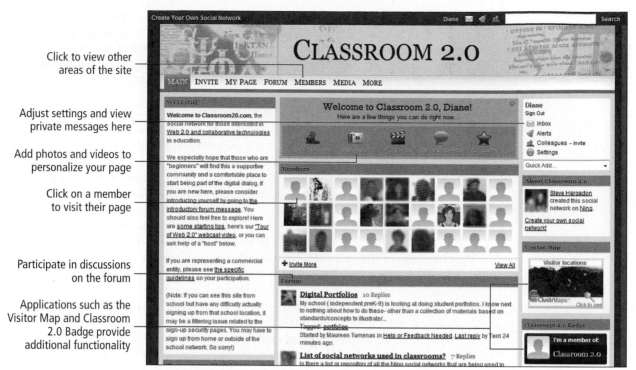

The following labels appear around the figure:

Click to view other areas of the site

Adjust settings and view private messages here

Add photos and videos to personalize your page

Click on a member to visit their page

Participate in discussions on the forum

Applications such as the Visitor Map and Classroom 2.0 Badge provide additional functionality

Figure 5.2 Classroom 2.0, hosted by Ning, includes some of the typical features found on many social networking sites.

Objective 2

Describe the advantages and disadvantages of social networks

What are the advantages of a social network?

There are many reasons why you might want to join a social network. As with most Web 2.0 applications, one of the primary reasons for using a social network is the ability to easily and affordably communicate with others. Although some sites offer advanced capabilities and features for a fee, most of the basic services are free. Most social networks are fairly straightforward, so members can develop an online presence without any knowledge of web design or coding. Because the learning curve is not steep, new members can begin connecting with others right away. Another advantage is the ability to add new people to your network, reconnect with old friends, and continue to expand your circle of friends and colleagues over time. Some people have extensive networks consisting of hundreds of contacts, while others prefer to keep their networks smaller and more personal. No matter what size your network is, each new contact can put you in touch with others who have similar interests. It's not unusual for new college students to check out potential roommates on social networking sites ahead of time. Starting an online friendship can help to make the transition from home to dorm (or apartment) an easier and smoother process.

Using social networks can also help to develop and improve your writing and technical skills. A study of low-income urban high school students conducted by the University of Minnesota in 2008 found that 77 percent of the respondents were members of a social network. The study determined that students using such sites were developing communication and technical skills that could help them to become successful in the future. Social networks are good tools for promoting your own business and expanding your professional networking opportunities. No matter what type of business you are in, chances are that there's a group of like-minded individuals on a social network site. Because most social networks are global in scope, you can also develop friendships with people from all over the world.

What are some disadvantages of a social network?

One of the most immediate disadvantages of a social network that you might encounter is the amount of time you'll spend there. Social networking sites can quickly become a distraction. In fact, a recent Pew Internet Project survey reported that 48 percent of teens visit social networking sites at least once a day, with nearly half of them reporting multiple visits. Some users actually report symptoms resembling addiction, including the need to repeatedly log on to sites to check their profile pages, neglecting other responsibilities and activities, and experiencing distress and anxiety when they are unable to access their sites. Another disadvantage involves privacy issues. Information, photos, and videos posted to your profile page or on a friend's page can have far-reaching consequences. Although you may have enabled privacy settings on your own page, it is very easy for someone who has access to your site to copy materials and post them elsewhere. Once this happens, you may have little or no control over how this information is used (Figure 5.3). Sadly, what you may have posted all in good fun can easily be misinterpreted by people who don't know you, and this can lead them to form a negative impression before they have ever met you. Although you may not think that those silly party pictures or sarcastic comments on your profile are inappropriate, many colleges and employers may disagree. College admissions personnel and human resource managers are beginning to use social networking sites to screen potential candidates, and the information they find could easily lead them to change their minds about you. In fact, one out of five employers routinely search sites such as Facebook and MySpace when screening

Figure 5.3 As shown in the popular cartoon *Zits*, it can be difficult to maintain your privacy on social networking sites.

prospective employees, with one-third reporting that the information they have found has caused them to drop a candidate from the running. Items that caused the most concern included information about alcohol and drug use, inappropriate text or photos, poor writing and communication skills, and bashing former employers or coworkers.

Another concern surrounding social networks involves individuals using these sites to engage in unethical or illegal activities, such as cyberstalking and cyberbullying. *Cyberstalking* is defined as threatening or harassing behavior that is facilitated by the use of the Internet and online tools such as email and online social networks. *Cyberbullying* is similar to cyberstalking but involves children, pre-teens, or teens rather than adults. A recent McAfee/Harris survey reported that 20 percent of teens have engaged in some form of cyberbullying behavior. Individuals who are victims of cyberstalking or cyberbullying may report being teased, humiliated, threatened, or frightened. They may receive intimidating emails or text messages, become the victims of online rumors or cyberpranks, or be threatened by humiliating or disturbing pictures. This behavior may not be limited to an online presence but could escalate to real-world situations as well. A *cyber predator* might also be a cyberstalker and is typically an adult who preys on children or other hapless individuals, attempting to lure them into sexual—or otherwise unsafe—situations. A well-known example of this type of behavior occurred in 2006 in St. Louis, Missouri. A 13-year-old girl, Megan Meier, hung herself in response to upsetting messages she received from a boy she befriended on her MySpace page. It was later learned that the boy did not exist; instead, he was a fictional character created by Lori Drew, the mother of a former friend of Megan's. Drew, Drew's daughter, and another woman initially developed the fictitious character as a hoax, but the malicious prank went badly astray. Based on Missouri law, it was determined that Drew had not engaged in any criminal activity relating to Megan's harassment and death. However, Drew was eventually found guilty of three counts of computer fraud for creating the fictitious MySpace account and faces three years in prison and a $300,000 fine. Various surveys reveal that parents consider online predators to be as much of a threat to children as drinking and drugs; however, new reports indicate that this belief may be highly exaggerated. According to a recent study, only two children out of 1,500 interviewed reported being sexually victimized by someone they met online. In contrast, nearly one-fifth of teen or young adult drivers involved in fatal traffic accidents had blood alcohol levels above the legal limit. Although tragic, cases such as Megan Meier's appear to be the exception rather than the rule. While online safety is a valid concern, statistics show that drugs and alcohol represent a much greater risk for teens and young adults.

Cyberstalking Threatening or harassing behavior that is facilitated by the use of the Internet and online tools such as email and online social networks.

Cyberbullying A type of bullying, involving children, pre-teens, or teens, but not adults, that is done via online tools such as email or social networks as opposed to being done face-to-face.

Cyber predator An adult who, using the Internet, preys on children or other hapless individuals, attempting to lure them into a sexual, or otherwise unsafe, situation.

Objective 3

Take appropriate measures to maintain your safety and privacy

What can I do to use social networks safely?

There are several actions you can take to help make your experience with social networks a positive one. One of the easiest is to use common sense. Everyone has a different comfort level for disclosing personal information. You will need to decide how much or how little information you want to share with others. One thing you should never do is share your password with others. Before you post anything to your network, think about what this information reveals about you. If you wouldn't give this information to a stranger, you shouldn't post it online. Many people use public message areas to post their thoughts, write about their activities, or issue group invitations. Predators and stalkers may strike up an online friendship or lurk in the background, reading your updates over time and developing a good idea of your daily routine from these types of posts. Posting general updates that include few details is a safer way to use public message forums. The same concept holds true when posting photos or videos. As a general rule, you should avoid publishing images that easily identify where you live, work, or go to school. Although you have less control over items your friends might post, you should make your wishes known to them. If a friend posts something you are uncomfortable with, you shouldn't hesitate to ask them to remove it from their site. In return, you should also respect your friends' privacy and avoid posting personal information about them without their permission. Remember also that the information and images you post online can be copied and reused—either by well-meaning friends or by unscrupulous individuals. Once you've posted something online, it can be difficult, if not impossible, to get it back. The images that seem funny now could potentially be embarrassing a few years down the road when you are trying to impress a potential employer or convince a new romantic interest that your wild streak is years behind you.

Similarly, those rules you learned as a child about never talking to strangers or divulging personal information such as addresses, phone numbers, or email addresses are just as true for online social networks. You have the right to choose whom you want to include in your network. Although one of the goals of social networks is to expand your circle of contacts, you should use caution if you choose to accept a friend request from someone you don't know. Connecting with a friend of a friend can be a bit like a blind date, but connecting with a total stranger could be dangerous. Sites such as StaySafeOnline.org (www.staysafeonline.org), OnGuard Online (www.onguardonline.gov), and Microsoft Security at Home (www.microsoft.com/protect) provide plenty of advice and information about safeguarding your privacy and using the Internet safely.

Is there a way to limit access to my social network?

Most social networks provide several levels of privacy options. You can usually choose to allow anyone to view your information or limit access to just your contacts (Figures 5.4a and 5.4b). Another option might provide access to your friends' contacts also. And you can often apply different privacy levels to different features. For instance, you might let anyone view your profile page but only allow trusted friends to view your photos. You should adjust your privacy settings to match your comfort level.

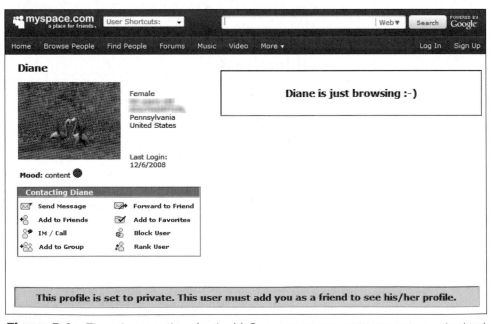

Figure 5.4a The privacy options for the MySpace page are set to prevent unauthorized individuals from viewing personal data.

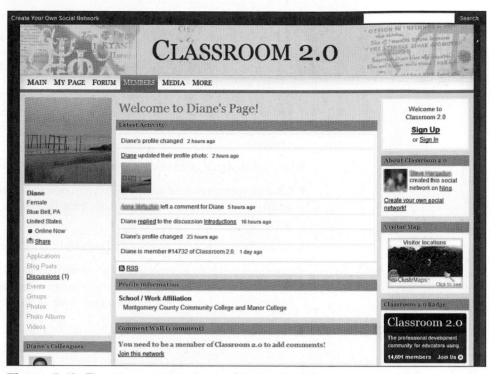

Figure 5.4b The privacy options for the Classroom 2.0 page are set to allow everyone to view the information posted there.

What other types of risks are there?

Unfortunately, social networking sites are not immune from the dangers that exist elsewhere on the Internet. You should make sure that you are using up-to-date antivirus and antispyware software and scan your computer regularly. It is possible to receive messages (similar to emails) that contain viruses, spyware, worms, or links to malicious sites. You should be very careful about opening messages from people you don't know. Even if a message appears to come from a friend, it could easily have been spoofed, or your friend's computer might have been infected. You should exercise caution if you receive a message asking you to download a file. Often, these files contain Trojan horses or other types of malware that can compromise your computer's security and threaten your privacy. In the last months of 2008, the Koobface virus struck many Facebook users. Members received messages with headers such as "You look just awesome in this movie" that contained a link leading to an online video site. Members that followed the link were notified that they needed to download a file in order to view the movie. Although Facebook reports that only a small percentage of members were affected, those members who followed the instructions may have found that their computers were subsequently infected with the virus, leaving them vulnerable to hackers. Infected computers may help spread the virus-infected messages, direct users to unsafe websites, or relay personal information to hackers.

There's also the possibility that those fun applications that you can add to your network page could be a security risk. Some security experts are concerned about external applications written by third-party developers. Although this has yet to become a serious problem, malicious applications have the potential to compromise your privacy and access confidential data on your computer. These applications are especially dangerous for two reasons. First, users tend to trust social networking sites and feel safe because they are in a closed environment, so they are more likely to download these programs without considering the consequences. Second, there is no easy way for a member to determine if an application is legitimate or malicious.

What else can I do to protect myself?

In addition to making sure that your computer is protected against viruses and spyware and has all the latest security updates, you should use the same safe computing practices on a social network that you use elsewhere on the Internet. Here are some other steps you can take:

- Check to see if your social network has a safety or security page that provides information about current threats or viruses, and visit it regularly to stay updated.

- Read your social network's privacy policy and be sure you understand it.

- Change your password periodically; and don't use the same password for other sensitive areas such as financial sites, email accounts, or your school or work network.

- Carefully review your privacy settings to be sure they reflect your preferences.

- Consider using an alternate browser—such as Mozilla Firefox—rather than Internet Explorer. Although alternate browsers are not invulnerable, much malware is still designed to work best with Internet Explorer, so using another browser might thwart an attack.

Objective 4

Set up an Orkut account and create your profile

Orkut (www.orkut.com) is a free social networking site owned by Google. Although it has been around for a while, Orkut is not that well known in North America. However, it has a very large following in Brazil and other Latin American countries and is also becoming popular in Asia.

Hands-On Exercises

For purposes of the Hands-On Exercises, Professor Schmeckendorf has decided to use Orkut because he believes it will integrate well with some of the other Google tools he is currently using. The Hands-On Exercise examples here will create an account using Professor Schmeckendorf's information; you will be creating an account for yourself and should add your own information where appropriate.

1 | Set Up an Orkut Account and Create a Profile

Steps: 1. Start Your Browser and Navigate to Orkut **2.** Create an Orkut Account
3. Fill Out Your Orkut Profile

Use Figures 5.5 through 5.8 as a guide in the exercise.

Step 1 **Start Your Browser and Navigate to Orkut**

Refer to Figure 5.5 as you complete Step 1.

a. Turn on the computer.

b. Start your preferred browser (Internet Explorer, Firefox, Safari, etc.). Type **www.orkut.com** in the address box of your browser and press **Enter**.

c. You can sign in to Orkut by using the Google account you created in Chapter 1 for your Blogger account. Type your email address and password for your Google account in the appropriate boxes.

To always remain logged in to your Google account on the particular computer you are using, click the checkbox next to **Remember Me on This Computer** to select it. If you are using a shared computer (such as a computer in a lab at school) or a notebook computer that could easily be stolen, *do not* choose this option.

d. Click the **Sign In** button to access your Google account.

C – Enter your email and password in the boxes

D – Click the Sign In button

Figure 5.5 Hands-On Exercise 1, Step 1.

 Step 2 **Create an Orkut Account**

Refer to Figures 5.6 and 5.7 as you complete Step 2.

The next screen you will see may ask you to complete some additional information, depending upon how much you provided when you first created your Google account. Your screen may differ slightly from the image shown in Figure 5.6. If necessary, you should provide the required details.

a. In the **Get Started with Orkut** section, click the **Continue** button.

Most social networks require you to verify that you meet their minimum age requirement. The Orkut network requires members to be 18 years of age or older. You should also make it a point to read Orkut's Community Standards to ensure that you are familiar with the site's policies and procedures.

A – Click Continue to proceed

Figure 5.6 Hands-On Exercise 1, Step 2a.

 Tip **Protect Your Identity**

Although you need to provide a birth date to verify that you meet a social network's age requirements, it may not be necessary to provide your true date of birth. Your birth date is a critical piece of information for identity thieves. If your social networking site is hacked into or compromised in some other way, this information may be readily available. Some experts recommend creating an alternate birth date for use when registering for online sites. You should check a site's Terms of Use to be sure that you are not violating any policies if you choose to do this.

b. Click the **Birthday** drop-down arrows to select the month and day of your birth.

c. In the **Birth Year** text box, type the year of your birth.

d. Click the checkbox to confirm that you are over 18 and agree to Orkut's Community Standards.

e. Click the **Accept Terms** button to proceed.

 Alert!

If you are under 18, you will be unable to join the Orkut social network. Check with your instructor for suggestions for an alternate activity. Individuals who are 13 or older may join MySpace or Facebook.

C – Type your year of birth   B – Select your birth date

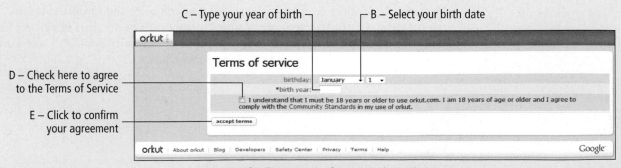

D – Check here to agree to the Terms of Service

E – Click to confirm your agreement

Figure 5.7 Hands-On Exercise 2, Steps 2b through 2e.

Step ③ Fill Out Your Orkut Profile

Refer to Figure 5.8 as you complete Step 3.

The **Edit Profile** screen allows you to add information about yourself. You are required to complete any field that has an asterisk in front of it, but the other fields are optional. The drop-down boxes on the right side of the page display key icons. These boxes are used to indicate your privacy settings. You have four choices: 1) myself, 2) only my friends, 3) friends of friends, or 4) everyone. At this time, Professor Schmeckendorf prefers that his birth year and college/university information only be visible to himself. He will allow the other two fields to be visible only to his friends. You will need to decide what privacy level you are comfortable with and which optional fields you wish to complete. Note that any field that does not include a privacy setting is visible by everyone. You should think carefully about what you choose to display in these text boxes.

a. Add your personal information to the following mandatory fields:

- **First Name** – Type your first name in the text box
- **Last Name** – Type your last name in the text box
- **Gender** – Click the appropriate option button
- **Country** – Click the drop-down arrow and select your country

b. In the **Company/Organization** text box, type **Ginormous State University**.

c. In the **Interested In** section, click the **Business Networking** checkbox to select it.

Orkut has already added the **Birth Day** and **Birth Year** you entered when you registered for your account to your profile. You will see privacy settings for these two fields and two other fields on the right side of the page.

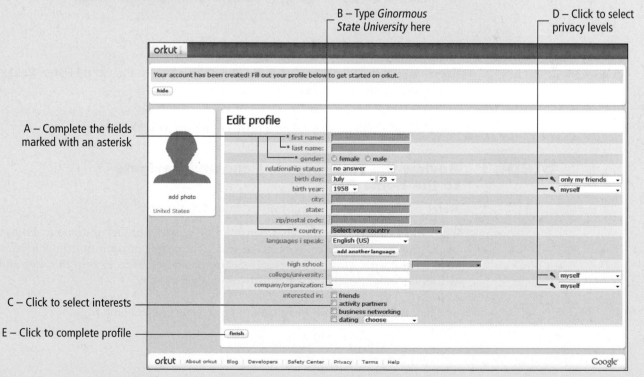

Figure 5.8 Hands-On Exercise 1, Step 3a through 3e.

d. Adjust the privacy settings for the following fields by clicking the **drop-down** arrow and selecting a setting. Use the suggested settings or select your own.

- **Birth Day** – Select **Only My Friends**
- **Birth Year** – Select **Myself**
- **College/University** – Select **Myself**
- **Company/Organization** – Select **Only My Friends**

e. Click the **Finish** button to complete your profile.

Leave your Orkut account open to complete the next exercise.

Objective 5

Invite a friend to join your Orkut network

Orkut provides several ways to add people to your network. If you have a Gmail, Hotmail, or AOL email account, you can use Orkut's Find Friends feature to import contact information contained in your address book and then locate people who are already Orkut members. If you choose not to import your contact information, or if you use a different email provider, you can use Orkut's search feature to locate individuals or communities. You can also invite friends from your home page.

Hands-On Exercises

2 | Invite a Friend to Join Orkut

Steps: 1. Review the Find Friends Page and Navigate to the Home Page **2.** Identify the Components of the Home Page and Invite a Friend

Use Figures 5.9 through 5.15 as a guide in the exercise.

 Step 1 **Review the Find Friends Page and Navigate to the Home Page**

Refer to **Figure 5.9** as you complete Step 1.

The **Find Friends** page appears when you first create your Orkut account. From this page, you can import email contacts or search for people or communities you might wish to link with. However, Professor Schmeckendorf prefers to skip this step and will invite only specific individuals to join his network.

a. Click the **Go to Home Page** link to go to your Orkut home page.

Click this link to search for
friends or communities

Log in to your email and
import your contacts

A – Click here to go
to your home page

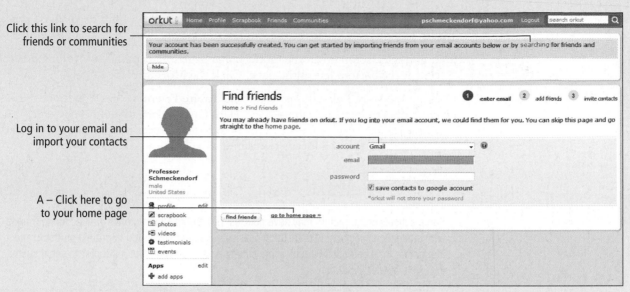

Figure 5.9 Hands-On Exercise 2, Step 1a.

Step 2 Identify the Components of the Home Page and Invite a Friend

Refer to Figures 5.10 through 5.15 as you complete Step 2.

Your home page provides a way for you to access all the different areas of your network from one place. Because Professor Schmeckendorf has just joined Orkut, there is not much to see on his home page now, but as he becomes more involved, more detailed information will be displayed here. Your home page should look similar to the one shown in Figure 5.10. At the top right of the page is the **My Friends** section. This area displays any contacts with whom you are already connected. The **Add Friends** button here will lead you to the Orkut search page where you can search for existing Orkut users, communities, or topics. But you can't invite non-Orkut

Existing friends appear here

Lists of communities
you have joined

Your updates and updates
from friends will appear here

Links to applications

Links to messages and settings

A – Click here to invite a friend

Figure 5.10 Hands-On Exercise 2, Step 2a.

members to join your network from this section; instead, you'll need to use the **Invite Friends** section at the bottom left of the page.

a. If necessary, scroll down the Orkut home page to locate the **Invite Friends** section at the bottom left of the page. Click the **More** link.

Clicking the **More** link will lead you to the **Invite Friends** page. Professor Schmeckendorf wishes to invite his lab assistant, Hans Grindeldorf, to join his network. You should select one or more friends to invite to join your network. Be sure to invite at least one other person from your class to ensure that you can continue with this exercise.

> **Alert**
>
> Some schools or instructors may have policies that prohibit instructors from becoming friends with students on social networks. Such policies have been instituted to protect students and instructors from potentially troublesome situations. Check with your instructor to see if such a policy exists at your institution.

b. In the **Friends to Invite** text box, add the email address for one of your classmates. You may invite more than one person by adding a comma, space, or new line after each email address.

c. Click the **Full Message** link to reveal the automated message Orkut will send as an invitation.

d. Although the default Orkut message is fine, you might want to personalize your invitation. Click the **Optional Message** text box and type:

Hi, I've joined Orkut as part of a class exercise. I hope you'll join my network.

Your optional message will appear above Orkut's automated message when your friend opens the email.

e. Type the information shown in the CAPTCHA box to confirm that you are a person and not an automated spammer. Note that your CAPTCHA text will be different from the text shown in Figure 5.11.

f. Click the **Submit** button to send the invitation.

Figure 5.11 Hands-On Exercise 2, Steps 2b through 2f.

Your **Invite Friends** page will now display the responses to your invitations. If a person you invited is not an Orkut member, you will see their email address and a note indicating that an invitation has been sent. You can't do anything further until the person you've invited accepts your invitation and joins Orkut.

g. If the person you invited is already an Orkut member, click the checkbox next to the email address and click the **Submit** button to add this person to your network.

G – Click to select, then click Submit

Figure 5.12 Hands-On Exercise 2, Step 2g.

After you add someone to your network, the **Invite Friends** page will display the current status of any invitations you have sent.

h. Click the **Friends** link at the top of the page to proceed to your **Friends** page.

H – Click to proceed to the Friends page

Status updated

Figure 5.13 Hands-On Exercise 2, Step 2h.

The **Friends** page allows you to view and manage your friends in Orkut. Clicking on a friend's name or profile picture will take you to their profile page. Orkut separates people into two categories: friends and contacts. Friends are those individuals you have added to your network. You can interact with these people directly through Orkut. Contacts are people whose contact information has been added to your network but who have not become members of your network. In essence, the Contacts area acts as an address book. Your contacts cannot interact with you through Orkut. You can sort your friends into various groups in the **Friend Groups** area. Orkut has created several default groups, such as best friends, family, school, and work, but you can also create your own groups. The **Open Requests** area allows you to view any invitations you have received, as well as any invitations you have issued that are still pending. The **Manage Contacts** area can be used to find additional friends, edit your contact information, and export your contact information for use elsewhere. Professor Schmeckendorf has added Hans Grindeldorf to his network. Note that Hans has not yet accepted the professor's invitation. He will need to read his email invitation and click a link to complete the process. In this next step, Professor Schmeckendorf will add Hans to the **School** group and then view Hans' profile. You should perform the same steps with the friend you added to your network.

i. Click the checkbox in front of your friend's name to select it.

j. Click the **Actions** drop-down arrow, and from the **Add to Group** section, click **School**. Notice that the **Friend Groups** will update to show your changes.

k. Click the link for your friend's name to view your friend's profile page.

Sort friends into groups ⎯

J – Choose an action to perform ⎯

K – Click to view your friend's profile

I – Click to select a friend ⎯

View open invitations you have received or sent

Manage your contacts here

Figure 5.14 Hands-On Exercise 2, Steps 2i through 2k.

l. From your friend's profile page, locate the **Logout** link in the top right corner. Click **Logout** to exit out of your Orkut account.

Your friend's profile page

L – Click to exit your Orkut account

Figure 5.15 Hands-On Exercise 2, Step 2l.

Objective 6

Modify your Orkut account settings

Like many other social networks, it is possible to add a brief statement to your profile, indicating your current status. This might be an accurate reflection of what you are currently doing, or it could be a humorous saying, a comment on current events, or some other sort of observation. Such a statement is optional and can be updated whenever you choose. Additionally, Orkut gives you the opportunity to create a very detailed profile. Although you may have provided some information when you originally created your profile, there is much more that you can add if you choose to do so. Whatever you decide to post, you should remember that unless there is a privacy setting associated with a particular field, anything you add to your profile is available to be viewed by anyone who accesses it. Orkut separates your information into different categories, including social, professional, and personal.

Hands-On Exercises

3 | Modify Orkut Account Settings

Steps: 1. Set Your Status **2.** Navigate to the Profile Page **3.** Edit Your Profile and Save Your Changes

Use Figures 5.16 through 5.22 as a guide in the exercise.

Step 1 Set Your Status

Refer to Figures 5.16 and 5.17 as you complete Step 1.

a. If necessary, open your web browser and navigate to **www.orkut.com**.

b. Sign in to your Orkut account.

c. Your Orkut account opens with the home page displayed. Your status appears at the top of the page. To update your status, click in the **Set Your Status Here** text box or click the **Edit** button to the right of the text box.

Your home page ────

C – Click the text box or the Edit button

Figure 5.16 Hands-On Exercise 3, Step 1c.

Emoticon A small graphical icon (e.g., a smiley face or sad face) used to display a mood.

The status area changes to display **Update** and **Cancel** buttons below the status text box. A drop-down arrow with an *emoticon*, a small graphical icon used to display a mood (e.g., a smiley face or sad face), appears in place of the **Edit** button.

d. Type a brief comment of your choice in the text box.

e. If you wish, you can also add an emoticon to your status. Click the **Add Smileys** button to the right of the text box and select an appropriate icon from the palette.

f. Click the **Update** button to set your status.

E – Click to select an emoticon

D – Type a comment

F – Click to update your status

Figure 5.17 Hands-On Exercise 3, Steps 1d through 1f.

Step 2   Navigate to the Profile Page

Refer to Figures 5.18 through 5.20 as you complete Step 2.

Orkut refers to the profile information you entered when you created your account as your *general* information. This general information represents an overview of details derived from the various categories you can complete. The categories reflect the various ways members use Orkut. Some people use Orkut to communicate with friends or for entertainment purposes, others use it to create a network of professional connections, while still others use it as a type of dating site.

a. There are two ways to access your profile from your home page. Click the **Profile** link at the top of the page or click the **Profile** link on the left side of the page.

A – Click either link to access your profile

Figure 5.18 Hands-On Exercise 3, Step 2a.

The profile page initially appears in an abbreviated form that can be expanded to show additional details. You can choose to see how your page will appear when you view it or when others view it. Professor Schmeckendorf wants to check his privacy settings, so he will set his profile to show how it will appear to everyone.

b. Click the **View Full Profile** link to expand the profile.

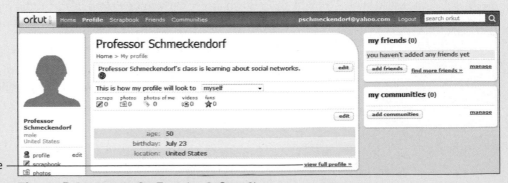

B – Click to expand profile

Figure 5.19 Hands-On Exercise 3, Step 2b.

Note that three tabs display on your profile: social, professional, and personal.

c. Click the profile tabs to review the information listed in each section. Note that the profile is still set to the default setting and shows how your profile will look to you. Depending upon the information you entered when you created your Orkut account, your profile page may appear different from Professor Schmeckendorf's.

d. Click the **This Is How My Profile Will Look to** drop-down arrow. Select **Everyone** from the list. Notice how the profile page has changed.

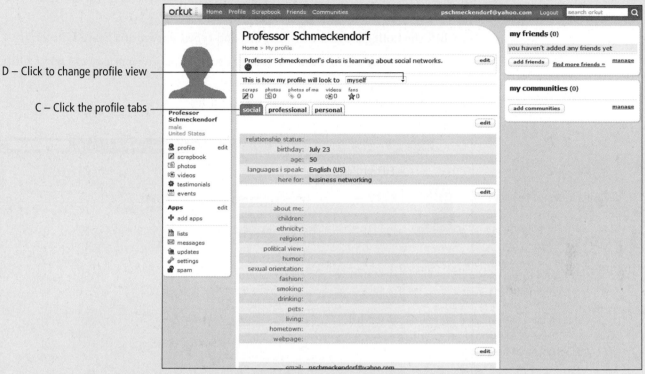

D – Click to change profile view

C – Click the profile tabs

Figure 5.20 Hands-On Exercise 3, Steps 2c and 2d.

Step 3 Edit Your Profile and Save Your Changes

Refer to Figures 5.21 and 5.22 as you complete Step 3.

Professor Schmeckendorf has decided to add information about his state—but not his city or zip code—and his college. He will also adjust the privacy setting.

a. With the **Social** tab selected, click the first **Edit** button to go to the **Edit Profile** page.

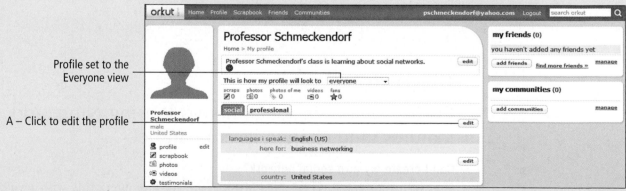

Profile set to the Everyone view

A – Click to edit the profile

Figure 5.21 Hands-On Exercise 3, Step 3a.

There are five tabs on the **Edit Profile** page. The **General** tab should be active.

 Alert !

If the **General** tab is not the active tab, you may have clicked on a different **Edit** button. Simply click the **General** tab to make it the active tab.

b. With the **General** tab active, click the **State** text box and add the two-letter abbreviation for your state.

c. Click the **College/University** text box and type **Ginormous State University**.

d. Click the **College/University Privacy Setting** drop-down arrow and select **Only My Friends**.

e. Click the **Update** button to revise your profile.

Figure 5.22 Hands-On Exercise 3, Steps 3b through 3e.

If you wish to add additional information, use the techniques you've just learned to update the fields in the other tabs. You will need to click the **Update** button for each tab to accept any changes you might make.

f. Click the **Logout** button to exit your Orkut account. Close your browser.

Objective 7

Create your own social network using Ning, add features, and change its appearance

Can I create my own social network?

Sites such as Orkut, Facebook, and MySpace are good for interacting with a wide variety of people and groups. It's possible to connect with people you already know, make new friends, or join groups of people with similar interests. But what if you'd like to be part of a smaller community? Sites such as Ning (www.ning.com), KickApps (www.kickapps.com), and CrowdVine (www.crowdvine.com) provide free hosting and tools to help you develop your own social network. Most of these sites don't require you to have any web design experience, but if you do, it's often possible to tweak your online community. Although there may be no charge to create your own community, many hosting companies will place ads on your network as a way for them to generate revenue. For a fee, you can eliminate the ads (or sponsor your own), obtain your own customized website address, or access other premium features.

What do I need to do to create my social network?

Success is often in the details. Take some time before you begin to determine your objectives for your network and plan accordingly. By doing so, you'll improve your chances of creating a useful online community that people will want to join and participate in. Following are some of the things you should consider:

- **Who will host the social network?** As mentioned previously, there are a number of sites that you can choose from. You should take some time to explore your options. Some are good for beginners, others are geared towards professional or business uses, and still others are meant to be used with existing websites. Check the About Us page for sites you are considering, review their privacy policies, and, if possible, examine some of the networks already using their services. Don't forget to think ahead: If your social network becomes successful, will the site you've selected still be able to support your members? Does it offer advanced features, and if it does, at what price?

- **Who will join the community?** You should have a clear idea of who you are building the community for. Will it be for people who share an affinity for a particular hobby or sport? Will it be a professional network for coworkers or your colleagues in a specific industry? Will it be a social network for your friends? In each instance, knowing who the members of your social network will be and considering their needs and preferences can help you decide how you'd like your site to appear and what features you'd like to include. A casual, fun type of theme may be fine for a social group but might prevent your site from being taken seriously if you were hoping to attract professional colleagues.

- **What features should be included?** There are a variety of features you can add to your social network: message areas, discussion forums, blogs, chats, photo and video sharing, etc. Explore the hosting site you have selected to see what's available for your network. You might decide to start out with just a few basic features and add more features as the site grows.

- **How will the site be moderated?** How can you protect your site from unwanted visitors such as hackers and spammers? What privacy levels are available to your members? It can be difficult to balance the desire to share information and ideas with the need for privacy and security, but you should have a plan in place to protect your members. Be sure you know how to work with the hosting site to handle any problems that might arise.

Professor Schmeckendorf has decided to create a social network that can be used by his former and current students. He believes that the networking opportunities of such a community will be beneficial to everyone. His former students will be able to reconnect with their classmates and provide updates on their current activities. His current students will be able to work with one another and have opportunities to find mentors among the former students. Professor Schmeckendorf has reviewed several sites that allow individuals to create their own social networks and has decided to use Ning because it appears easy to use and is free. For this Hands-On Exercise, you should follow the instructions to create your own social network. You might choose to create a social network for your class, school, or a club, to support an outside interest such as a group or hobby, or for some other purpose. Check with your instructor for further instructions for selecting a topic. Alternatively, you can follow the directions in these exercises to create a duplicate of the social network Professor Schmeckendorf will create. If you do, be sure to substitute your name and information in place of Professor Schmeckendorf's.

Hands-On Exercises

4 | Create a Social Network Using Ning

Steps: 1. Create a Ning Account **2.** Name Your Social Network and Create a URL
3. Describe Your Social Network, Add Features, and Change Its Appearance

Use Figures 5.23 through 5.31 as a guide in the exercise.

Step 1 Create a Ning Account

Refer to Figures 5.23 and 5.24 as you complete Step 1.

Before you can begin to create a social network on Ning, you must first obtain a Ning ID. This user ID will permit you to join social networks hosted on Ning or create your own network.

a. Open your web browser and navigate to **www.ning.com**.

b. Click the **Sign Up** link at the top of the page to proceed to the Ning Sign Up page.

B – Click to begin the
registration process

Figure 5.23 Hands-On Exercise 4, Step 1b.

c. On the **Sign Up** page, click on the **Terms of Service** and **Privacy Policy** links to review Ning's policies. When you have finished reviewing these pages, use your browser's **Back** button to return to the **Sign Up** page.

d. Type your name in the **Name** text box.

e. Type your email address in the **Email Address** text box. This email address will become your Ning user ID.

f. Type a password in the **Password** text box. To ensure that you have typed the password correctly, retype your password in the **Retype Password** text box.

> **Tip** **Creating a Strong Password**
>
> To help keep your personal information safe, experts recommend using strong passwords that are changed frequently. A strong password should consist of at least 8 to 12 characters and use a combination of upper- and lowercase letters, numbers, and symbols. Your password should not be a word found in the dictionary or include information that would be easy for someone who knows you to guess (such as your birth date, street address, or favorite pet's name). Microsoft has more information about creating strong passwords and includes a password-checker tool on their website at **www.microsoft.com/protect/yourself/password/checker.mspx** so that you can see how strong your password is.

g. Click the **Birthday** drop-down arrows to select the month, day, and year of your birth. Remember that you can use an alternate birth date if you prefer.

h. In the **Type the Code on the Right** text box, type the CAPTCHA characters that appear in the box. Note that your CAPTCHA characters will differ from the ones shown in Figure 5.24.

i. Click the **Sign Up** link at the bottom of the page.

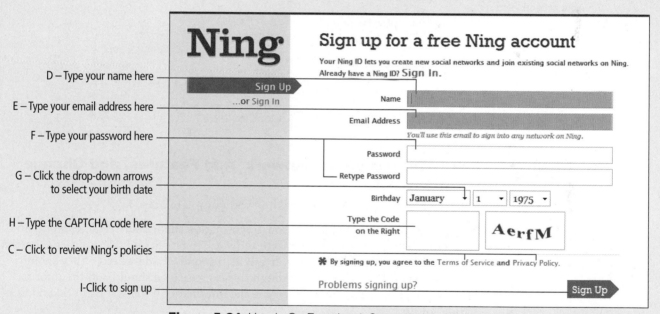

Figure 5.24 Hands-On Exercise 4, Steps 1c through 1i.

 Name Your Social Network and Create a URL

Refer to Figure 5.25 as you complete Step 2.

If you are following these instructions to create your own social network, you should think of an appropriate name for your network. You will also create a URL that will uniquely identify your site. The URL is your social network's website address and is what people will type into the browser's address box to reach your site. Ideally, your URL should be the same as, or similar to, your network's title. However, it is best if the URL is concise and easy to remember. Your URL also needs to be unique—something no one else has chosen. Unless you select a premium service, the Ning domain name will become part of your URL. If at some point you become unhappy with the network's name or URL, you have some decisions to make. You can change the name of your network whenever you wish; but for branding purposes and to avoid confusing your network's members, this is probably not a good idea. It is not possible to change the URL for your network. If you need to change the URL, you have to create a new network and select a new URL. Obviously, planning ahead when selecting your network's name and URL is a good idea.

a. Click in the **Name Your Social Network** text box and type the name you have selected. Professor Schmeckendorf has decided to call his network *Schmeckendorf's Students*.

b. Click in the **Pick a Web Address** text box and type the URL you have selected. Note that your URL must have at least six letters. Professor Schmeckendorf has selected "schmeckendorfstudents" for his URL. The complete URL for his site will be **www.schmeckendorfstudents.ning.com**.

c. Click the **Create** button to complete this process.

A – Type a name for your network here

B – Type the URL here

C – Click to create your network

Figure 5.25 Hands-On Exercise 4, Steps 2a through 2c.

 Step 3 **Describe Your Social Network, Add Features, and Change Its Appearance**

Refer to Figures 5.26 through 5.31 as you complete Step 3.

In this step, you will provide additional information about your social network, add features to help members communicate and work together, and select a theme for the network. The description you provide can help people decide whether they should join your network. As you work through this exercise, you should add the information that pertains to your network or use the information Professor Schmeckendorf is adding for his.

On the **About Your Network** page, you will adjust the privacy settings, create a tagline, include a brief description of your community, list some keywords, and select the language for your network. A *tagline*, or slogan, is typically a catchy phrase or short sentence or two that describes your network and displays as a subtitle at the top of the page.

Tagline A catchy phrase, slogan, or short sentence or two that describes your network and displays as a subtitle at the top of the page.

a. In the **Privacy** section, click the **Private** option button. Professor Schmeckendorf wants his social network to be a closed community. Members must be invited to view the site or to join.

b. Click the **Tagline** text box and type a brief slogan to describe your network. Professor Schmeckendorf has chosen *Connecting with Technology.* for his tagline.

c. Click the **Description** text box and type a description of up to 140 characters explaining the purpose of your network. Professor Schmeckendorf's description is:

A gathering place for former and current students of Professor Schmeckendorf's computer classes at Ginormous State University.

d. Click the **Keywords** text box and type a word or words that describe your network. Key words should be separated by commas. Professor Schmeckendorf has decided to add the following key words:

- Schmeckendorf
- Ginormous State University
- GSU

e. If necessary, click the **Language** drop-down arrow to select **English (U.S.)**.

f. Click the **Next** button at the top or bottom of the page to continue.

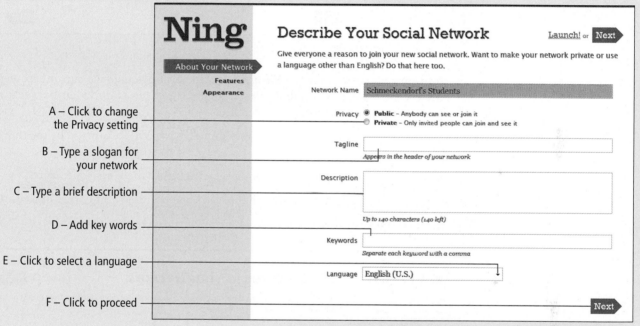

Figure 5.26 Hands-On Exercise 4, Steps 3a through 3f.

On the **Features** page, you can select which features to add to your network and decide where to locate them. The **Layout** area already includes some features that have been added by default and can be repositioned or removed. There are also three features in the shaded area on the right, which are locked and will always appear on your site unless you select a premium service.

g. Professor Schmeckendorf is happy with the positions of the default features; however, he wants to review all of the available features. Click the **View All Features** link to display the rest of the features.

Professor Schmeckendorf has decided to add the **Photos**, **Videos**, **Forum**, and **Get Badges** features to his social network. You may wish to add others to your network or position them differently. Use the techniques in the steps below to select and position your features. Be careful not to add too many features, because this may clutter your network's interface and make it difficult for the members to navigate through the network.

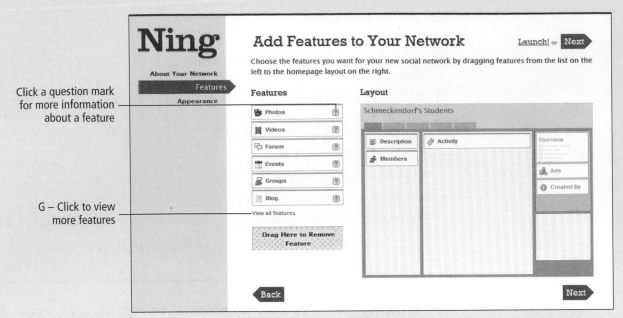

Click a question mark for more information about a feature

G – Click to view more features

Figure 5.27 Hands-On Exercise 4, Step 3g.

h. Position your cursor over the **Photos** feature and notice that the cursor becomes a 4-headed arrow. Click and drag the **Photos** feature beneath the **Members** feature in the left column to position it there.

i. Using the technique described in Step 3h, move the **Videos** feature below the **Photos** feature.

j. Move the **Forum** feature to the center section, below the **Activity** feature.

k. Move the **Get Badges** feature to the space in the bottom right corner of the site.

l. Click the **Next** button at the bottom or top of the page to continue.

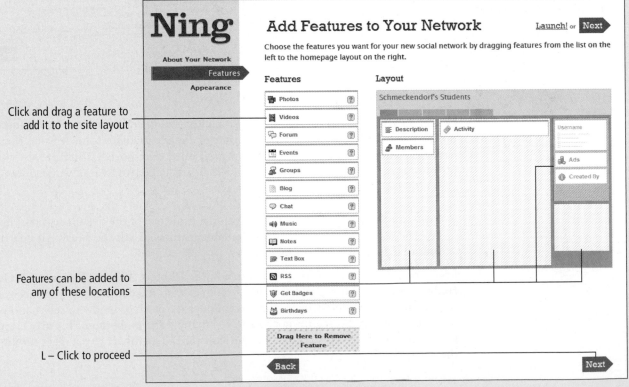

Click and drag a feature to add it to the site layout

Features can be added to any of these locations

L – Click to proceed

Figure 5.28 Hands-On Exercise 4, Step 3l.

On the **Appearance** page, you can select a predesigned theme for your social network and then customize it further by adjusting the various **Theme Settings**. Professor Schmeckendorf has decided to apply the **Blue Jeans** theme to his network and keep the default **Theme Settings**. You can sample various themes and see an approximation of how your network might appear by viewing the thumbnail image at the bottom right of the page.

m. Click the **Blue Jeans** theme—or another theme that you prefer—to apply it to your network.

n. Click the **Launch** button at the bottom or top right of the page.

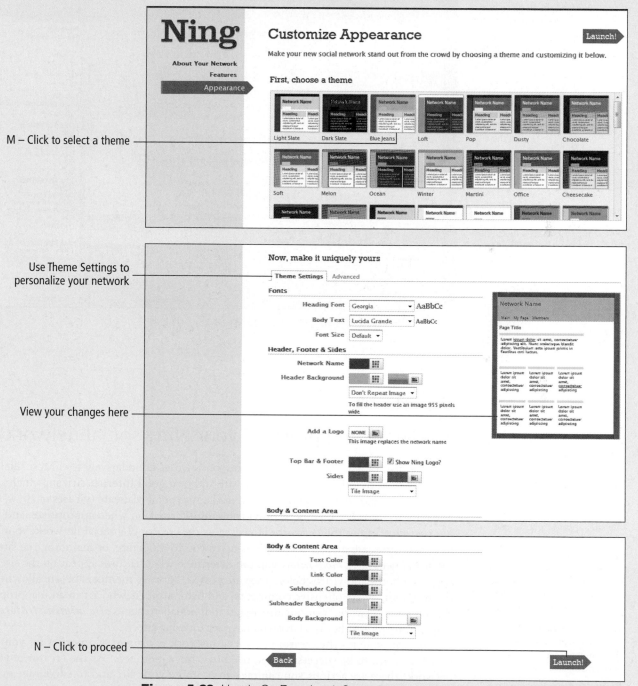

M – Click to select a theme

Use Theme Settings to personalize your network

View your changes here

N – Click to proceed

Figure 5.29 Hands-On Exercise 4, Steps 3m and 3n.

Congratulations! You've now created your own social network. Depending upon how closely you followed the steps in the exercise, your site may look similar to Professor Schmeckendorf's site (Figure 5.30).

o. On the right side of the page, below your name, click the **Sign Out** link to log out of your social network. Close your browser.

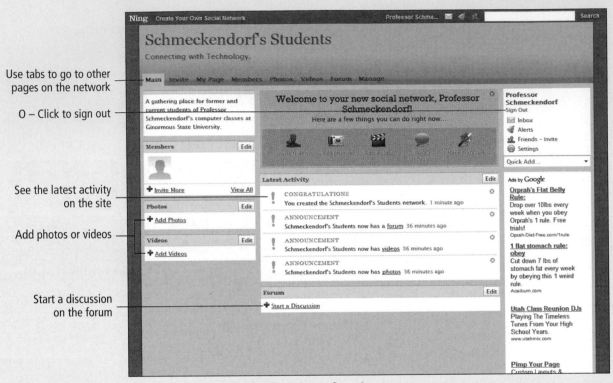

Figure 5.30 Hands-On Exercise 4, Step 3o.

Objective 8

Moderate and promote your Ning social network

As a member of a social network, your responsibilities are relatively few. Most likely, you only need to follow the rules of the site and be a good Internet citizen, which means don't send spam or knowingly spread any type of malware (viruses or spyware), be polite to the other members, provide useful information when appropriate, and have fun participating in the network. However, as the creator of a social network, your responsibilities are greater because it is up to you to moderate, or maintain, the site. As the social network's *moderator*, you can determine what features appear on the site, approve photos and videos before they are posted, approve members before allowing them to join, delete offensive comments, and ban members who act in an inappropriate way on your network. You can also assign individuals to act as *site administrators* and help you maintain the standards you have set for your site.

Another role for the creator of a social network is *promoter*. In order for your social network to be successful, you need to attract members. As the creator of your network, there are actions you can take to promote your site and to encourage others to help you spread the word.

In this next Hands-On Exercise, Professor Schmeckendorf will handle some basic moderator tasks and begin to promote his network.

Hands-On Exercises

5 | Moderate and Promote Your Social Network

Steps: 1. Log In to Your Social Network **2.** Adjust the Settings **3.** Invite a New Member and Create an Administrator **4.** Create a Badge

Use Figures 5.31 through 5.48 as a guide in the exercise.

 Step 1 **Log In to Your Social Network**

Refer to Figures 5.31 through 5.36 as you complete Step 1.

a. Open your web browser and navigate to **www.ning.com**.

b. Click the **Sign In** link.

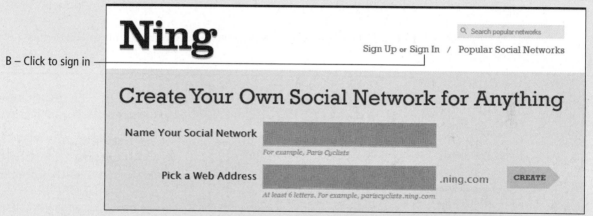

Figure 5.31 Hands-On Exercise 5, Step 1b.

c. Type the email address and password you selected to use as your Ning ID in the appropriate text boxes.

d. Click the **Sign In** link.

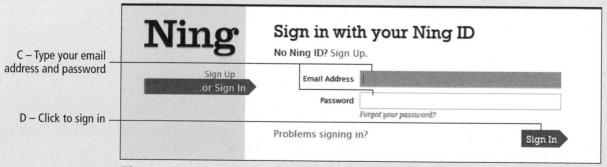

Figure 5.32 Hands-On Exercise 5, Steps 1c and 1d.

You've now signed in to the Ning site and need to access the social network you created.

e. Click the **My Social Networks** link to display the social networks you have joined on Ning.

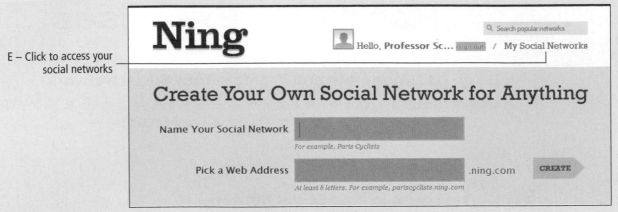

E – Click to access your social networks

Figure 5.33 Hands-On Exercise 5, Step 1e.

If you are a member of any other social networking sites hosted by Ning, you may see a list of those sites on the next page. Since this is Professor Schmeckendorf's first experience with Ning, he is not a member of any other networks. Your **My Social Networks** page may differ slightly from the one shown in Figure 5.34.

f. Click the **View Social Networks You Created** link to locate your network.

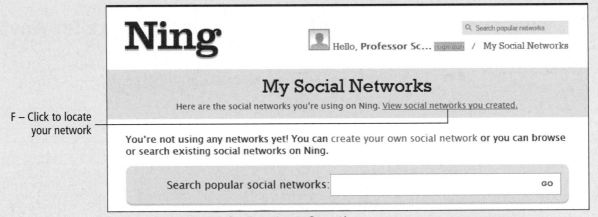

F – Click to locate your network

Figure 5.34 Hands-On Exercise 5, Step 1f.

The next page displays a list of social networks that you have created. Figure 5.35 displays the link to Professor Schmeckendorf's network. Your screen will display a link to the network you created previously and any others you may have also created.

g. Click the link for the social network that you created for this chapter.

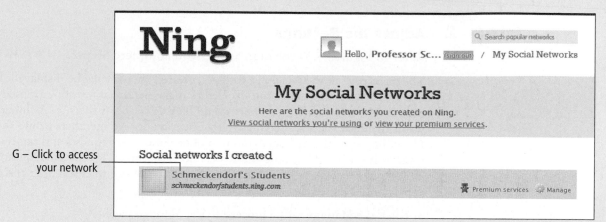

G – Click to access your network

Figure 5.35 Hands-On Exercise 5, Step 1g.

Because this is a closed community, members must log in again using their Ning ID before they can access any of the information in Professor Schmeckendorf's network. This helps to protect the privacy of Professor Schmeckendorf's current and former students and prevents unwanted or unauthorized individuals from viewing the site.

h. Type the email address and password you selected to use as your Ning ID in the appropriate text boxes.

i. Click the **Sign In** button to proceed.

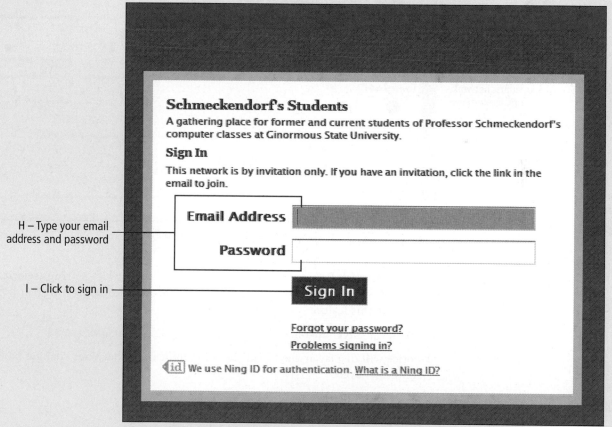

H – Type your email address and password

I – Click to sign in

Figure 5.36 Hands-On Exercise 5, Steps 1h and 1i.

Step 2 Adjust the Settings

Refer to Figures 5.37 through 5.40 as you complete Step 2.

The main page of the social network you created should now be displayed. Previously, Professor Schmeckendorf decided to make his social network a closed community so that only invited members would be able to access the site. As moderator, he wants to adjust the site's settings so that he can approve members before they join. He will receive an email notifying him of new member requests and can review a prospective member's profile before deciding whether to accept the request. He also wants to moderate any photos that are posted to the site to ensure that the content is appropriate and does not violate any copyright laws.

a. Click the **Manage** tab to proceed to the **Manage** page.

b. In the **Your Members** section, click the **Network Privacy** icon.

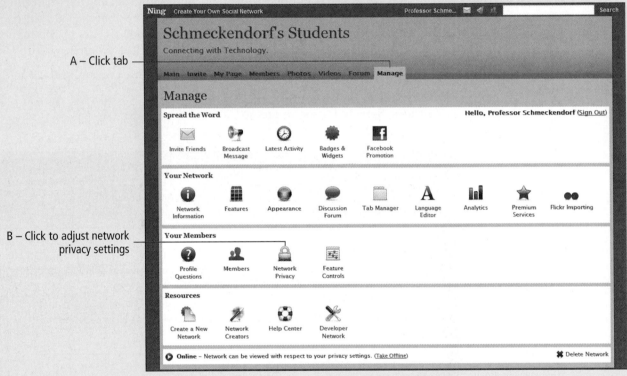

Figure 5.37 Hands-On Exercise 5, Steps 2a and 2b.

c. The **Network Privacy** page displays, showing the privacy settings selected previously. Click the **Approve New Members Before They Can Join** text box to activate this feature.

d. Click the **Save** button.

A notice will display at the top of the page, indicating that your changes have been successfully saved.

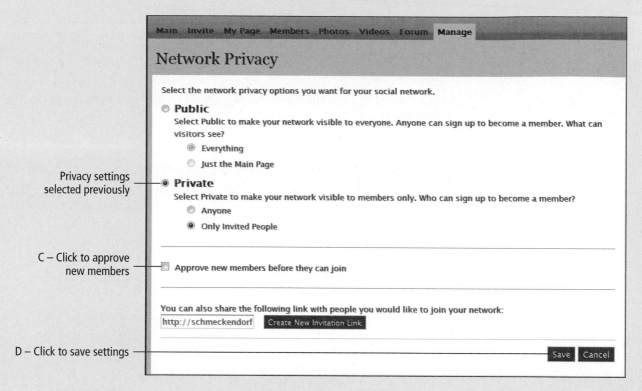

Privacy settings
selected previously

C – Click to approve
new members

D – Click to save settings

Figure 5.38 Hands-On Exercise 5, Steps 2c and 2d.

e. Click the **Manage** tab to return to the **Manage** page.

f. In the **Your Members** section, click the **Feature Controls** icon.

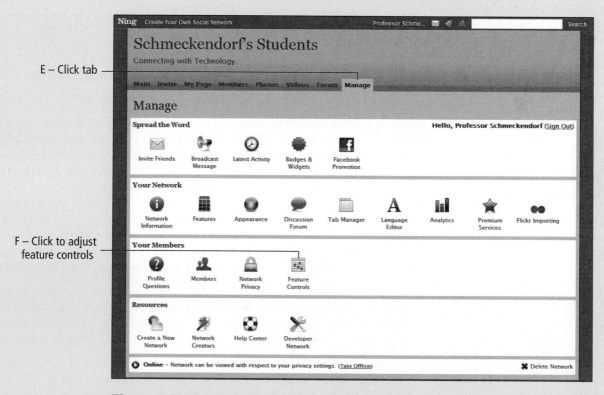

E – Click tab

F – Click to adjust
feature controls

Figure 5.39 Hands-On Exercise 5, Steps 2e and 2f.

g. The **Feature Controls** page displays with your previous settings already displayed. In the **Photos** area, click the **Approve Photos Before They Appear** checkbox.

h. Click the **Save** button.

A notice will display at the top of the page, indicating that your changes have been successfully saved.

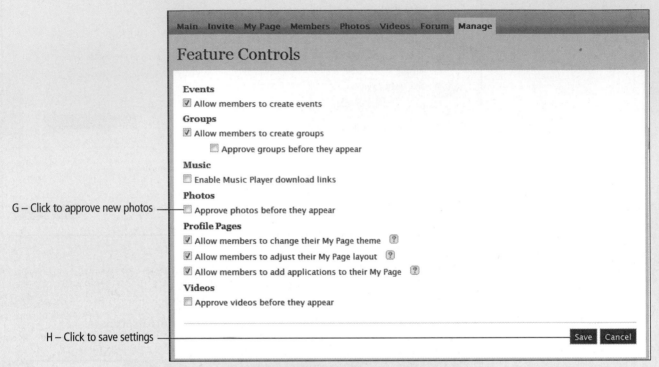

Figure 5.40 Hands-On Exercise 5, Steps 2g and 2h.

Step 3 Invite a New Member and Create an Administrator

Refer to Figures 5.41 through 5.44 as you complete Step 3.

Professor Schmeckendorf is concerned that his moderator duties may take up too much of his time. He has decided to assign his lab assistant, Hans Grindeldorf, as an administrator. However, before he can do this, Hans needs to become a member. You will need to select a trustworthy friend or classmate to act as the administrator for your social network in the next part of this exercise. A site administrator does not have as many rights as the site creator. For instance, an administrator cannot assign administrator privileges to another member, delete the network, or access network information, privacy settings, or feature controls. Only the network creator can complete these tasks. However, a site administrator can delete objectionable content, approve members, and approve photos before they are posted to the network.

a. Click the **Invite** tab to navigate to the **Invite** page. You can invite members by: importing addresses from a web-based email account such as Gmail, AOL, or Hotmail; entering email addresses manually; or importing from an address book application such as Outlook. For this exercise, you will enter an email address manually.

b. Click the **Enter Email Addresses** link to expand this section.

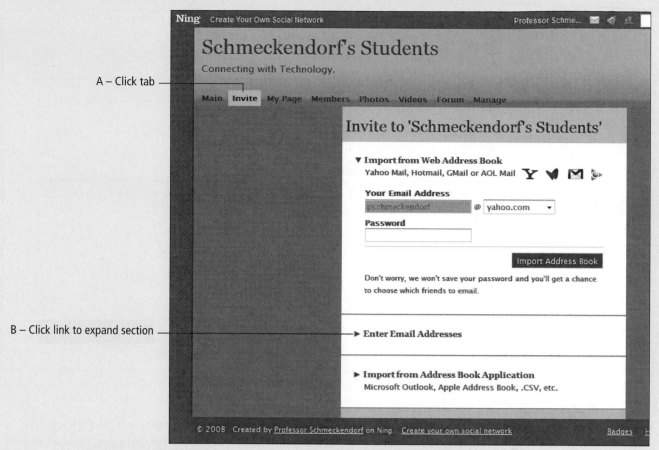

A – Click tab

B – Click link to expand section

Figure 5.41 Hands-On Exercise 5, Steps 3a and 3b.

c. In the **Send To** text box, type the email address for the person or persons you wish to invite to join your network. Separate multiple email addresses with a comma.

d. Although you do not have to include a message, it is a good idea to do so. In the **Your Message** text box, type the following:

Hi, I'd like you to become a member of my social network and take on the administrator role too. Thank you.

e. Click the **Send Invitations** button to send the invitation.

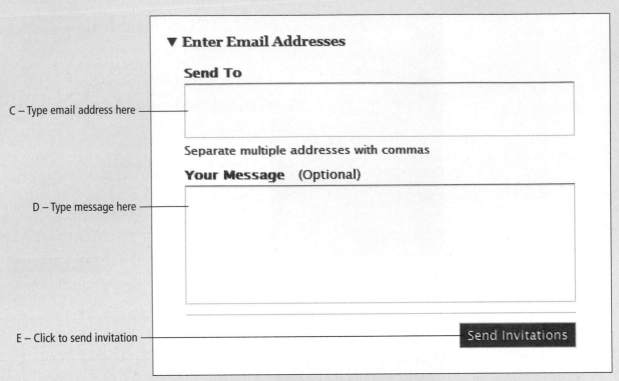

C – Type email address here

D – Type message here

E – Click to send invitation

Figure 5.42 Hands-On Exercise 5, Steps 3c through 3e.

A message displays, indicating that your invitation has been sent. Before you can proceed to the next step of this exercise, the person you invited must respond to the invitation. The invitation will appear in the recipient's email box with the subject line "Come Join Me on Schmeckendorf's Students"—or whatever name you have given your network. The email includes a link to join the network. Clicking the link will take the recipient to a sign in page. The recipient may either sign in using an existing Ning ID or can complete a brief sign up form and answer several short profile questions. Check the email account you used to sign up for Ning. You will receive a confirmation email once the person you invited joins the network, and then you can proceed with the rest of the exercise.

f. Click the **Manage** tab to go to the **Manage** page.

g. In the **Your Members** section, click the **Members** icon to display the list of members in your network.

F – Click tab

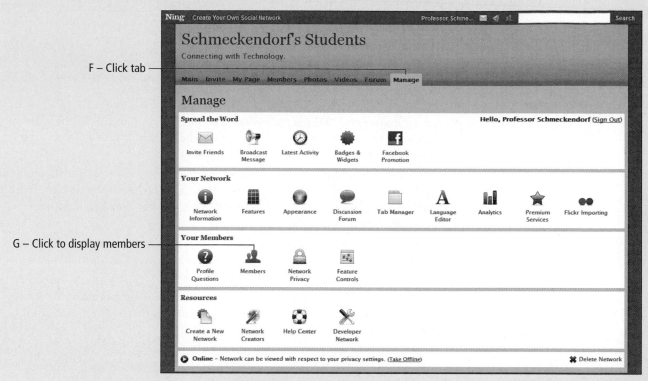

G – Click to display members

Figure 5.43 Hands-On Exercise 5, Steps 3f and 3g.

The Members page contains a tab for **Members** and a tab for **Administrators**.

h. If necessary, click the **Members** tab to select it. Click the checkbox next to the name of the person you invited to select it.

i. Click the **Promote to Administrator** button.

j. A message indicating that your change was successfully saved will appear. Click the **Administrators** tab and confirm that the member has been added as an administrator.

J – Click tab

I – Click to promote a member

H – Click to select a member

Figure 5.44 Hands-On Exercise 5, Steps 3h through 3j.

Step 4 Create a Badge

Refer to Figures 5.45 through 5.49 as you complete Step 4.

Ning provides several ways for you to promote your social network. These methods include:

- Send an invitation – This is the easiest and quickest way to spread the word about your site. Go to the Invite page, enter the email addresses of your friends and colleagues, and invite them to join your network.

- Share network content – When a video, photo, discussion thread, or blog post is added to the network, it includes a Share link. You can click the link to email it to individuals who are not in the network. This is a good way to let others see what your network is all about.

- Embed content – Some features include code that can be embedded in other sites, such as a website or another social networking site. This provides another way to generate interest in your online community.

- Create a Facebook application – This feature may be a bit more advanced, but Ning provides assistance for developing applications that will promote your social network on Facebook.

- Create a badge or widget – Similar to embedding code on a website, badges and widgets provide icons that you can post on other websites or social networking sites to improve your network's visibility. A *badge* is a small graphic that links to your social network. A widget is a small application that displays video or photos—or that plays music—and will also lead back to your site when it is clicked.

Badge A small graphic that links to your social network.

Professor Schmeckendorf and Hans will take care of inviting the current and former students for whom they have valid email addresses. However, Professor Schmeckendorf likes the idea of including a badge on other websites. Because the site is still under development, he does not want to deploy a badge on another site at this time, but he has learned that it is possible to customize badges. In this step, you will customize a badge for later use in promoting Professor Schmeckendorf's social network.

a. Click the **Manage** tab to go to the **Manage** page.

b. In the **Spread the Word** section, click the **Badges & Widgets** icon.

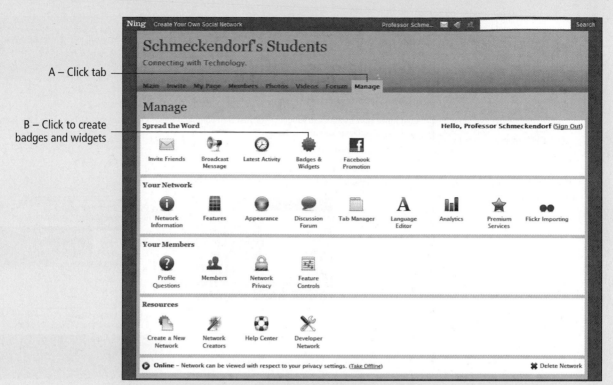

A – Click tab

B – Click to create badges and widgets

Figure 5.45 Hands-On Exercise 5, Steps 4a and 4b.

c. If necessary, click the **Customization** tab to display options for customizing badges and widgets.

d. In the **Background Image & Color** section, click the **Open Color Picker** button to reveal the **Pick a Color . . .** color pallet.

e. Click a color swatch of your choice or, if you know the hexadecimal code for the color you wish to use, type it in the text box. Click **OK** to apply your color choice. The badge and widget will refresh to display the selected color. Professor Schmeckendorf wants to use a color that is used in the border of his social network, so he will replace the current color by typing *#528097* in the **Pick a Color . . .** text box and then clicking **OK**.

> ### Tip ⭐ Identifying Colors on the Web
>
> If you've ever gone to a paint store to buy white paint, you know how many different shades of white exist. Do you want bright white, flat white, cream, eggshell, ivory, off-white, or one of the many other choices? To specify the right color on web pages, web designers use the hexadecimal color system. The hexadecimal system consist of 16 characters, including the numbers 0, 1, 2, 3, 4, 5, 6, 7, 8, and 9 and the letters A, B, C, D, E, and F. Hexadecimal codes, or *hex codes*, can be used to identify 16.7 million colors. A hex code is composed of the # symbol, followed by six digits grouped into three pairs. The first pair represents the red color value, the second pair represents the green color value, and the third pair represents the blue color value, with 0 being the lowest value and F being the highest value. Thus, the hex code for black is #000000 and the hex code for white is #FFFFFF, with other colors having some value between these two. For more information about working with color on the web, visit the HTML Goodies site (www.htmlgoodies.com/tutorials/colors). To generate your own hex codes, visit the Color Schemer site (www.colorschemer.com/online.html).

C – Click tab

D – Click to select a color

E – Type hexadecimal code
or click a color and click OK

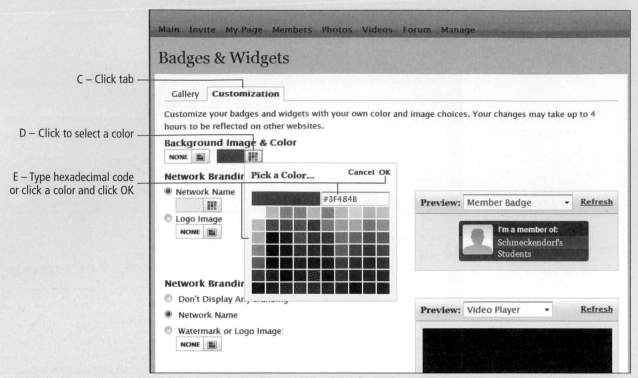

Figure 5.46 Hands-On Exercise 5, Steps 4c through 4e.

f. Click the **Badge** or **Widget** drop-down arrow to preview the different types of icons available.

g. Compare the settings on your screen with the settings shown in Figure 5.47 to be sure they match. Click the **Save** button to save your settings. A message will display at the top of the page, indicating that your changes were successfully saved.

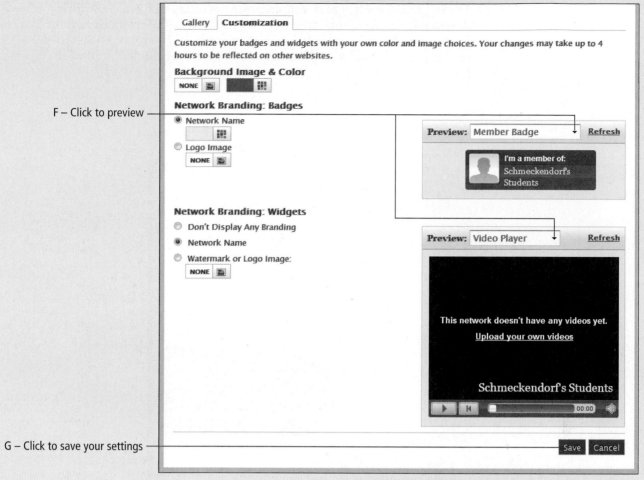

F – Click to preview

G – Click to save your settings

Figure 5.47 Hands-On Exercise 5, Steps 4f and 4g.

h. Click the **Main** tab to return to the **Main** page of the network. Scroll down to the bottom of the page to view the badge that was placed there when you first created the site. Notice that the colors of this badge have changed to reflect the new colors you chose in the previous step.

H – Click tab

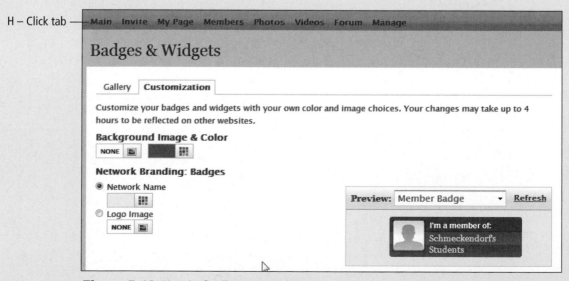

Figure 5.48 Hands-On Exercise 5, Step 4h.

The badge on the Main page will update dynamically to show the current membership count for the network. Members can click the **Get More Badges** link to go to the Badges and Widgets Gallery and select the type of badge or widget they would like to share in other locations to help spread the word about this network (Figure 5.49).

Badge on main page has changed to display new colors

Members can access additional badges from this link

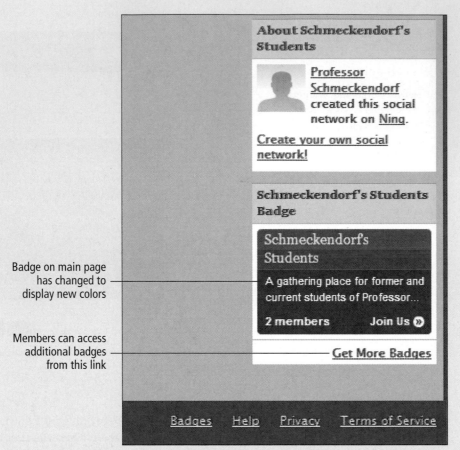

Figure 5.49 Updated badge displayed on the main page of Professor Schmeckendorf's site.

You may now log out of your Ning network and close your browser.

Objective 9

Describe Internet resources that educate people about social networking

The collaboration and communication features of a social network give you more ways than ever to interact with people all over the world. Whether you decide to participate in an existing social network or create your own, there are a number of resources that can provide additional information to help you get the most from this experience. Some of the following sites may be of interest:

- David Lee King (www.davidleeking.com) – This blog from David Lee King, a public librarian in Topeka, Kansas, explores emerging digital technologies as they relate to libraries. His blog includes a number of posts on social networking.

- Ning: Network Creators (http://networkcreators.ning.com/notes/The_Perfect_Social_Network) – This social network hosted by Ning provides advice and tutorials for individuals who have created their own social networks on Ning.

- Mashable: 10 Most Beautiful Social Networks (http://mashable.com/2007/07/09/beautiful-social-networks) – Mashable has created a list of social networks that they believe are well designed. Check them out if you're looking for inspiration for your own network.

- Find a Social Network (http://findasocialnetwork.com) – Use this search engine to locate social networks that match your interests. Submit your own social network to help others find your site.

- Social Networking (www.whatissocialnetworking.com) – This site provides a simple primer explaining the basics of social networking in a clear and easy-to-understand manner.

- Social Networking in Plain English (www.youtube.com/watch?v=6a_KF7TYKVc) – The folks at Common Craft have created an entertaining video that explains the concepts of social networking.

- StaySafeOnline.org (www.staysafeonline.org) – This website of the National Cyber Security Alliance has been developed to educate the public about good online safety practices and covers various topics, including social networking.

Summary

In this chapter, you have learned a number of the basic skills needed to participate in a social network and for creating your own network. We've looked at the advantages and disadvantages of social networking and provided information on how to maintain your safety and security as a member of a network, as well as how to help maintain your members' privacy if you create your own network. To be successful, social networks need to attract members who will participate and add value, because collaboration and communication are the key features of social networks.

Key Terms

Multiple Choice

1. A catchy phrase that appears at the top of a social networking site as a subtitle is known as a(n):

    (a) subheading.

    (b) badge.

    (c) tagline.

    (d) emoticon.

2. Which of the following is an example of a professional network?

    (a) LinkedIn

    (b) Orkut

    (c) Twitter

    (d) Digg

3. Which of the following activities is *not* the responsibility of a site administrator?

    (a) Deleting the network

    (b) Removing objectionable content

    (c) Approving new members

    (d) Approving photos and video

4. Widgets that are created by third-party developers are known as:

    (a) internal applications.

    (b) moderated applications.

    (c) profile applications.

    (d) external applications.

5. Which of the following is an example of an issues-focused social network?

    (a) Bebo

    (b) Plaxo

    (c) Flickr

    (d) Change.org

6. The main difference between cyberbullying and cyberstalking is:

    (a) cyberstalking never involves email.

    (b) cyberbullying is less serious than cyberstalking.

    (c) cyberbullying involves children, preteens, or teens rather than adults.

    (d) cyberstalking only involves adults.

7. Which of the following is *not* a way to add people to your Orkut network?

    (a) Use the Find friends feature.

    (b) Use the address export tool.

    (c) Use the Orkut search feature.

    (d) Invite friends from your home page.

8. Which of the following is *not* a method used to create awareness of a social network?

    (a) Issue invitations.

    (b) Set the privacy settings so that only invited individuals can see the content.

    (c) Share network content.

    (d) Post a badge on another website or social network.

9. Which of the following sites can be used to create your own social network?

    (a) Facebook

    (b) YouTube

    (c) Classmates

    (d) CrowdVine

10. The social network created using Ning in the Hands-On Exercises is an example of a(n):

    (a) closed community.

    (b) open community.

    (c) hybrid community.

    (d) private community.

Fill in the Blank

1. A(n) _____ is a graphical icon that can be added to your status area in Orkut.

2. The creator of a social network can assign an individual to act as the _____ _____ to help moderate the site and maintain the network's standards.

3. An adult who uses social networks and other online tools to lure children or adults into unsafe situations of a sexual or illegal nature is known as a(n) _____ _____.

4. _____ are applications that can be added to your social network and allow you to do things such as play games, listen to music, promote causes, and track events.

5. A social network that is visible to anyone and permits people to join without being invited is a(n) _____ _____.

Practice Exercises

1. **Create a Scrap on Orkut**

   Social networks give their communication areas different names. Facebook calls their area the *Wall*. Orkut calls it the *Scrapbook*, and the messages you create are called *scraps*. You can write a message for your scrapbook or create a scrap for a friend. The message can include text, graphics, images, video, audio, or html code. In this exercise, you will create a scrap for your own scrapbook and create another scrap for a friend. You need to have completed Hands-On Exercise 2 to complete this exercise, and the friend you invited in that exercise needs to have accepted your invitation.

   a. Open a web browser.

   b. Navigate to **www.orkut.com**.

   c. Log in to the Orkut network using the Google account information that you created previously.

   d. After logging in, click on the **Scrapbook** link at the top of the page.

   e. Click the **Scrap Tips** link for more details about creating scraps.

   f. Click in the **Scrapbook** text box at the top of the page and, in your own words, type a brief message describing the purpose of this exercise.

   g. Click the **Preview** button to see how your scrap will look.

   h. Make any necessary changes to your scrap by revising the text in the text box. Once you are happy with it, click the **Post Scrap** button to add this comment to your Orkut home page.

   i. Print out a copy of this page or capture it by taking a screenshot.

   j. Next, you will send a scrap to a friend. Click the **Friends** link at the top of the page to display your friends on Orkut. If the friend you invited in Hands-On Exercise 2 did not accept your invitation, you can ask them to do so now or invite someone else.

   k. Click on the name of a friend to go to your friend's home page.

   l. Click the **Scraps Icon** beneath your friend's name or click the **Scrapbook** link in the left column to open your friend's Scrapbook.

   m. Click in the **Scrapbook** text box and type a brief message to your friend to welcome them to Orkut. Using the steps above, preview your scrap, and then post it.

   n. Print out a copy of this page or capture it by taking a screenshot.

o. Submit the printouts (or screenshots) you produced in Step i and Step n to your instructor.

p. Log out of the Orkut network and close your browser.

2. **Change the Privacy Settings on Orkut**

Now that you have begun using scraps on Orkut, you should consider who you want to be able to view them. Orkut's default setting lets anyone view your scraps. In this exercise, you will change the privacy settings for the Scrapbook.

a. Open a web browser.

b. Navigate to **www.orkut.com**.

c. Log in to the Orkut network using the Google account information that you created previously.

d. After logging in, click on the **Scrapbook** link at the top of the page.

e. In the **My Scrapbook** area, click on the **Change Settings** link on the right side of the page.

f. The **My Settings** page displays with the **Privacy** tab open. If the **Privacy** tab is not the active tab, click it to make it the active tab.

g. Scroll down to the **Allow Content to Be Accessed By:** section. There are six content areas that you can modify. You can set each area to be visible to 1) only my friends, 2) friends of friends, or 3) everyone.

h. Click the drop-down arrows and change the privacy setting for each area as follows:
   - **View Scrapbook** friends of friends
   - **Write in Scrapbook** only my friends
   - **Videos** only my friends
   - **Testimonials** friends of friends
   - **Feeds** only my friends
   - **Albums** only my friends (Note that you can also set the permissions for each album individually.)

i. Click the **Save Changes** button to accept the privacy changes.

j. Print out a copy of this page or capture it by taking a screenshot.

k. Click the **Scrapbook** link at the top of the page to return to your scrapbook. Notice that the new privacy settings are displayed.

l. Print out a copy of this page or capture it by taking a screenshot.

m. Submit the printouts (or screenshots) you produced in Step j and Step l to your instructor.

n. Log out of the Orkut network and close your browser.

3. **Upload Photos to Your Ning Social Network**

Professor Schmeckendorf would like to add some photos to the social network he has created for his students. He has photos of an older-style classroom and a more modern classroom. You should use the Ning social network you created in Hands-On Exercise 4 to complete this exercise. You may add your own photos to your network or download the two files provided for this exercise (Classroom Now.jpg and Classroom Then.jpg).

To download the files, open your browser and navigate to www.pearsonhighered.com/nextseries. From the list of books provided, point to the title of this book, click the active link, and then follow the instructions as specified on the website to download the Chapter 5 files.

a. Open a web browser and navigate to **www.ning.com**.

b. Log in to your Ning account, using the email address and password you used to create your Ning ID.

c. Click the **My Social Networks** link, and on the next page, click the **View Social Networks You Created** link.

d. Click the link for the social network you created. If you successfully created the privacy settings in the Hands-On Exercises in this chapter, you will be asked to sign in to your network again using your Ning ID.

e. Locate the **Photos** area on your home page. If you used the same layout as Professor Schmeckendorf in the Hands-On Exercises, this area should be on the left side of the page.

f. Click the **Add Photos** link. If a **Warning – Security** dialog box appears, click **Run**.

g. The photo uploader tool appears on the **Add Photos** page. This tool resembles Windows Explorer. The left side of the pane displays folders on your computer. Navigate to the folder where you have saved your Chapter 5 files: **Classroom Now.jpg** and **Classroom Then.jpg**. If you are using different images, locate them now. If the files are not stored in the Documents folder (at the top of the folder list), click the drop-down arrow to select the correct location. Double-click to open a folder in the list and reveal subfolders or files.

h. Once you have located the files, Ctrl-click to select both of them. Drag the photos to the **Drag Photos Here** area.

i. Click the **Next** button to proceed.

j. You can add or edit information for all photos at one time or add information to each photo individually. If necessary, click the **Edit Information for All Photos** link to expand the selection. You will add the photo information in this section rather than for each image. If you are using your own images, adjust the instructions below to suit your images as appropriate.

k. Since each of the photos provided by Professor Schmeckendorf already displays a title, leave the **Title** text box in the **Edit Information for All Photos** section blank.

l. Click the **Description** checkbox and then, in the text box, type **Classrooms from yesterday and now.**

m. Click the **Tags** checkbox and then, in the text box, type: **classroom, desks, chairs, blackboard.**

n. Click the **Can Be Viewed by** checkbox, and then click the **Anyone** option button. Because Professor Schmeckendorf's network is a closed community and these images do not portray any personal information, he feels comfortable allowing these photos to be viewed by anyone. If you prefer a higher level of privacy, select the option of your choice.

o. Click the **Apply This Info to the Photos Below** button.

p. Print out a copy of this page or capture it by taking a screenshot.

q. Click the **Upload** button to begin the upload process. Note that if you are using your own photos, you should follow Ning's Terms of Service and ensure that you are not in violation of copyright. If you are posting images of other people, you should at the very least have their permission and may need to obtain a model release.

r. Click the **Main** tab and notice that a post in the **Latest Activity** area indicates that you have added photos. The **Photos** area displays the photos as a slideshow that visitors can view.

s. Print out a copy of this page or capture it by taking a screenshot.

t. Submit the printouts (or screenshots) you produced in Step *p* and Step *s* to your instructor.

u. Log out of the Ning network and close your browser.

4. Add Profile Questions to Your Ning Network

It is possible to add one or more profile questions that new members must answer when they join your network. Ning provides two default questions: Gender and Location. By default, members are not required to answer these two questions. Professor Schmeckendorf wants to make these questions required, and he would also like to know when each member graduated. This will be a required question also. If a member does not answer a required question, the member cannot join the network. However, Professor Schmeckendorf will add a privacy setting to the graduation question so that only the member, any site administrators, and the site creator will be able to view the answer. It will not be visible to other members.

a. To log in to your Ning network, repeat Practice Exercise 3, Step *a* through Step *d*.

b. On your home page, click the **Manage** tab.

c. On the **Manage** page, in the **Your Members** section, click the **Profile Questions** icon.

d. On the **Profile Questions** page, the **Gender** and **Location** questions are already set up. Click the **Required** checkbox next to each.

e. For the third question, click in the **Question Title** text box and type **What year did you graduate?**, then click the **Required** checkbox and the **Private** checkbox.

f. Print out a copy of this page or capture it by taking a screenshot.

g. Click the **Save** button to save your settings.

h. Submit the printout (or screenshot) you produced in Step *f* to your instructor.

i. Log out of the Ning network and close your browser.

Critical Thinking

1. Are you a member of one or more social networks, other than the Orkut and Ning networks you worked on during this chapter? If so, what networks do you participate in? Why did you choose to join? How much time do you spend using social networks? What do you think is the greatest advantage of a social network? What is the biggest disadvantage? Answer these questions in a brief one- or two-page paper explaining your reasons, and submit it to your instructor.

2. Before you read this chapter, were you aware that various types of malware and scams existed on social networking sites? Security experts are concerned about the threats posed by social networks. Because members are receiving information from people they "know," they may not exercise the same level of safety when opening messages, clicking on hyperlinks, or following directions. Have you experienced any trouble with a virus, spyware, or a scam resulting from your use of a social network? Do you think this is a serious problem? Research this issue on the Internet and locate an article discussing a current security threat on a social network (within the last 6 months or as determined by your instructor). Write a synopsis of the article and your responses to these questions, and then submit the paper to your instructor.

Team Projects

1. As discussed in this chapter, it is possible to find social networks developed for a wide range of topics and interests. Split your group into two teams and visit the issues-focused social networks on Change.org (www.change.org). Each team should pick two topics and review the associated networks. Compare and contrast the two networks

and create a chart listing your findings. Consider items such as included features, number of members, site design, and ease of use. Include a brief review of your impression of each network.

2. As a team, explore the professional networks LinkedIn (www.linkedin.com) and Plaxo (www.plaxo.com). Sign up to join both sites and explore the features offered by each. As a college student, how would you use these sites? Conduct a search on each and see if anyone you know is a member of one of the sites. Do you think that one of these sites is better than the other? If so, why? Would you consider inviting an instructor to be your contact? Why or why not? Do you think an instructor would be more inclined to accept your invitation from a professional networking site than from a site like Facebook or MySpace? Create a brief paper that explains your team's findings on each site and that supports your opinions.

Glossary

Advertising programs Programs that allow you to display ads on your blog and pay you based on the number of people who click on the ads and how many of those clicks turn into actual purchases.

Affiliate programs Programs that pay you for referring your blog readers to other sites where they can purchase goods or services.

Aggregator A type of software that is specially designed to go out and check the Internet for new content from websites, blogs, or podcasts to which you subscribe.

Badge A small graphic that links to your social network.

Beta version Software that is still being tested and evaluated.

Blog Short for *web log*, a type of web page that features entries that provide a commentary on a single subject or a particular genre.

Blog archive A list of posts to the blog organized by date.

Blog carnival A type of online magazine (or newsletter) that is usually published on a blog on a regular basis (weekly, monthly, etc.).

Blog comments Written commentaries left by readers pertaining to a certain blog post.

Blog directories Listings of blog sites, usually organized by topic.

Blog posts The text, images, and/or videos that provide information to blog readers. Posts contain a title and the date they were posted to the blog site and are listed in reverse chronological order.

Blog search engine A specialized type of search engine that focuses on indexing and returning search results for information posted on blogs.

Blog spam Comments that are posted to a blog by automated programs to specifically promote a product or website.

Blogger A person who creates and maintains a blog.

Blogosphere The entire collection of all blogs on the web.

Blogroll A list of hyperlinks to other blogs that the blog creator feels will be of interest to his or her readers.

CAPTCHA A program that helps protect websites from having software programs, or bots, execute procedures on the sites.

Cease and desist letter A request to immediately stop an alleged copyright infringement.

Closed community A social network to which members typically must be invited by the site organizer or pre-existing members.

Contextual A type of ad in which the topic is related to the content of the website on which it is displayed.

Contributory infringement A type of infringement in which you do not commit the original infringement by posting copyrighted material. But you link to the material while aware that the content you are linking to is copyrighted, and your link to the content materially contributes to the infringement.

Copyright The legal protection granted to authors of "original works of authorship."

Copyright infringement The use of copyrighted material without the permission of the copyright holder.

Cyber predator An adult who, using the Internet, preys on children or other hapless individuals, attempting to lure them into a sexual, or otherwise unsafe, situation.

Cyberbullying A type of bullying, involving children, pre-teens, or teens, but not adults, that is done via online tools such as email or social networks as opposed to being done face-to-face.

Cyberstalking Threatening or harassing behavior that is facilitated by the use of the Internet and online tools such as email and online social networks.

Dot-com bust A period of time between late 2000 through 2002 in which many dot-com companies with unworkable business ideas went out of business.

Dot-coms Companies that do most or all of their business on the Internet.

Emoticon A small graphical icon (e.g., a smiley face or sad face) used to display a mood.

External applications Features that can be added to a social network that are created by third-party developers, sometimes for commercial purposes.

External links Hyperlinks that connect to web pages that are located outside of the wiki.

Extracted Files which have been unzipped, or restored, to their original size.

Gadget A section of your blog that contains code that results in some type of functionality for your blog.

GNU General Public License A license that specifies that a software program can be distributed to and modified by anyone, even for commercial purposes.

Header Section of a blog that contains the title of your blog and can contain a subtitle in certain templates.

Hyperlink Text or an image that connects to another document on the web or to another location on the same web page.

ID3 tags Pieces of information that are attached to MP3 audio files.

Internal applications Features that can be added to a social network that are developed by the creators of the network.

Internal links Hyperlinks that connect one wiki page to another point within the wiki.

Internet trolls Individuals who write inflammatory, controversial, or irrelevant content in online communities such as Wikipedia, just to provoke emotional responses from readers.

IP address A unique number assigned to devices connected to the Internet.

Issues-focused network A social action network that provides members with information and opportunities to help with causes that range from global warming and animal rights to fair trade and peace in the Middle East.

Labels Topics or categories that are created by you to describe your blog posts.

Moderator A social network role in which you can determine what features appear on the site, approve photos and videos before they are posted, approve members before allowing them to join, delete offensive comments, and ban members who act in an inappropriate way on the network.

Notifications Emails sent out by your wiki provider to alert you when changes are made to your wikis.

Open community A social network in which anyone is free to join, regardless of their interests or who they might know.

Page views The number of times a web page is loaded in a browser.

Paid-to-blog programs Companies that pay bloggers to blog.

Peer review A process by which experts in a given field review another author's scholarly work to determine that the output is valid and substantially correct.

Podcast A group of audio or video files, usually issued in a series or sequence, that can be subscribed to and downloaded from the Internet.

Podcatcher Software that is specially designed to go out and check the Internet for new episodes of the podcasts to which you subscribe.

Pop filter A mesh screen that is placed directly in front of a microphone to disrupt the fast flow of air as it speeds towards the microphone.

Professional network A social network that connects business people and other professionals in an online community and allows them to showcase their talents and skills.

Profile A feature of a social network that is used to provide information about a member.

Promoter A person who promotes a social network site and encourages others to help spread the word.

Public domain Works which may be reproduced, distributed, or modified by anyone due to the expiration of copyright.

Really Simple Syndication (RSS) A popular type of web feed that is used to syndicate content on the Internet.

Refereeing A process by which experts in a given field review another author's scholarly work to determine that the output is valid and substantially correct.

Revision history page A chronological listing (most recent first) of the edits to a wiki page.

Search engines Websites that are designed to search the web for information and create an index of that information.

Server A computer that provides services to other computers upon request.

Sidebar A feature of PBwiki; this is a small section that is always visible (by default) on the right side of your wiki no matter what page of the wiki you are viewing.

Site administrators People who are assigned to maintain the standards set for a social networking site.

Social network A community made up of people, groups, or organizations that are connected by one or more common interests.

Sponsored ads Clickable advertisement buttons or banners that advertisers will pay you to place on your website.

Storyboard A panel, or series of panels, arranged in sequence to portray the action or events that will occur in a video.

Sync The process of connecting your PMP to your computer to update its contents.

Tagline A catchy phrase, slogan, or short sentence or two that describes your network and displays as a subtitle at the top of the page.

Terms of use The terms governing use of copyrighted material.

Traffic The amount of visitors to a blog or web page.

Transitions Effects that take place in between media clips.

Unique visitors The number of different people who visit a website within a specific time period.

Venture capitalists Investors who specialize in funding new, high-growth ventures in exchange for shares of stock in a company.

Vidcast A video podcast.

Vodcast A video podcast.

Watchlist A list of web pages that are being monitored.

Web 2.0 An expression used to describe the changes that have taken place in the usage and applications available on the Internet (specifically the World Wide Web) over the past five to seven years.

Web feed A data format for a web page that enables it to provide information when the page's content is updated.

Widgets Applications or features which can be added to a web site such as a blog or social network.

Wiki A collection of web pages that are designed to be edited by groups of individuals.

Wiki community The users and contributors to a wiki.

Wiki farm A server (or a group of connected servers) that runs wiki software and is designed to host multiple wikis at the same time.

Wiki page One page on a wiki.

Wiki vandals Individuals who deface pages in a wiki by deleting legitimate information, inserting irrelevant or nonsensical information, violating the policies of the wiki (such as adding content that is speculative on Wikipedia), or inserting links to commercial sites in an attempt to sell products or services.

Wikipedia An online encyclopedia that is deployed in many languages and is accessible at no cost to its users.

Zipped files Groups of files that have been compressed using special file compression software to condense the files so that they are smaller in size and can be downloaded quickly.

Zipped folders Groups of files that have been compressed using special file compression software to condense the files so that they are smaller in size and can be downloaded quickly.

Index

Illustration Credits

CHAPTER 1

Fig. 1.1 Wikipedia product screen shot(s) reprinted with permission from Wikipedia.

Figs. 1.19-1.23 Microsoft product screen shot(s) reprinted with permission from Microsoft Corporation.

Fig. 1.25 Microsoft product screen shot(s) reprinted with permission from Microsoft Corporation.

Fig. 1.26b Microsoft product screen shot(s) reprinted with permission from Microsoft Corporation.

CHAPTER 2

Fig. 2.4 Plantronics® • Audio™.

Fig. 2.5 Courtesy of Dean Sabatino www.deansabatino.com

Figs. 2.6-2.15 Audacity ® software is copyright © 1999-2008 Audacity Team. Web site: http://audacity.sourceforge.net/. The name Audacity ® is a registered trademark of Dominic Mazzoni.

Figs. 2.16-2.21 Microsoft product screen shot(s) reprinted with permission from Microsoft Corporation.

Figs. 2.22-2.24 Audacity ® software is copyright © 1999-2008 Audacity Team. Web site: http://audacity.sourceforge.net/. The name Audacity ® is a registered trademark of Dominic Mazzoni.

Fig. 2.25 Microsoft product screen shot(s) reprinted with permission from Microsoft Corporation.

Fig. 2.26-2.32 Audacity ® software is copyright © 1999-2008 Audacity Team. Web site: http://audacity.sourceforge.net/. The name Audacity ® is a registered trademark of Dominic Mazzoni.

Figs. 2.33-2.35 Microsoft product screen shot(s) reprinted with permission from Microsoft Corporation.

Figs. 2.36-2.39 Microsoft product screen shot(s) reprinted with permission from Microsoft Corporation.

CHAPTER 3

Figs. 3.9-3.13 Technorati, Inc.

Fig. 3.16 Technorati, Inc.

Figs. 3.34-3.35 Microsoft product screen shot(s) reprinted with permission from Microsoft Corporation.

Fig. 3.38 Microsoft product screen shot(s) reprinted with permission from Microsoft Corporation.

Fig. 3.56 Microsoft product screen shot(s) reprinted with permission from Microsoft Corporation.

Figs. 3.82-3.90 © Amazon.com, Inc. or its affiliates. All Rights Reserved.

Fig. 3.95 © Amazon.com, Inc. or its affiliates. All Rights Reserved.

Chapter 5

Figs. 5.3a-5.3b ZITS © ZITS PARTNERSHIP, KING FEATURES SYNDICATE